Our Lady of Guadalupe and
Saint Juan Diego

Celebrating Faith

Explorations in Latino Spirituality and Theology

Series Editor: Virgilio Elizondo

This series will present seminal, insightful, and inspirational works drawing on the experiences of Christians in the Latino traditions. Books in this series will explore topics such as the roots of a Mexican-American understanding of God's presence in the life of the people, the perduring influence of the Guadalupe event, the spirituality of immigrants, and the role of popular religion in teaching and living the faith.

The Way of the Cross: The Passion of Christ in the Americas
edited by Virgil P. Elizondo
Faith Formation and Popular Religion: Lessons from Tejano Experience
by Anita De Luna
Border of Death, Valley of Life: An Immigrant Journey of Heart and Spirit
by Daniel G. Groody
Mexican Spirituality: Its Sources and Mission in the Earliest Guadalupan Sermons
by Francisco Raymond Schulte
The Virgin of Guadalupe: Theological Reflections of an Anglo-Lutheran Liturgist
by Maxwell E. Johnson
The Treasure of Guadalupe
edited by Virgilio Elizondo, Allan Figueroa Deck, and Timothy Matovina
Our Lady of Guadalupe and Saint Juan Diego: The Historical Evidence
by Eduardo Chávez

Our Lady of Guadalupe and Saint Juan Diego

The Historical Evidence

Eduardo Chávez

Translated from Spanish
by Carmen Treviño and Veronica Montaño

ROWMAN & LITTLEFIELD PUBLISHERS, INC.
Lanham • Boulder • New York • Toronto • Oxford

ROWMAN & LITTLEFIELD PUBLISHERS, INC.

Published in the United States of America
by Rowman & Littlefield Publishers, Inc.
A wholly owned subsidary of The Rowman & Littlefield Publishing Group, Inc.
4501 Forbes Boulevard, Suite 200, Lanham, Maryland 20706
www.rowmanlittlefield.com

PO Box 317
Oxford
OX2 9RU, UK

British Library Cataloguing in Publication Information Available

Library of Congress Cataloging-in-Publication Data

Chávez, Eduardo, 1956–
[Virgen de Guadalupe y San Juan Diego. English]
Our Lady of Guadalupe and Saint Juan Diego : the historical evidence / Eduardo
Chávez ; translated from Spanish by Carmen Treviño and Veronica Montaño.
p. cm. — (Celebrating faith)
Includes bibliographical references and index.
ISBN 13: 978-0-7425-5104-6 (cloth : alk. paper)
ISBN 10: 0-7425-5104-0 (cloth : alk. paper)
ISBN 13: 978-0-7425-5105-3 (pbk. : alk. paper)
ISBN 10: 0-7425-5105-9 (pbk. : alk. paper)
1. Juan Diego, Saint, 1474–1548. 2. Guadalupe, Our Lady of. I. Title. II. Series.

BT660.G8C4813 2006
232.91'7097252—dc22   2005029159

Printed in the United States of America

∞™ The paper used in this publication meets the minimum requirements of
American National Standard for Information Sciences—Permanence of Paper for
Printed Library Materials, ANSI/NISO Z39.48-1992.

I want to dedicate this work to each of the people who with sincere and humble hearts take Holy Mary of Guadalupe and Saint Juan Diego into their souls. He is Her humble messenger who marked history.

Contents

Acknowledgments

I am deeply thankful to so many people who have collaborated so that this work could be possible: to them I dedicate it, especially to Most Holy Father Benedict XVI; to Cardinal Norberto Rivera Carrera; to each one of the Episcopal Bishops and Vicars; to the Basilica of Guadalupe; to presbytery and the faithful of the Archdiocese of Mexico. Also, to the Mexican Episcopacy, to the Congregation for the Cause of the Saints, to my family, to Mrs. Carmen Treviño, who had the patience to translate this book, and Ms. Verónica Montaño, who edited this work.

Abbreviations

AAEE	Archivo de Asuntos Eclesiásticos Extraordinarios [Special Ecclesiastic Affairs Archives]
AHBG	Archivo Histórico de la Basílica de Guadalupe [Historical Archives of the Basilica of Guadalupe]
ACCM	Archivo del Cabildo y Catedral de México [Chapter and Cathedral of Mexico Archives]
ACM	Archivo de la Ciudad de México [Mexico City Archives]
AGN	Archivo General de la Nación [National General Archives (Mexico)]
AGI	Archivo General de Indias [General Spanish American (Indias) Archives]
AGS	Archivo General de Simancas [General Simancas Archives]
AHAM	Archivo Histórico de la Arquidiócesis de México [Historic Archives of the Archbishopric of Mexico]
AHMNA	Archivo Histórico del Museo Nacional de Antropología [Historic Archives of the National Museum of Antropology]
AHMV	Archivo Histórico de Manuscritos de Viena [Historic Archives of the Vienna Manuscripts]
AHNAM	Archivo Histórico Nacional, Madrid [National Historic Archives, Madrid]
AI	Archivo Iberoamericano [Latin American Archives]
ARAHE	Archivo de la Real Academia de la Historia de España [The Royal Academy of the History of Spain Archives]

ARSI	Archivo Romano de la Sociedad de Jesús [The Roman Archives of the Society of Jesus]
ASV	Archivo Secreto Vaticano [The Secret Vatican Archives]
BAV	Biblioteca Apostólica Vaticana [The Vatican Apostolic Library]
BBG	Biblioteca Lorenzo Boturini de la Basílica de Guadalupe [Lorenzo Boturini Library of the Basilica of Guadalupe]
BMAH	Biblioteca del Museo de Antropología e Historia [The Museum of Anthropology and History Library]
BNP	Biblioteca Nacional de París [The National Library of Paris]
BNM	Biblioteca Nacional de México [The National Library of Mexico]
BNV	Biblioteca Nacional de Viena [The National Library of Vienna]
CELAM	Conferencia del Episcopado Latinoamericano [Latin American Episcopacy Conference]
CEM	Conferencia del Episcopado Mexicano [Mexican Episcopacy Conference]
CJBM	Colección Juan Bautista Muñoz [The Juan Bautista Muñoz Collection]
NYPL	New York Public Library

Presentation

On August 27, 1529, my venerable predecessor, Friar Juan de Zumárraga, wrote to the King of Spain a distressed letter in which he assured him that "if God does not provide a remedy from His hand the Earth is about to lose itself totally." Everything he saw in the Mexico in that moment—abuses, murders, violence—took him to that devastating conclusion. Two years later, on Saturday, December 9, 1531, he received the unusual visit of a humble Indigenous who presumed to bring a message from the Queen of Heaven, who requested a temple, "a sacred small house." In only three days more, that same Indigenous brought convincing proof to him of Mary's message, and Zumárraga agreed to raise a modest hermitage. He never imagined the immense importance that hermitage was going to have, but now we see its importance and we, his successors, thank him.

This message can be verified, with abundant information and scientific proof, by anyone who reads this book that we have the pleasure to present, and whose author, Eduardo Chávez, Doctor in History of the Church and who I have named Postulator before the Holy See to the canonization of that humble Indigenous Juan Diego, who brought so much joy to my predecessor, and through whom we today see how abundantly "God provided with the remedy of His hand" for our mother country and the world. How much we owe to him, the human instrument to grant us that gift, and how responsible we are to share it with "all the other various images of men."

Although all Mexicans know his name, and we all feel loved and welcomed like him by our Most Holy Mother, we do not know much about him.

My immediate predecessor, Cardinal Ernesto Corripio, wanted to begin to settle the debt which all Mexicans contracted with him, by obtaining his beatification. As for me, joyfully conscious of that same obligation and debt as the successor of Cardinal Corripio and of Zumárraga, I have asked for this book, that, although brief and easy to read, has cost its author and his collaborators years and years of investigation. He has based this book faithfully on what we know for sure about that admirable man Juan Diego Cuauhtlatoatzin.

Mexico-Tenochtitlan, July 2003

+ Cardinal Norberto Rivera Carrera
Archbishop Primate of Mexico

~

Prologue

Holy Mary of Guadalupe and Juan Diego: History or Myth?

The "Guadalupan Event" as a key to reading the history of Evangelization in the New World or in the American continent appears with increasing force in numerous pontifical documents related to the Latin American world and in the episcopals of the same continent in the last two centuries, especially after the Latin American Plenary Council of 1899[1] until the magistracy of John Paul II at the Special Synod of American Bishops. These documents invoke Holy Mary of Guadalupe as the Mother of our faith. In his time Pope Leo XIII and the bishops trusted the future of the Latin American Church to Her intercession.

Long before that in the eighteenth century, the Holy See recognized the Most Holy Virgin of Guadalupe as Patroness of Mexico and all the territories of the then Spanish Empire.[2] The patronage of Holy Mary of Guadalupe had

---

[1] Cfr. *Actas y Decretos del Concilio Plenario de la América Latina celebrado en Roma*, 1906, pp. LXXXVI, CXL, 7.

[2] Benedict XIV granted the Most Holy Virgin of Guadalupe Her own Mass and Office (celebrated on December 12); with a decree signed by Card. Prefect of the Congregation of Rites and by the Secretary of same congregation, on April 24, 1754, in ASV, *Decrt. Sac. Rit. C. ab anno to 1754 ad annum 1756*, f. 124. Extension of the concession for the other domains of Spain (1757), on file at the Basilica of Guadalupe (without indication of coloc. of file). Benedict XIV with the brief *Non est equidem*, on May 25, 1754, confirms the concession of the Mass and Office and declares the Virgin of Guadalupe the main Patroness of the Kingdom of New Spain and grants other particular thanks and indulgences, in *Collection of Works and Opuscules*, Impr. Lorenzo de S. Martín, Madrid 1785, pp. 1–60. Office of the Town Hall of Saint Peter of Rome for the Coronation of Our Lady of Guadalupe, on June 11, 1740, in History of Basilica of Guadalupe Archives (without indication of coloc. of file).

entered the hearts of Mexicans. She had accompanied them with force in the risky days of independence from the mother country and throughout all of the nineteenth century. In 1894, Leo XIII granted a new liturgical office in honor of Holy Mary of Guadalupe; he would even compose Latin verses that were placed in a mosaic at the foot of the main altar in the old Collegial Church of Guadalupe (February 26, 1895), as requested by the Bishop of Tehuantepec, D. José Mora y del Río.

In the new liturgical texts in honor of Holy Mary of Guadalupe the historical aspect of the appearances to the Indigenous Juan Diego was emphasized. Soon it was granted that the *tilma* with the Image of the Most Holy Virgin of Guadalupe be crowned canonically in 1895 in a gesture deeply felt by all the Mexican bishops and all the Catholic people.[3] Numerous bishops from the rest of the continent participated to emphasize "patronage" of Holy Mary of Guadalupe all over the continent. A few years later, the bishops of the American continent asked the Holy Father Pius X to proclaim the Virgin of Guadalupe "Patroness of America;" the bishops of the Philippines, whose Christian history is inseparable to the one of Mexico did the same. The unanimous request would be renewed years later to Pope Pius XI, who was so kind in the matters concerning Mexico. The reasons given on these different occasions insist on the nexus between the Virgin of Guadalupe and the history of Evangelization of America and the Philippines.

Those repeated requests were welcomed on the part of the Holy See. The Virgin of Guadalupe found greater response every day, a more precise historical reference in all Latin American Episcopal documents and in the Pontifical Magistracy. Has She been and is She a mere ideological position or a reference to a precise historical fact and therefore of objective value?

In these last years it has been a constant preoccupation of the ecclesiastical hierarchy to want to accurately indicate the historical roots of the evangelizing path followed in this continent, of the method used by God in this concrete salvific history, of its constants and their meaning. Thus, during the years that preceded the celebrations of the Fifth Centennial of the beginnings of Evangelization in America, they wanted to go deeper into the issue; the founding Evangelization in Latin America was the subject, for example, of a seminar that the CELAM and the Episcopal Commission of Education and Culture of Mexico celebrated then. John Paul II, on March 9, 1983, invited the Latin American bishops reunited in Port-au-Prince to commit themselves

---

[3] All the documentation on the subject is in *Álbum de la Coronación de la Sma. Virgen de Guadalupe*, Mexico 1895.

to this issue. On October 12, 1984, he confirmed this mission by opening a novena to them of the Fifth Centennial in Santo Domingo, on the land where the Cross of Christ stood for the first time and where the "Our Father" and the "Hail Mary" were prayed for the first time in a "new Evangelization."[4] A new perspective on the historical data was needed for this, with a realistic historical point of view, without ideologies.

One such realistic historiographical perspective we found already studied in the meeting of the CELAM on "Popular Religiousness" (in Bogota in 1976) and manifested in the document of the Latin American Episcopacy in Puebla in 1978, that proposed a renewed Evangelization appealing to the "Christian memory of our people," because "with deficiencies, and in spite of the always present sin, the faith of the Church has sealed the soul of Latin America, marked its essential historical identity, constituted a cultural matrix on the continent, of which new peoples were born. It is the Gospel, incarnated in our people, which congregates them in a cultural historical originality which we call Latin America. That identity is symbolized very luminously in the *mestiza* countenance of Mary of Guadalupe, who rose at the beginning of Evangelization."[5]

Nevertheless, some writers, influenced by diverse ideologies, as early as the nineteenth century to the present time have wanted to eliminate the Guadalupan Event in diverse ways: trying to turn it into a kind of cultural mask of a religious syncretism, a continuation of old rites under new forms and appearances, reducing it to a simple cultural symbol, imagining it as part of a catechistic "theater" instrument fabricated by the evangelizing friars, or turning it into a Catholic religious symbol created by a *criollismo* to sustain their legitimate patriotism.

Sometimes, without trying, the opinions of the authors who maintain in several ways these diverse attitudes have cooperated to spread explicitly, or implicitly, the image of three original sins that would weigh, according to them, on the history of the Catholic Evangelization of Latin America: the Conquest, Latin American Catholicism, and the crossing of races, seen as a degenerating mixture of racial components opposing the racial purity that would occur in other places on the continent, and that in Catholic countries has been brutally destroyed.[6] For that reason some Protestants have considered Latin

---

[4] John Paul II, in *Insegnamenti di Giovanni Paolo II*, Vatican Ed. Bookstore. VIII/2, 88s.

[5] Conferencia del Episcopado Latinoamericano (Celam), *Documentos de Puebla*, rm. 445–446.

[6] Cfr. on these positions the acute analysis of the well-known Peruvian literary Mario Vargas Llosa about the Peruvian case, but with many references to Mexico and other Latin American countries: Vargas Llosa, Mario, *La utopía arcaica. José María Arguedas y las ficciones del indigenismo*, Ed. FCE, Mexico 1996.

American Catholicism as a confused syncretistic form of pre-Christian traditional religiousness and a poorly assimilated Catholicism. They even try to explain here the roots of Latin American political and economical problems.

Because of such positions the Guadalupan Event is neither understood nor accepted in its real meaning. The proponents of these positions exclude from their analysis some of the conditions that must be respected as actuality in all study of historical fact and in its respective analysis: realism (the method must be imposed by the object of our study and not by a previous ideology), rationality, and morality. To present the Guadalupan Event as a poetic, idyllic, or dramatically ideological fact immediately, without resorting seriously to the historical data or documenting what has happened in this way, the meaning of the miracle of Guadalupe would therefore be totally unrealistic. The historian must not say something that is false, but must reminded either hide something that is true, as Cicero said: It is necessary to approach facts with the humility of truth, without false triumph or modesty, only looking at the truth.[7]

The Miracle of the Guadalupe Virgin and Juan Diego

What has been and continues to be the miracle of Guadalupe? After the immediate first stage of rejecting the Indigenous cultures and imposing Christianity, explicable if you consider the formation and the cultural temperament of the missionaries, an enculturation of the faith was obtained, overcoming the walls of division and racial hatred through intense intermarrying which gave birth to the Mexican people in a literal sense, and to the Latin American in a figurative sense. The most perfect symbol of this encounter is indeed precisely the one of Guadalupe, carried out by Juan Diego, which Latin American bishops, reunited in Puebla in 1979,[8] expressly recognized as a birth certificate or as the seal of this alliance. Without the miracle of the Gospel, expressed in force in Guadalupe, this alliance would have been impossible; even the self-criticism that today is made of the same evangelizing process initiated by the missionaries after the famous homily of the Dominican Friar Antonio de Montesinos on the fourth Sunday of Advent of 1511 in Santo Domingo ("La Española"), would have never occurred. The

---

[7] Cfr. John Paul II, "Discurso para la apertura del 'Novenario' de años promovido por el CELAM: Fidelidad al pasado, mirada a los desafíos del presente, compromiso para una nueva evangelización," Sto. Domingo, October 12, 1984, in *Insegnamenti di Giovanni Paolo II*, Libreria Ed. Vaticana, VII/2, p. 889.

[8] Conferencia del Episcopado Latinoamericano (Celam), *Documentos de Puebla*, nn. 445–446.

Guadalupan Event, with all its historical complexity, aids in understanding the gift of this evangelizing process. It is not easy for a historian to distinguish the scope of nature and the scope of Grace. Normally historians tend to separate history and theology distinctly as two parallel roads in two levels that do not touch or do not interfere with each other. The true danger in a partial reading of the history shaped by Christians is in not distinguishing between nature and Grace. As already Saint Augustine advised against Pelagius, "Common to all is nature; not so is grace. . . . That one receives nature must not be refuted as grace." This not distinguishing allows another "nondistinction," between the facts of the world and the particular history generated by a particular event; the consequence is the sacralization of human history. Not too long ago some Catholics even identified the history of Grace with the struggle of classes in a Marxist-matrix influence.

These identifications destroy not only the faith that is born precisely as an encounter, as a particular event which is humanly impossible or at least incomprehensible at first, and nevertheless true. They also destroy the freedom of God to shape history according to His own modalities, like using an individual to communicate a Grace and to construct the universal history of salvation (the common method that we see used by God in all the Bible and that has its culmination in the Incarnation of the Word in the womb of Mary of Nazareth). It also destroys the real freedom of man to welcome or to adhere totally to the Grace that God offers to him. If it were not thus, the true drama of the person would not exist; only a type of unstoppable, determined, and fatidic historical march would occur, with no responsibility on the part of man. The consequence would be to take away from the Mystery of the Incarnation of the Son of God, Jesus Christ, in one time in history, in a concrete place in Palestine, in the womb of the woman, Mary of Nazareth, in its historical concretion; Most Holy Virgin Mary would be reduced to the pure symbol of "Virgin Mother," nonexistent in history. Everything that does not enter this dimension is reduced to a pure symbol, without the context of a real event, to an abstract story or a comfortable invention to support preconceived theses. In the same order, miracles, talents, prophecies, "charismas" (gifts given by the Holy Spirit to the Church), and all other possibility of divine intervention in history is denied a priori.

On the contrary, Christianity is always a historical occurrence in its diverse manifestations. It is always a particular event; precisely because of its particularity, it surpasses all determinist and fatalistic conceptions of history—it creates freedom. Christianity thus understood promotes an awareness of what is meant by Grace. The power of God is revealed by facts and events that constitute a new reality within the world, a live reality, in movement and, therefore, an exceptional and unforeseeable event in man's history. Under this perspective it is necessary to read many pages of the history of the Church; particularly in America we read thus the records of the Guadalupan Event.

The Meaning of the Guadalupan Event

The historical records speak to us of a dramatic situation at the beginning of the history of Evangelization in America: the hopelessness and tragic frustration on the part of the Indigenous and the difficulty in transmitting the Evangelical Announcement on the part of the Spanish missionaries. Then something unexpected happens: one of those interventions of the Lord in time, an unexpected Grace, of which the history of the Church is rich.

According to Indigenous, mixed, and "Spanish" sources, in the first days of December 1531, on the hill of Tepeyac (or Tepeyacac), a hill consecrated to the cult of the Aztec goddess Tonantzin and a cultural place according to the religious conceptions of the old Mexican people, near the great Mexican lake, the Mother of God appears to an Indigenous, a Christian neophyte about 50 years old, Juan Diego Cuauhtlatoatzin ("Cuauhtlatoa" in the Náhuatl language means "the eagle who speaks"), who was going to the city or the Franciscan mission. Juan Diego may have been one of the first Indigenous baptized by the first Franciscan missionaries of Mexico. The visionary was the messenger of Holy Mary to Zumárraga, the bishop-elect of Mexico, who asked for proof of the authenticity of the message. The proof that the Virgin gave him is well known: the roses gathered by Juan Diego on that hill, in his *tilma*, where the creole mixed Image of Our Lady would be painted by Herself. That Image has been since then a missionary catechism through the cultural elements of the valley of Anáhuac. In the transformed *tilma* of Juan Diego the Indigenous could read the meaning of that Event. It was like the birth of a new era and the beginning of a new Christian cultural tradition, totally enculturated in the Mexican people, and more in the Latin American people.

A question arises and it prevails immediately: Do we find ourselves before a historical event, regardless of the poetic and cultural elements around it, or only a cultural symbol created for Evangelization purposes, and later, patriotic ones? The answer to this question has also been the objective of the historical investigation carried out on the occasion of the canonization process for Juan Diego and whose documentation is presented in the book *The Encounter of the Virgin of Guadalupe and Juan Diego.*

The Guadalupan Event was the response from God to a humanly impossible situation: the relationship between the world of the Indigenous and that of the newly arrived Spaniards. The Christian Indigenous, Juan Diego, was the link between the non-Christian, old Mexican world and the Christian missionary proposition which arrived through the Hispanic mediation. The result was the enlightenment of a new Christianized people. Juan Diego was neither a Spaniard arriving with Cortés, nor a Spanish Franciscan missionary; he was a native belonging to that old world rich in culture. A sculptural group that today can be seen on the hill of Tepeyac, where we find in contemplation before Holy Mary of Guadalupe the Indigenous Juan Diego, the Bishop Juan de Zumárraga, and other men, women, and children, almost in a kind of procession contemplating Holy Mary, expresses with a strong plasticity this fact and this message. This is the particularity of the ecclesial mediation of Juan Diego, the "ambassador envoy of Holy Mary of Guadalupe," as the *Nican Mopohua* calls him. Juan Diego was therefore the missionary of this encounter in which Christ was to become embodied in a concrete cultural humanity through the mediation of Holy Mary. One of the 12 Franciscan Apostles of Mexico, Friar Toribio Paredes de Benavente, Motolinia (Motolinia meaning "the poor man"), in one of his letters to the king of Spain saw the encounter as humanly impossible, if it were not by the work of the Grace of God. For that reason the Indigenous neophytes invoked the friars along with Virgin Mary for such a miracle. The miracle was to happen as a totally unimaginable and unexpected Grace and it would be a liberating reality.

Those two worlds, until then strangers to each other and enemies, with all premises for hatred or the fatalistic acceptance of defeat on the part of one, for the scorn or the exploitation on the part of others, for ambitions and rivalries and civil wars among all, began to recognize in Holy Mary of Guadalupe the Mother of all. She requested through Juan Diego to be constructed in that place a house, home for all. Thus the Christian faith totally took root in the Mexican cultural world. It is the birth of the Mexican and Latin American Catholic people. Forgetting this story can always produce new ruptures and old antagonisms. Only the Christian Event can constantly illuminate a people. Guadalupe and Juan Diego remind us of this Event.

The Consequences of Such an Encounter

The consequences of such an encounter in the history of Christianity are numerous and important. First of all, from the statistical point of view, Catholics of Spanish and Portuguese languages constitute the statistical majority of members of the Catholic Church. The fact of the missionary methodology in the history of Christianity is that the Christian missionaries belonged to the side of the invaders and had to defend the human rights of the invaded. Also, being consistent with the Gospel, frank and strong in its message, the Catholic missionaries did not choose one of these two worlds over the other. They presented the Christian Event as a significant fact for both. In this, God mysteriously arranged the Guadalupan Event as a confirmation of the essential methodology of the Christian announcement and the effective impulse of the same in those initial dramatic moments. This demonstrates to us how Christianity is a phenomenon capable of dialogue with man from the first moment in which it makes contact with a human situation, dramatic as it may be.

There is a mural painted in the beginning of the seventeenth century in the old Franciscan convent of Ozumba that represents the beginning of the Christian history of Mexico: the arrival of "12 Apostles," Franciscan missionaries in Tenochtitlán, in June 1524, the three adolescent Indigenous protomartyrs of the American continent, the Apparitions of Holy Mary of Guadalupe, and the Indigenous Juan Diego with the holy halo. Putting aside a discussion on the date of this painting's composition, the painting clearly shows the unity and continuity of this initial Christian history of Mexico.

The Image of Holy Mary before whom the Indigenous Juan Diego and the Archbishop Friar Juan de Zumárraga knelt together, is the link that was to unite both worlds represented there. This is the aspect that Pope John Paul II emphasized in his second visit to Mexico in the month of May in 1990 when proposing Juan Diego as the authentic apostle of his people and messenger of Holy Mary of Guadalupe. This is the meaning of his canonization.

The miracle performed at Guadalupe created in Latin America, and Mexico in particular, such awareness of Christian tenets that it has become known for having numerous incidents, frequently dramatic, in its history. In spite of everything, we see how the Virgin Holy Mary of Guadalupe keeps a people alive and gives it the real dimension of its destiny. The liberal Mexican thinker Ignacio Manuel Altamirano recognized this in his own way:

> If there is a truly old, national, and universally accepted truth in Mexico, it is the one that refers to the Apparition of the Virgin of Guadalupe. . . . There is nobody, either among the wildest Indigenous, nor among the most ignorant *mestizos* that doesn't know about the Apparition of the Virgin of Guadalupe. . . . Not only do all the races that live on Mexican ground coincide with Her, but what is more surprising still is that all the political parties which have covered the country with blood during half a century do also. . . . Lately, in the worst cases, devotion to the Mexican Virgin is the only tie that unites them . . . the deep social division . . . also disappears, only before the altars of the Vir-

gin of Guadalupe. There they are all even, *mestizos* and Indigenous, conservatives and liberals, aristocrats and plebeians, poor and rich. . . . The authors (of the Guadalupan tradition) were the Spanish Bishop Zumárraga and the Indigenous Juan Diego who agreed together in the social banquet, in the occasion of the Apparition, and who appear in the popular imagination, kneeling before the Virgin on the same step. . . . In every Mexican there is always a more or less great dose of Juan Diego.[9]

The Spaniard Zumárraga and the Indigenous Juan Diego kneeling before the Virgin on the same step, and the part of Juan Diego in each Mexican and each Latin American, synthesize the dimensions of the Guadalupan Event and the consequences of that encounter, which is that the Christian Event still continues to grow against all the attempts to lead it to ideological reductions, ruptures, or oppositions.

Dr. Eduardo Chávez's work, based on the historical records widely studied and presented in other previous publications among which *El encuentro de la Virgen de Guadalupe y Juan Diego* [*The Encounter of the Virgin of Guadalupe and Juan Diego*] stands out (already in its fourth edition), offers a wonderful synthesis of the messenger of Holy Mary, easy and pleasant in its reading, absent of novel brushstrokes and with the information offered by strict historical documentation, frequently mentioned in the various essential notes of the book. The book is for that reason, and without false pretenses, a noble instrument to approach the Guadalupan Fact and its meaning through the figure of its messenger ("prophet," in the sense of this Biblical word that means "to speak in name of another one") and apostle (which in its evangelical meaning is "the one that is chosen to be sent"), the Indigenous Juan Diego Cuauhtlatoatzin.

R. P. Dr. Fidel González, MCCJ

---

[9] Ignacio Manuel Altamirano, *La Celebración de Guadalupe*, Mexico 1884, pp. 1130–33.

Commentaries

Little can be said after the excellent introductions by Norberto Cardinal Rivera, Archbishop of Mexico, active in the canonization cause for Juan Diego Cuauhtlatoatzin, and by R. P. Dr. Fidel González, MCCJ., President of the Historical Commission, named by the Congregation for the Cause of the Saints in order to review everything with regard to this case. Cardinal Rivera points out the historical veracity of the studies, while Dr. González, in his prologue, outlines the essence of the circumstances, now and at that time, in which Juan Diego's life and his canonization have to be situated.

We all know about the discussion of whether this is a real person: a man of flesh and bone that lived in our world, faced problems and situations like ours or worse, and solved them with exemplary virtue, or on the contrary, is he a fiction, a character in a beautiful story, a Christian or patriotic symbol, the protagonist of a nice myth, founder of American Christianity, or later, of the Mexican patriotic conscience?

Father Fidel González's question touches directly on the basis of the issue: "Do we find ourselves before a historical event, regardless of the poetic and cultural elements around it, or only a cultural symbol created for Evangelization purposes, and later, patriotic ones?" which he himself answers: "The Guadalupan Event was the response from God to a humanly impossible situation: the relationship between the world of the Indigenous and that of the newly arrived Spaniards. The Christian Indigenous, Juan Diego, was the link between the non-Christian, old Mexican world and the Christian missionary proposition which arrived through the Hispanic mediation. The result was the enlightenment of a new Christianized people."

These new people are not only "new" in their Christianity, they are new in their very anthropological essence because they became the Mexico of "mestizos," children born of Indigenous and Spanish parents, profoundly human, not only wounded by sin and its consequences, but also enriched by the divine favor to live out their love through the maternal tenderness of our Most Holy Mary of Guadalupe, love to which She corresponds with an uncontainable fervor, passed on to us after that founding protagonist, Juan Diego Cuauhtlatoatzin, about whom everyone speaks, and with whom we all identify in some way, but, paradoxically, whom few of us know.

This book by the Pbr. Dr. Eduardo Chávez, who as Postulator of the Cause has obtained the Canonization of Juan Diego, centers on his concrete figure, contributing with scientific evidence, as Cardinal Rivera points out, "what we know for sure about this admirable man," as a historical concrete person, as well as in his Christian holiness, manifested by his virtues and life. However, it is by all means pertinent to note that one would not understand these virtues and life if we did not frame them within the dramatic and most particular circumstances of his world, or better said, of both his worlds, because he was born, grew up, lived, matured, and almost reached old age in his ancestral American Indigenous culture, and then must have had a very dramatic and painful adjustment, to be born again, grow up, live, and reach the maturity of his exemplary Christian holiness.

Thus, the only thing left is to recommend the readers of this work, for a better evaluation of this unique person presented here, to turn also to the sources, both Indigenous as well as Spanish, or perhaps another book, also by Dr. Eduardo Chávez in collaboration with Dr. Fidel González and myself: *El Encuentro de la Virgen de Guadalupe y Juan Diego*, which is the summary that the Congregation for the Cause of the Saints presents, applying scientific methodology of the convergence of these documental sources, proofs they gathered, analyzed, and approved. This book has not been translated yet; we hope that soon it will be.

So, Juan Diego is neither a myth nor a legend, but a historical person by whom we have known the message of Our Lady of Guadalupe. He is one of the main protagonists of the model Event for "*a perfectly inculturated Evangelization.*"[1]

Villa de Guadalupe, June 29, 2005
Mgr. José Luis Guerrero
Director of the Instituto Superior de Estudios Guadalupanos

---

[1] John Paul II, *Ecclesia in America*, 11.

~

Introduction:
Juan Diego, Messenger of Hope

In order to draw close to a humble man, as was Juan Diego, one of the main protagonists of the Guadalupan Event, it was necessary to go deeper into the various investigations that have taken place for centuries: to look in libraries and archives in various parts of the world; to analyze commentaries and studies which have been deepening from different aspects this event; to investigate from the continuous and uninterrupted oral tradition that has been kept in the memory of the people to historical documentary sources of great importance, such as maps, codexes, testaments, songs, old narrations such as the *Nican Mopohua* and *Nican Motecpana*, *Información de 1556*, *Informaciones Jurídicas de 1666*, the important manuscripts of the first missionary friars, and many other documents that contribute very valuable news and information about this great Event. Then we processed all this with a historical scientific method that proposes the convergence of the historical documental sources.

If it is not possible to close off a supernatural phenomenon, such as the Apparition of the Virgin Mary, in temporal history, it is possible to demonstrate evidence of the manifestations of such an event, and also possible to know the people who lived that moment, their lives, occupations, customs, education, behavior, society, and so on. All this leaves a clear trace and marks history. If it is not possible to measure the degree of faith or the grade of conversion within the heart and soul of a human being, it is possible to know and confirm some of their expressions through history.

In December 1531, what is called the Guadalupan Event took place. In other words, Our Lady of Guadalupe appeared to Juan Diego Cuauhtlatoatzin (which means "eagle that speaks"),[1] a humble Indigenous, from the ethnic Indigenous *Chichimecas*. He was born around 1474, in Cuauhtitlán, which at that time belonged to the kingdom of Texcoco, and was baptized by the first Franciscans in approximately 1524.[2] In 1531 he was a mature man, about 57 years old. He edified others with his testimony and his word; in fact, they would go up to him, as we shall see later, so that he would intercede for the needs, petitions, and prayers of his people, because "everything that he asked for was granted by the Lady from Heaven."[3] Juan Diego never neglected the opportunity to narrate the manner in which the marvelous encounter with Holy Mary of Guadalupe occurred, and the privilege that Her message had been.

He was an authentic missionary. Because of the extraordinary encounter which he experienced, Juan Diego is called different names that marked his mission and his condition: the humble and obedient Indigenous, the good Indigenous, the good Christian, the Holy Man, the Pilgrim, the humble Ambassador of the Virgin, Our Lady's Visionary, Holy Mary of Guadalupe's Messenger. For that reason the simple people recognized him and venerated him as a true saint, and used him as an example for their children. This coincides with the document *Nican Motecpana*, where it tells us about the exemplary life of Juan Diego: "If only we would serve Her and withdraw ourselves from all the disturbing things of this world, so that we too could obtain the eternal joy of Heaven!"[4] Juan Diego died in 1548,[5] a little after the death of another im-

---

[1] "Cuauhtlatoatzin," Juan Diego´s Indigenous name, Cfr. Carlos de Sigüenza y Góngora, *Piedad Heroica de don Fernando Cortés*, Talleres de la Librería Religiosa, second edition of "La Semana Católica," Mexico 1898, p. 31. Also in Xavier Escalada, S.J., *Enciclopedia Guadalupana*, Ed. Enciclopedia Guadalupana, Mexico 1997, T. V.

[2] "Testimonio del P. Luis Becerra Tanco," in *Informaciones Jurídicas de 1666*, AHBG, Ramo Histórica, f. 158r: "and having been baptized Juan Diego in the year 1524, which is when the religious of Mister Saint Francis came (and whose parish he belonged to). It is certain that he was baptized at the age of 48."

[3] Fernando de Alva Ixtlilxóchitl, *Nican Motecpana*, AHCM; published in Ernesto de la Torre Villar and Ramiro Navarro de Anda, *Testimonios Históricos Guadalupanos*, Ed. FCE, Mexico 1982, p. 305.

[4] Fernando de Alva Ixtlilxóchitl, *Nican Motecpana*, p. 305.

[5] Cfr. Fernando de Alva Ixtlilxóchitl, *Nican Motecpana*, pp. 304–5. Also in Xavier Escalada, S.J., *Enciclopedia Guadalupana*, Ed. Enciclopedia Guadalupana, Mexico 1997, T.V. Also in *Anales de Puebla y Tlaxcala* or *Anales de los Sabios Tlaxcaltecas* or *Anales de Catedral*, AHMNA, AAMC, No. 18, 1, which says, "*Year of 1548, omomiquili in Juan Diego in oquimotenextilitzino in tlazo Cihuapili Guadalupe México*"(Year of 1548, Juan Diego died honorably, to whom the precious Lady of Guadalupe appeared). Also in *Analejo de Bartolache* or *Manuscrito de la Universidad*, BNAH, Archivo Histórico, Archivo de Sucs. Gómez de Orozco, which says: "Texcia 1548, Omomiquili Juan Diego in oquimonextilli in tlazocihuapili Guadalupe México. Otecihuilo niztac tépetl" (Tecpatl year, 1548 Juan Diego died honorably, [to whom] the Beloved Lady of Guadalupe appeared. It hailed on the white hill). Also in "Testimonio del P. Luis Becerra Tanco," in *Informaciones Jurídicas de 1666*, f. 158r: "Juan Diego died at the age of 74 in the year 1548." This was also declared and confirmed by Jerónimo de León, Gaspar de Praves, and Pedro Ponce de León, all of them great and important men, reporters for Luis Becerra Tanco; "for example, it is known that Pedro Ponce de León

portant protagonist of the Event, the Archbishop of Mexico, Friar Juan de Zumárraga. As Fernando de Alva Ixtlilxóchitl pointed out: "After serving the Lady of Heaven there for 16 years, he died in 1548, at the time that the Bishop died. . . . He was also buried in the temple. He was 74 years old."[6]

All of the successors of Friar Juan de Zumárraga have uninterruptedly promoted the Guadalupan Event. Likewise, the Episcopacy of Mexico has been one of the strongest supporters, motivating scientific investigation as well as the Evangelization and the popular devotion in an integral pastoral. The Episcopacy of Mexico declared on October 12, 2001, "The truth of the Apparitions of the Most Holy Virgin Mary to Juan Diego on the hill of Tepeyac has been, from the beginning of Evangelization to the present, a constant tradition and a deep-rooted conviction among us Mexican Catholics, not unfounded but based on documents of the time and on rigorous official investigations verified in the following century, by persons who had lived with those that were witnesses and protagonists in the construction of the first Hermitage."[7] Further on it is mentioned that "We consider it also our duty to manifest that the history of the apparitions needs to go with the recognition of the privileged visionary speaker of the Virgin Mary."[8]

The popes, understanding the great importance of the Guadalupan Event, have granted graces, privileges, and indulgences to the Guadalupan Sanctuary of the Tepeyac. One of the most antique documentary examples is the one of 1573, where Pope Gregory XIII[9] granted graces and plenary indulgences to the faithful who visited the Church of the Blessed Virgin Mary of Guadalupe to recite there pious prayers.[10] This was only 25 years after the death of Juan Diego, and in 1576, the pope revalidated and prolonged these graces.[11] The Archbishop of Mexico at the time, Pedro Moya de Contreras,

---

was an Indigenous, born in 1546 and died in 1626, who became a priest and graduated with a degree in Theology in the Pontific University of Mexico, and served in the parish of Zumpahuacan. He was an expert in the Náhuatl culture and wrote a valuable book which describes his survival at the time. This book is the second part of the *Chimalpopoca Codex* or *Anales de Cuauhtitlán*, dated 1892. The author was a friend and reporter for Becerra Tanco, one of the first writers of Guadalupan History." *Diccionario Porrúa. Biografía y Geografía de Mexico*, Ed. Porrúa, Mexico 1995, p. 2768.

[6] Fernando de Alva Ixtlilxóchitl, *Nican Montecpana*, p. 305. Also the death of Friar Juan de Zumárraga in the *Codex Vaticanus*, in BAV, Fondo Vaticano, Vat. Lat. 3738, f. 94r.

[7] Mexican Episcopacy. *El Acontecimiento Guadalupano hoy en el aniversario de la dedicación de la actual Basílica de Guadalupe y el traslado de la Sagrada Imagen*, México, D. F., October 12, 2001, no. 3.

[8] Mexican Episcopacy, *El Acontecimiento Guadalupano hoy*, no. 9.

[9] Gregory XIII (1572–1585).

[10] Gregory XIII, *Ut Deiparae semper virginis*, Vatican Secret Archives, Sec. Brev. 69, ff. 537v–538v; 70, ff. 532v–533v.

[11] Everardo Mercuriano, Gen., *Letter to the Archbishop of México, Pedro Moya de Contreras*, Rome, March 12, 1576, ARSI, Mexican No. 1, f. 9r; Published in Félix Zubillaga (Editor), *Monumenta Mexicana, Monumenta Historica Societatis Iesu*, Rome 1956, T. I, 1570–1580, pp. 192–193.

thanked him explicitly.[12] Another example of the devotion of the pontiffs to Our Lady of Guadalupe of the Tepeyac was when Pope Benedict XIV granted, in 1754, proper Mass and Office to celebrate Holy Mary of Guadalupe on December 12, extending that privilege to the rest of the Spanish territories on July 2, 1757. This was after extensive studies, inspections, and scientific investigations were performed.

Up until now the pontiffs have recognized that the Guadalupan Event has left an evident sign of a fact that occurred in history and which is manifesting Evangelization fruits. Pope Pius XII, for example, offered an Allocution for the fiftieth anniversary of the Pontific Coronation of the Image of Our Lady of Guadalupe of Mexico, which was transmitted by radio on October 12, 1945. The Holy Father said, "And so it happened, as the Hour of the Lord sounded for the numerous regions of Anahuac. The world had just opened up when, near the lake of Texcoco, the miracle bloomed. On the 'tilma' of the poorest Juan Diego, as the tradition states, paint brushes that were not from down here, left the sweetest Image painted, and which the corrosive work of the centuries would respect marvelously."[13]

Also, on October 12, 1961, the celebration of the fiftieth anniversary of the Patronage of the Virgin of Guadalupe over all of Latin America, Pope John XXIII declared:

> The always Virgin Saint Mary, Mother of the true God, for Whom one lives, pours out Her tenderness and maternal delicateness on the hill of Tepeyac, trusting to the Indigenous Juan Diego Her message with some roses that fell from his "tilma," while upon it Her sweetest portrait, that no human hands painted, remains. Thus, Our Lady wanted to continue demonstrating Her calling as a Mother: She, with Her *mestiza* face, between the Indigenous Juan Diego and the Bishop Zumárraga, as if to symbolize a kiss of two races. . . . First Mother and Patroness of Mexico, then of America and of the Philippines;[14] and so the historical sense of Her message was acquiring its fullness, while She opened Her arms to all horizons in a universal desire of love.[15]

---

[12] *Letter from the Archbishop of México, Pedro Moya de Contreras, to Pope Gregory XIII*, Vatican Secret Archives, AA-Arm. I. XVIII, s. f.

[13] Pius XII, "Alocución Radiomensaje," October 12, 1945, in AAS, XXXVII (1945) 10, pp. 265–66.

[14] Our Lady of Guadalupe was declared Patroness of the Philippines on July 16, 1935. Cfr. PIUS XI, Apostolic Letter "B.V. sub titulo de Guadalupa Insularum Philippinarum Coelestis Patrona Declaratur," in AAS, XXVIII (1936) 2, pp. 63–64.

[15] John XXIII, "Ad christifideles qui ex ómnibus Americae nationibus Conventui Mariali secundo Mexici interfuerunt," for the fiftieth anniversary of, Rome, October 12, 1961, in AAS, LIII (1961) 12, pp. 685–87.

Pope Paul VI, on October 12, 1970, the seventy-fifth anniversary of the Pontific Coronation of the Image, exclaimed, "The devotion to the Most Holy Virgin of Guadalupe, so deeply rooted in the heart of every Mexican and so intimately united to Her historical nation after four centuries, continues preserving among you, Her vitality and Her value, and it must be a constant and particular demand of an authentic Christian renovation for everyone."[16]

Pope John Paul II has always declared the great importance of the Guadalupan Event as the historical fact which has given fruits of salvation. Since his first pastoral visit to Mexico in 1979, he was direct and precise when he spoke about Holy Mary of Guadalupe as the one who lit the road to Evangelization. He said on that occasion, "Our Lady of Guadalupe, venerated in Mexico and in all the countries as the Mother of the Church in Latin America, is for me joy and a fountain of Hope. Star of Evangelization, let Her be your guide."[17] Also, for the Holy Father, Juan Diego performed a very important mission at the beginning of this Event. The Holy Father said, "Since the Indigenous Juan Diego talked about the sweet Lady of Tepeyac, You, Mother of Guadalupe, enter, in a true sense, into the Christian life of the people of Mexico."[18]

For a long time, the bishops of Mexico as well as of Latin America had been asking for the canonization of Juan Diego, but it was not until the Archbishop of Mexico, Ernesto Corripio Ahumada, started the procedures that the process was initiated. On January 7, 1984, in the National Basilica of Guadalupe, he presided over the ceremony in which the Canonic Process for the Servant of God, Juan Diego, the humble Indigenous messenger of the Virgin of Guadalupe, was begun. He concluded his procedures on March 23, 1986. A short time later all of the documentation was turned in to the Congregation for the Causes of the Saints, which approved the work.[19] In addition, Archbishop Corripio united 21 specialists in history, investigators and experts on the Guadalupan Event, myself among them, with the abbot of that time—Mgr. Guillermo Schulenburg—to discuss all the aspects in favor as well as against the Cause for Juan Diego. This took place on October 9, 1989, in the conference hall of the Archdiocese of Mexico. It was important

[16] Paul VI, "Allocution Radio Television," October 12, 1970, in AAS, LXII (1970) 10, p. 681.

[17] John Paul II, "Allocution for the III General Conference of the Latin American Episcopacy," January 28, 1979, in AAS, LXXI 3, p. 205.

[18] John Paul II, "Alocución a los Obispos de América Latina," First Apostolic Trip to Mexico, Mexico D.F. January 27, 1979, in AAS, LXXI (1979) 3, p. 173.

[19] Cfr. Letter from the Congregation for the Causes of the Saints to Ernesto Cardinal Corripio Ahumada, June 8, 1982, Prot. N. 1408–2/1982, pp. XVI–XXIV; XIX.

to know all the different points of view in order to analyze not only Juan Diego's personality but also the opportunity to continue the Cause. One could express whatever opinion with total freedom, either in favor or against, and the conclusion was: "No opinion was uttered against the physical existence of the Servant of God. His reputation, virtues and veneration were deeply discerned and confirmed positive."[20]

The *Positio*, approved in 1990, was elaborated according to the norms and guidelines of the Congregation for the Causes of the Saints,[21] after having gone through a long road of examinations and courts, especially those of historians, theologians, bishops, and cardinals who confirmed that Juan Diego was venerated from "time immemorial." This has been manifested by all types of objects, such as images and designs of Juan Diego in which he is represented with a halo on chalices, pulpits, altars, paintings of miracle testimonies, and offerings. There are several documents which say that Juan Diego was a good and holy Christian Indigenous, as we shall see later. In 1746, Cayetano de Cabrera y Quintero, in his book *Escudo de Armas*, expressed it thus: "Even the same Indigenous who would visit the Sanctuary trusted in the prayers of their countryman, alive and later dead and buried. They saw him as an intercessor before Most Holy Mary to obtain their petitions."[22]

On April 9, 1990, in the Decree of Beatification, the Holy Father John Paul II recognized the life of holiness and veneration attributed to Juan Diego from time immemorial. During his second Apostolic visit to Mexico, on May 6, the Holy Father presided in the Basilica of Guadalupe over the solemn celebration in honor of the blessed Juan Diego, inaugurating the manner of liturgical veneration which should be rendered to the humble and obedient Indigenous, messenger of the Virgin of Guadalupe.

The Holy Father affirmed that

> Juan Diego is an example for all the faithful because he shows us that all the followers of Christ, whatever their condition or state, are called by the Lord to the perfection of holiness by which the Father is perfect, each in his own way.[23] Juan Diego, carefully obeying the momentum of Grace, faithfully followed his vocation and submitted totally to the will of God, according to the way in which he felt called by the Lord. Doing this was outstanding in his tender love for the Most Holy Virgin Mary, whom he held constantly present and vener-

---

[20] Joel Romero Salinas, *Juan Diego, su Peregrinar a los Altares*, Ed. Paulinas, Mexico 1992, p. 54.
[21] Cfr. *Relatio et Vota* of the Historical Consultants on June 30, 1990, and of the Theological Consultants on March 30, 1990.
[22] Cayetano de Cabrera y Quintero, *Escudo de Armas*, Imp. del Real, Mexico 1746, p. 345, no. 682.
[23] *Conc. Vat. II, Const. Dogm. Lumen Gentium*, no. 11.

ated as Mother, and he submitted himself to the care of Her house with a humble and filial attitude. It is not surprising that many faithful people saw him as a saint while he was still alive and asked him to help them with his prayers. This reputation of holiness continued after his death, so there are many testimonies of their veneration, which demonstrate sufficiently that Christians referred to him as a saint, and known as such, he was given the signs of veneration that are usually reserved for the Beatus and the Saints. This is also evident in the monuments, in which the figure of Juan Diego can be seen adorned with a halo and other signs of holiness. It is true that such signs of veneration were more apparent above all right after Juan Diego's death, but nobody can deny that they still continue until today. So for sure, there is congruent testimony of a peculiar veneration given without interruption to Juan Diego. Having many bishops and laical Christians, principally Mexicans, requested so, the Congregation for the Causes of the Saints tried to collect the documents which illustrate the life, virtues and reputation of the holiness of Juan Diego and they showed the veneration that he was given, which rightfully investigated, concluded with the *Positio* about the holiness of Juan Diego, of his virtues and veneration that was given him from immemorial time.[24]

The work of the Congregation for the Causes of the Saints is highly professional. The greatest specialists on the subject work there, doing all procedures in a meticulous and detailed manner, not leaving any doubt unclear, any question unanswered, even if it means going beyond the normal procedure as written. As in all the cases that have been presented along history, the Congregation did not neglect any of the doubts or objections that were presented in the Cause of the Canonization of Juan Diego. So it was arranged that, along with the Archdiocese of Mexico, a historical commission be formed, which would lead an investigation in accordance with the historical scientific method and under the norms of the Congregation. This commission was lead by P. Dr. Fidel González, doctor in history of the Church, consultant of the Congregation for the Causes of the Saints, professor of the Pontific Gregorian University and the Pontific Urbanian University, specialist in history of the Latin American Church; myself, P. Dr. Eduardo Chávez, doctor in history of the Church, academic director of studies at the Mexican Pontific College, member of the Mexican Society of Ecclesiastic History, founding member of the Superior Institute of Guadalupan Studies, and specialized investigator of the Archdiocese of Mexico; and Mgr. José Luis Guerrero, canon in the Basilica of Guadalupe, lawyer in civil and canonic law, investigator and professor, a man with a vast education and a

---

[24] AAS, LXXXII (1990), pp. 853–55.

great specialist in the Guadalupan Event, and director of the Superior Institute of Guadalupan Studies.

This historical commission collected all that was done for centuries, investigated again in the archives and libraries in various parts of the world, analyzed not only doubts and objections which some posed under their own interests, but also studied and analyzed the continuous and uninterrupted oral tradition which is still kept today in the minds of the people, to documental sources such as maps, codexes, annals, testimonies, songs, antique narrations, the so-called *Nican Mopohua* and *Nican Motecpana*, the *Información de 1556*, the *Informaciones Jurídicas de 1666*, the important writings of the first missionary friars, and many more documents. Just as doubts and objections were taken into consideration, so were the new contributions and affirmations in favor of this historical fact, coming from the most various investigators, scientists, and experts of the Guadalupan Event. The work was an effort of several years, analyzing, studying, and investigating under the historical scientific method, and putting every historical source in its proper value and nature in its convergence. Under the precise norms of the Congregation for the Causes of the Saints, the results of the scientific investigation were approved on October 28, 1998, stating and confirming the truth about the Guadalupan Event and about the mission of the humble Indigenous, Juan Diego, model of holiness, who after 1531 diffused the message of Our Lady of Guadalupe by his word and by the exemplary testimony of his life.

One more step was given, asking the Congregation that the essential and most important results of the investigation by the historical commission be published. Thanks to this the book, under the title *El Encuentro de la Virgen de Guadalupe y Juan Diego*,[25] was published in 1999.

The Congregation entrusted some doctors and professors in history of the Church from the most prestigious pontific universities, specialists in Mexico and Latin America, to analyze this book slowly and meticulously. Their acceptance was unanimously positive and laudatory, in the essence of the history of the Guadalupan Event, especially about Juan Diego, as well as about the scientific methodology used in the investigation.

P. Alberto Gutiérrez, S.J., Doctor in history of the Church, for example, declared,

This is a colossal effort to gather all the written and oral [traditions] documentation about the fact of the apparition of the Most Holy Virgin and the vi-

---

[25] Fidel González, Eduardo Chávez, and José Luis Guerrero, *El Encuentro de la Virgen de Guadalupe y Juan Diego*, Ed. Porrúa, Mexico 1999, XXXVIII, 564 pp. Currently, it is in its fourth edition.

sionary, Juan Diego Cuauhtlatoatzin. In addition to the exemplary file consultation, and as far as one may say, an exhaustive and vast bibliography on the subject of Guadalupe [in favor and against the apparitions and the existence of Juan Diego]. The documents of Indigenous, Spanish, and mixed origin are presented in order and without prejudice or premeditated selection or interpretation. I believe that it should be affirmed that these sources lead to an undeniable historical certainty about the fact of the Apparitions of the Virgin Mary to a real person, who was the Indigenous Juan Diego, not only because of their variety and convergence but also because of the transparent manner in which they are presented and contextualized.[26]

Another great specialist, professor and doctor in history of the Church, is P. Eutimio Sastre Santos, who after a long elaboration of all of the elements that compose his judgment of the investigation that took place, said in conclusion, "To the question, if with such documentation one can have a significant confirmation of the history of Juan Diego, I respond: Affirmative."[27]

P. Willi Henkel, one of the most well-known historians in the international circle, also gave his conclusions after the publication of the scientific investigation, as we mentioned, in the book *El Encuentro de la Virgen de Guadalupe y Juan Diego*. He affirmed strongly that

Whether the sources are Indigenous or Spanish, they show us that from the beginning of the second half of the sixteenth century, valid historical elements about the apparitions and the person of Juan Diego have existed. The book, *El Encuentro*, has presented sufficient sources. There has existed a continuity of oral and written traditions since 1531. The apparitions of Our Lady of Guadalupe were well known in the sixteenth century. Veneration grew in the course of time and arrived in Rome, where Pope Gregory XIII granted indulgences in 1573. In the course of the following centuries the veneration continued always to grow. Juan Diego is inseparably united to the veneration of Our Lady of Guadalupe. Such knowledge is based on solid history. Various Popes, like Gregory XIII, Benedict XIV, Leo XIII, and John Paul II have recognized and confirmed the veneration of Our Lady of Guadalupe. They have trusted the protection of the Latin American people to Our Lady of Guadalupe.[28]

---

[26] Alberto Gutiérrez, S.J., review of the book *El Encuentro de la Virgen de Guadalupe y Juan Diego*, by the authors Fidel González, Eduardo Chávez, and José Luis Guerrero, Ed. Porrúa, Mexico 1999, Rome, November 18, 1999, in the Archives of the Congregation for the Causes of the Saints.

[27] Eutimio Sastre Santos, review of the book *El Encuentro de la Virgen de Guadalupe y Juan Diego*, by the authors Fidel González, Eduardo Chávez, and José Luis Guerrero, Ed. Porrúa, Mexico 1999, Rome, November 2, 1999, in the Archives of the Congregation for the Causes of the Saints.

[28] Willi Henkel, review of the book *El Encuentro de la Virgen de Guadalupe y Juan Diego*, by the authors Fidel González, Eduardo Chávez, and José Luis Guerrero, Ed. Porrúa, Mexico 1999, Rome, November 6, 1999, in the Archives of the Congregation for the Causes of the Saints.

Several of the historical documents tell us about the importance of the Sanctuary of Guadalupe, the veneration of the Image that is impressed or stamped on the *tilma* of Juan Diego. They are also an important part of the convergence of the historical sources which tell us about the existence of Juan Diego, as well as his reputation of holiness, and must be taken into account. One can see the importance of this centenary devotion.

Certainly the pontiffs have confirmed along the centuries the importance of the Guadalupan Event, which marked history.

In 1999, Pope John Paul II affirmed again with great force the importance of the message of Guadalupe conveyed by Juan Diego and confirmed the perfect Evangelization that has been given to us by Our Mother, Mary of Guadalupe. The Pope declared: "And America, which has historically been and is a melting pot of people, has recognized in the *mestizo* countenance of the Virgin of Tepeyac, . . . in Holy Mary of Guadalupe, . . . a great example of Evangelization, perfectly enculturated. . . . For that reason, not only in the center and in the south but also in the north of the continent, the Virgin of Guadalupe is venerated as the Queen of all America."[29] The pope confirmed the force and the tenderness of God's message by way of the Star of Evangelization, Holy Mary of Guadalupe, and Her faithful, humble, and true messenger, Juan Diego, in whom She deposited all Her trust: a historical moment for the Evangelization of the people. The Holy Father reaffirmed that "The apparition of Mary to the Indigenous Juan Diego, on the hill of Tepeyac, in 1531, had a decisive repercussion on Evangelization. This influence goes beyond the limits of the Mexican nation, reaching out to all the continent. . . . Most Holy Mary is invoked as 'Patroness of all America and Star of the first and new Evangelization.'"[30]

In order to better understand this great Guadalupan Event and Juan Diego's mission, it is important to have in mind the context in which it took place, which was in a certain sense tragic but at the same time full of hope. In other words, amidst the tremendous Indigenous depression, in the dramatic moment of the conquest and the uneasy consciousness of the Spaniards of that time, a new nation arose. It was precisely at that moment that the devotion to the Virgin of Guadalupe and Her role in human history developed, and as Pope John Paul II saw it, made this Event a model of "per-

---

[29] John Paul II, *Ecclesia in America*, Mexico, January 22, 1999, Libreria Editrice Vaticana, Vatican City, 1999, no. 11, p. 20. The Holy Father literally quoted the *IV General Conference of the Latin American Episcopacy*, Santo Domingo, October 12, 1992, 24. Also see in *AAS*, 85 (1993) p. 826.

[30] John Paul II, *Ecclesia in America*, p. 20, no. 11.

fectly enculturated Evangelization." Her message is full of hope and Juan Diego was its bearer.

But let us enter, if only by means of some sketches, into the recognition of the initial steps that the Evangelization accomplished with the first friar missionaries, a little after the dramatic and shocking moments that the conquest signified.

CHAPTER ONE

∽

During the Trauma of the Conquest and the Death of Their Idols, the First Steps of Evangelization Were Being Given

Without a doubt, in the first effort to evangelize Mexico the work of the missionaries was extraordinary.[1] However, the trauma of the Conquest lasted, inevitably, a long time among the natives. The specialist in the Náhuatl culture, Miguel León-Portilla, tells us that "They who thought themselves invincible, the people of the sun, the most powerful in Middle America, had to accept their defeat. Their gods were dead, lost was their government and authority, fame and glory; the experience of the Conquest meant more than a tragedy, it was nailed in their souls and its memory became a trauma."[2] The echoes of the sad and gloomy *Canto Mexicano* sounded in the desolate Anáhuac:

> The cry spreads, the tears drop there in Tlatelolco.
> The Mexican left by water;
> They seem like women, the flight is general.

---

[1] Cfr. Friar Gerónimo de Mendieta, *Historia Eclesiástica Indiana*, Ed. Porrúa (=Col. Biblioteca Porrúa, no. 46), Mexico 1980. Also Friar Toribio Motolinia, *Historia de los Indios de la Nueva España*, Ed. Porrúa (=Col. "Sepan cuantos" no. 129), Mexico 1973. Also Friar Bernardino de Sahagún, *Historia General de las Cosas de la Nueva España*, Ed. Porrúa (=Col. "Sepan cuantos" no. 300) Mexico 1982.

[2] Miguel León-Portilla, *El Reverso de la Conquista*, Ed. Joaquín Mortiz, Mexico 1970, pp. 21–22.

Where can we go? Oh, friends! Then, was it true?
Now they abandon the city of Mexico.
The smoke is rising, the fog is spreading . . .
Cry my friends,
understand that with these facts
we have lost the Mexican nation.
The water is sour, the food is sour!
This is what the Giver of Life has done in Tlatelolco.

Thus, with great pain and profound depression, did the Indigenous nation
yell to the wind soon after the Conquest. Miguel León-Portilla says that "The
way in which the ancient nation of Mexico was lost is remembered with
dramatism."[3]

And with anguish, some Indigenous priests moaned:

What are we to do then,
we who are small men and mortals;
if we die, let us die;
if we perish, let us perish;
the truth is that the gods also died.[4]

Here the great work and the great challenge that the missionaries had to
face is summed up, since they had to do something so that the Indigenous
would survive and, at the same time, take away the Indigenous idols, which,
from the missionaries' perspective, were the fountain of their perdition.

Friar Gerónimo de Mendieta tells us about the preoccupation of the friars,
since the beginning of the Evangelization, in removing the idols from the Indigenous. The missionaries tried thousands of ways to make themselves understood but "neither the Indigenous understood what was told to them in
Latin, nor did their idolatries stop, nor were the Friars able to reprimand
them for it, nor to use convenient methods of getting rid of the idols because
they did not know their language. And this kept the missionaries very un-
happy and worried."[5] Mendieta wrote that the missionaries were convinced
that if the idolatry continued, their work would be in vain. They complained
that while the Indigenous were sent to construct houses for the Spaniards,
idolatry continued with no solution. The friars warned that "For this reason,
business was as usual, the idolatry remained; and, above all, we saw that,

[3] Miguel León-Portilla, *El Reverso*, p. 62.
[4] This is the answer of the wise Mexican priests to 12 Franciscans who arrived in 1524. Vatican
Secret Archives, Misc. Arm-I-91, f. 36r. Also in Miguel León-Portilla, *El Reverso*, p. 25.
[5] Friar Gerónimo de Mendieta, *Historia Eclesiástica*, p. 219.

while the temples of the idols remained, it was a waste of time and they worked in vain."[6]

The 12 Franciscans had not been in the New World one year when they decided, with great boldness, motivated by their religious fervor, that they themselves would destroy the temples and the idols, even if this cost their own lives. And so they did, with great determination, taking advantage of the darkness of the night and being helped by the children and the young people whom they catechized in their classes. On January 1, 1525, they started their religious destruction in Texcoco, and later continued in Mexico, Tlaxcala, and Huejozingo. Motolinia offers us details of that first "battle" against the idols:

> Idolatry was as big as ever, until the first day of 1525, which was on a Sunday. The greater number and biggest *teocallis*, temples of devils, were in Texcoco and it was also the fullest of idols. There were many popes and ministers. On that night, from 10 at night until daybreak, three Friars frightened and expelled all those who were in the devils' houses and halls. That day, after Mass, a talk was given, regretting the killings very much, and ordering them, on behalf of God and the King, not to do that again, otherwise they would be punished according to how God commanded such to be punished. This was the first battle against the devil, and then in Mexico and its surroundings, and in Coauthiclan [Cuauhtitlán].[7]

With this we can see that to destroy, from the foundation, the claws of ignorance and the devil, which the Indigenous idolatry represented to them, was the challenge, not only for the religious, but also for all good Spanish Catholics in the sixteenth century because if the Indigenous continued the adoration of false gods, their efforts to evangelize would be in vain.

Within this context one can better understand why the first missionaries remained silent about the Guadalupan Event, since they were before the phenomenon of the Apparition of a Virgin Mother in the precise place where the mother of the gods was venerated: Coatlicue Tonantzin, an old Aztec deity, who had her temple in Tepeyac. However, one of these first missionaries, Friar Bernardino de Sahagún, could not be quiet about what to him was definitely a "satanic invention, to palliate idolatry."[8]

---

[6] Friar Gerónimo de Mendieta, *Historia Eclesiástica*, p. 227.

[7] Friar Toribio Motolinia, *Historia de los Indios*, p. 22.

[8] Friar Bernardino de Sahagún, *Florentine Codex*, approx. 1564–1569, Manuscript 218–220 from the Palatine Collection in the Medicea Laurenciana Library, Book XI, f. 234r. Published in Friar Bernardino de Sahagún, *Historia General*, p. 705.

From our present-day understanding of what the Virgin of Guadalupe really is, the silence of those first missionaries as well as the direct attack of some of them, such as the Franciscan Friar Bernardino de Sahagún, whose most important fragment we already mentioned, or Friar Francisco de Bustamante, whom we shall analyze later, would seem apparently negative for our devotion. However, this is not so, this actually helps us understand and prove that the Image of Guadalupe was not brought over by the Spaniards, nor was it a devotion imposed by the devoted of the Guadalupana of Extremadura, Spain, on the Indigenous, but which actually emerges in Tepeyac.

The Franciscan Friars before the Antitestimony of Their Catholic Countrymen

While the Franciscan missionaries, because of their religious fervor, destroyed Indigenous temples and idols, always justifying their paternal attitude, saying it was for the good and the salvation of the Indigenous, some of their Spanish countrymen, on the contrary, enslaved them, using the heartless argument that the Indigenous were not human beings, so they had no right to own anything, and that they should submit. For these Spaniards, who called themselves Christians, the Indigenous were only objects to use to obtain easy fortunes. This slavery had a great impact. The missionaries were aware of the negative and disastrous attitudes and the antitestimony of their countrymen.

After many incidents, on August 27, 1529, Friar Juan de Zumárraga himself wrote to the King and Emperor Carlos V with great anguish about how bad the situation was in New Spain, having witnessed outrages and injustices that were being committed by some Spaniards. (This was only one year and four months before the Apparition.) But let us see some of these news that Bishop Zumárraga transmitted:

> The natives are very sad and hurt, not only because their property has been taken away from them, but also because their town has been destroyed so that they must look for someplace else to live. In addition, they [the Spaniards] take away the water for the mill, it was theirs [the Indigenous] to irrigate their farmlands and patches. The poor Indigenous of that town—without the water, there is no way that they can survive. The lawyer Delgadillo has done the same thing—in the town of Tacuba he has taken a walled-in orchard with many trees and flowers, which belonged to another man, against the man's will. There he is building a very comfortable resting home. In the same town of Tacuba, the lawyer Matienzo has taken a place against the owner's will also,

where he now makes mills, incredible. I point this out, without many other things: ranches, places where they have their cattle on the best land, fall on who it may, be it as it may. Thus I conclude, saying that they are well-equipped with land, abundant Indigenous that serve them, slaves in the mines that take gold to them, and great possessions of sheep, cows, and horses.[9]

What's more, corruption was terribly common, even in the high positions. Zumárraga added that "Government positions have been given to friends, relatives and servants, who do not have the academic education or experience required. Most of them do not have the moral background required for the superiority of that position. This has been done to fill their hands, giving them an opportunity to steal and get rich quickly, and they have taken advantage of their jobs in order to obtain secret farms and other things that they run across."[10]

Zumárraga was not only unable to do anything with regard to the assaults and crimes of the Spaniards, but also he was threatened by them. The archbishop continued with his description of the happenings:

And because I think that nothing should be hidden from Your Majesty, I tell you that the Lords of Tlaltelolco came to me, crying so, that I felt sorry for them. They complained that the President and judges had asked for their daughters, sisters, and relatives who were good-looking and another man told me that Pilar had asked him for eight young girls who were well-disposed for the President. I told a Guardian Priest, who was my interpreter, to tell them not to give the girls to sin. As a consequence, supposedly, they wanted to hang one of these men. In addition to this, I told the Guardian Priest of the San Franciscan Monastery and he charitably told the President, who sent me a kind threat asking me if I thought it wise to be inquiring about his life and other things. And because I saw his disillusion with the warnings that I made in secret many times about the mistreatment of the Indigenous, thefts, bad government, and misuse of natural resources, they would take the position which Your Majesty granted me. Having placed myself before God and Your Majesty in my sermons, I would talk about all of these things in general sometimes, warning them that I would tell Your Majesty about it since you had ordered me to do so, and I had to tell the truth, and I got along well with Your Highness, whose intention was as I had already talked about. The President said that with many Christians at his table, he had said that if he were present, he would throw me out of the pulpit, and they said that because I usually rebuked them, they have

[9] *Carta de fray Juan de Zumárraga al rey de España*, Mexico, August, 27, 1529, Archives of Simancas, Bibl. Miss., III, 339, letter 13. Copy in Col. Muñoz, T. 78, f. 279r–279v.

[10] *Carta de fray Juan de Zumárraga al rey de España*, Mexico, August 27, 1529, f. 281v.

stopped going to my sermons. On Sundays, they usually go to banquets with a lot of people and go from house to house, calling women and forcing them out of their houses, and there many dishonest and unlawful things happen.[11]

Here you can see clearly why Friar Juan de Zumárraga, even though he was the bishop of Mexico City, felt impotent before all of these disasters and abuses committed by some of the Spaniards, especially by those who were in charge of the government of the capital. Thefts, crimes, and corruption were their laws, as was mistreating the Indigenous to satisfy all types of interests.

The bishop of Mexico, aware of the fact that there was no human solution, prayed for God to intervene, saying, "Likewise, I think it well to inform Your Majesty of what is happening now, because it is something that is so important, that if God does not provide a remedy from His hand, this land is about to be totally lost."[12]

Zumárraga was not the only one who thought this way or saw things like this. All of the first missionaries coincided on this issue, as did the Franciscan Friar Gerónimo de Mendieta, who also offers us his version of the facts, and comments in his work, *Historia Eclesiástica Indiana,* in book 1, chapter 9, which he titled *De la ocasión que los indios de Cumaná y Maracapana tuvieron para aborrecer los cristianos, y destruir los monasterios que tenían, matando los religiosos* [*About the occasion in which the Indigenous from Cumaná and Maracapana had to hate the Christians, and to destroy the monasteries they had, killing the religious*]. Mendieta said, "Unfortunately many Indigenous turned against the Friars, because the Spaniards tried to abuse them. Among the most cruel ones was Alonso de Ojeda, who settled close to the convent and whom the Friars received as they do to everyone, offering hospitality. He called Maraguay, the *cacique* of the town, and he asked for information from the Indigenous whom he pointed to. Ojeda asked if there were cannibals, which offended the Indigenous, but he said no. Ojeda took a boat and arrived to the town of Maracapana, and having been received by the Indigenous as if he were an angel, he told them that he wanted to buy things. With deceit, he took a load of corn with several Indigenous who expected their payment but the only thing he did was to tie them up and take them as slaves. Some who resisted were stabbed.[13]

---

[11] *Carta de fray Juan de Zumárraga al rey de España*, Mexico, August 27, 1529, f. 284r–284v.
[12] *Carta de fray Juan de Zumárraga al rey de España*, Mexico, August 27, 1529, f. 314v.
[13] Friar Gerónimo de Mendieta, *Historia Eclesiástica*, p. 43.

Mendieta continued describing in chapter 11, which he titled *De la consid-eración que se debe tener cerca de este desastrado acaecimiento y de otros seme-jantes, si han acontecido o acontecieren en Indias* [*From the consideration that one must have about this disastrous event, and others like it, if they have occurred or oc-curred in the Indies*]. The friar said, "Well do I know that not everyone can ac-cept or is pleased with this subject, and for this reason, in part, if it were pos-sible, I would like not to touch it; but I cannot avoid stumbling over it with each step that I take, being such a common business in the Indies, and which has totally prevented the conservation and the salvation of countless people who in a short time have been consumed."[14] Mendieta continued explaining firmly that the Indigenous were "the most meek, peaceful, and modest people that God created. In the beginning, when the Spaniards arrived in their land, they never ceased to receive them with the greatest love and benevolence, until the Spaniards enslaved them and the Indigenous learned."[15]

The Franciscan continued describing in book 3, chapter 50 of his work, which he titled *De las grandes persecuciones que los primeros religiosos padecieron por parte de sus hermanos españoles* [*From the great persecutions which the first religious suffered on behalf of their Spanish brothers*]. He said,

As the Spaniards at that time saw themselves as lords of such an extensive land, populated by countless people, and all of them subdued and obedient to what-ever the Spaniards wished to order, the Spaniards lived abusively, each one as he wished and fancied, exercising all types of vices. They treated the Indigenous with such harshness and cruelty that paper and time would not suffice to tell all the humiliations which they did to them in particular. Not being able to keep up with the Spaniards, they would sell the land they owned to usurer merchants [that there used to be among them]. They sold the children of the poor, who be-came slaves. . . . The Friars, seeing how inconvenient it was for the Indigenous to have to go through those humiliations and then to love our faith and Chris-tian religion, would preach against those vices and sins which were committed in public, and would rebuke them publicly and personally with full Christian liberty. When those who governed [that also participated in these crimes and other worse ones, such as to enslave people as they wished] saw this, they turned against the Friars as if they were terrible enemies, taking not only the alms which they previously gave, but in addition, trying to dishonor them and speak-ing badly of them to the people, also afflicting them in every way possible. Fear-ing that the Friars gave notice to the King about their tyrannies, they commis-sioned guards to interrupt all the roads and trails so that word could not get

---

[14] Friar Gerónimo de Mendieta, *Historia Eclesiástica*, p. 49.
[15] Friar Gerónimo de Mendieta, *Historia Eclesiástica*, p. 53.

through. In this way they prevented anyone from taking letters from religious men without reading themselves the letters first. They would visit the ships and check up everything, looking for letters from the Friars. Not happy with this, in case there were any doubt, at the cost of the innocent, so that they would not be blamed if one of their letters made it to the King, they would pretend to be the witnesses and write reports dishonoring the saintly Bishop and the Friars with ugly things beyond their imagination.[16]

The first missionaries truly did an admirable job defending the Indigenous, denouncing injustice, trying to evangelize the Indigenous with the Catholic principles of the sixteenth century. Many of the Indigenous were converted, thanks to the friars; their testimony and their great effort were bearing fruit. Their catechism and teachings took shape little by little. Remember that Juan Diego was converted to the Catholic faith thanks to them. Without a doubt, the first missionaries constituted one of the basic conditions for Evangelization of the inhabitants in the new lands recently discovered. But the job was immense and in many ways out of their control, not only with regard to the Evangelization of the Indigenous, but also, as we mentioned, the conversion of their same countrymen. It was a titanic job, and at the same time, understandably limited. For those reasons, what the Bishop of Mexico, Friar Juan de Zumárraga, said is very true: "if God does not provide a remedy from His hand, this land is about to be lost." The most complete darkness drizzled over the Anáhuac.

The knowledge of the essential points of this strong impact on everyone, the mixture of religious ideas, which are the central part of the Conquest, the marked characteristics of each culture, as well as the advanced military technology of the Spaniards and the disputes within the Indigenous groups all help us to understand more about and centralize the Guadalupan Event. In other words, the situation resulting from the Conquest and the discord existing among the Spaniards made it impossible to find a solution. The domination of one world over the other could have resulted between the Spaniards, who felt questioned by their conscience, and the Indigenous, who manifested in their pain a profound fatalism. Only an intervention of another magnitude could create a new people, a new race.

---

[16] Friar Gerónimo de Mendieta, *Historia Eclesiástica*, pp. 311–12.

CHAPTER TWO

~

The Star of Evangelization Appears in the Darkness

Ten years after the Conquest, Evangelization of these lands slowly began when on Saturday, December 9, 1531, very early in the morning, Juan Diego was walking to Saturday Mass for the Virgin Mary and Catechism in Tlaltelolco, attended by Franciscans from the first convent built then in Mexico City. He had been converted and been baptized only a few years before. He was born in Cuauhtitlán, married an Indigenous named María Lucía, and at that time lived in the town of Tulpetlac with his uncle Juan Bernardino.

When the humble Juan Diego arrived at the foot of the hill called Tepeyac, he suddenly heard beautiful chants, harmonious and sweet, coming from the top of the hill. They seemed to be a chorus of various birds answering back and forth in a concert of extraordinary beauty. He saw a shiny white cloud and he could see a marvelous rainbow of many colors.

The Indigenous was mesmerized, in astonishment, and he said to himself, "'Am I by luck worthy of what I see? Maybe I am just dreaming it. Maybe I just see it as if in between dreams. Where am I? Where do I see myself? Perhaps I am there where our old ancestors, our grandparents have said: in the land of the flowers, in the land of corn, of our flesh, of our sustenance, perhaps in the land of Heaven?' He was looking toward there, on top of the hill, on the side where the sun rises, from where the precious celestial chant is coming."[1]

---

[1] Antonio Valeriano, *Nican Mopohua*, translated into Spanish by P. Mario Rojas Sánchez, Ed. Fundación La Peregrinación, Mexico 1998, p. 27.

Still being in this rapture, suddenly the chant stopped and he heard how a woman, sweet and delicate, called him out by his name, precisely from the top of the hill. She called him: "Juanito, Juan Dieguito." Without any hesitation, the Indigenous decided to go where he was being called; joyfully and happily he started to go up the hill, and when he reached the top he found himself before a beautiful Maiden standing, waiting for him, and She called for him to get close. And when he got in front of Her, he realized with great astonishment, the beauty of Her countenance, Her perfect beauty: "Her dress shone as the sun, as if vibrating, and the stone where She stood, as if shooting rays. Her splendor was like precious stones, like a jewel, everything that is most beautiful, She was. The ground dazzled with the resplendence of the rainbow in the fog. The mesquites and the cacti and all the other plants that usually grow there looked like emeralds, the foliage like turquoises, and their stems and thorns shone like gold."[2] Everything manifested Heaven's presence.

Juan Diego prostrated himself before Her and he heard the voice of the sweet and gracious Lady from Heaven, as in the Mexican language, She said: "Listen, my son, the youngest, Juanito, where are you headed?" And he answered: "My Lady, Queen, My Little Girl, I go there, to your little house in Mexico, Tlaltelolco, to follow the things of God which are given to us, that we are taught, by those who are the image of Our Lord, our priests."[3] In this way, dialoguing with Juan Diego, the precious Maiden told him who She was and what She wanted:

Know, be certain, my son, the smallest one, that I am the perfect always Virgin, Holy Mary, Mother of the true God for whom one lives, Creator of people, Owner of the closer and the immediacy, the Owner of Heaven and Earth. I want very much, I desire very much, that my little sacred house be erected here, where I will show Him, I will exalt Him when I manifest Him, I will give Him to all the people in my personal love, in my compassionate sight, in my help, in my salvation; because I am truly your compassionate Mother, yours and those men in this land who are one, and the rest of the various nations of men, my lovers who cry out to me, who look for me, who trust in me, because there I will hear their cry, their sadness, to remedy, to cure all the different sufferings, their miseries, their pains. And to accomplish what my compassionate, merciful glance intends, go to the Bishop of Mexico's palace, and you will tell him how I sent you, you will let him know that I wish him to provide a house here for me, to build my temple on the flatland. You will tell him everything, all that you have seen and admired, and what you have heard.[4]

---

[2] Antonio Valeriano, *Nican Mopohua*, p. 29.
[3] Antonio Valeriano, *Nican Mopohua*, p. 30.
[4] Antonio Valeriano, *Nican Mopohua*, pp. 30–33.

And the Lady from Heaven made him a special promise: "Rest assured that I will be very grateful and that I will pay for it, for it I will make you rich, I will glorify you,[5] and a lot of it you will deserve. I will reattribute your fatigue, your service of going to ask for the matter that I send you."[6]

Thus, in such a sublime manner, the Lady from Heaven sent Juan Diego as Her messenger before the head of the Church in Mexico, the Bishop Friar Juan de Zumárraga. The humble and obedient Juan Diego prostrated himself before Her on the ground and soon started walking, straight to the city of Mexico, to fulfill the wish of the Lady from Heaven.

He arrived at the house of the bishop, the Franciscan Friar Juan de Zumárraga, and asked the servants and the household to tell the bishop that he brought a message for him, but they, seeing him so humble and so poor, simply ignored him and made him wait. With infinite patience, Juan Diego was set on accomplishing his mission, so he waited. When they let the bishop know, he asked that the Indigenous be brought to his presence. Juan Diego went in and knelt before him; immediately he told him all that he had admired, contemplated, and heard; he gave him the message from the Lady from Heaven, the Mother of God, word by word what She had sent him for and what Her will was. Skeptical of his words, the bishop listened to Juan Diego, judging that it was part of the Indigenous's imagination, mainly because he was recently converted, but even though he asked him many questions about what he had related, and he saw that the Indigenous had been consistent and clear in his message, the bishop did not give it too much importance, anyway. He dismissed Juan Diego with respect and cordiality but he did not believe what he had said. Still, the bishop took some time to think about the message. The Indigenous left the bishop's house very sad and grief-stricken, because he realized that his words were not believed and he had been mistrusted, and also because he did not accomplish the will of the Most Holy Mary.

Virgilio Elizondo gives us a reflection:

Fray Juan de Zumárraga was, along with many of the other missioners, one of the greatest evangelizers and defenders of the Indians. Yet he was equally one of the most fierce in destroying anything that hinted of paganism. In one of his famous letters (June 12, 1531), he wrote that he had destroyed more than 500 temples and 20,000 idols. He was convinced that he first had to destroy before he could build the new church. He was so busy destroying temples of the Indian

---

[5] I will glorify you: *nimitzcuiltonoz, nimitztlamachtiz;* both verbs are used to signify an extraordinary joy and happiness.

[6] Antonio Valeriano, *Nican Mopohua,* p. 34.

deities, and then, seemingly out of nowhere, this Indian, this *macehual*, wanted a temple built at Tepeyac, the site of the ancient Indian goddess Tonantzin. How utterly ridiculous! I'm surprised he didn't have Juan Diego flogged for such apparent nonsense.[7]

Juan Diego returned to the hill, to the same spot where the Mother of God had appeared to him:

> and as soon as he saw Her, he prostrated himself before Her, he threw himself on the ground, he said, "Little Patroness, Lady, Queen, my Daughter, the Youngest one, my Little Girl, I have already gone to where you sent me to fulfill your kind word. However, I barely entered the place of the Governing Priest, I saw him, I presented your word before him, as you ordered me. He received me kindly and he heard it perfectly but, judging by his answer, he may not understand it, he does not hold it as truth. He told me, 'Again you will come, I will listen to you patiently, from the very beginning I will see why you have come, your wish, your desire.'"[8]

Juan Diego understood that the bishop thought that he lied or fantasized, and with all humility he said to the Lady from Heaven:

> I beg you very much, my Lady, Queen, my Little Girl, that you send one of the noble persons, who is well-known, respected, honored, to take your kind word so it will be believed. Because I am truly a country man, I am a *mecapal*, I am a *parihuela*, I am a tail, a wing; I myself need to be led, carried, it is not my place to walk in nor to stop there where you have sent me.[9] My Little Virgin, my Youngest Daughter, Lady, Child, please excuse me, I will grieve your countenance, your heart with sorrow, I will befall your anger, your displeasure, Lady, my Mistress.[10]

The Queen of Heaven listened with tenderness and kindness, but responded firmly to the Indigenous:

> Listen, the smallest of my children, rest assure that my servers are not few, my messengers to whom I may entrust my word so that they carry out my will. But

[7] Virgilio Elizondo, *Guadalupe, Mother of the New Creation*, Ed. Orbis Books, Maryknoll, New York 2002, p. 55.

[8] Antonio Valeriano, *Nican Mopohua*, p. 37.

[9] *Mecapal, cacaxtli* (parihuela): implements used to carry, still in use in many parts of the country. The first is a strap of rope which passes around the forehead and helps to hold the load; the second is a wooden frame of twigs and tight ropes where a bundle is placed and it rests on the back of the porter. These are expressions of great humility, taken from sayings and ways of speaking of that time, folk talk, as if to say, "I am not more than an animal used for cargo, I need other people to lead me, I feel alien to those places where you sent me."

[10] Antonio Valeriano, *Nican Mopohua*, p. 38.

it is necessary that you, personally, go, beg, that through your intercession my wish, my will, be accomplished. And I beg you very much, my son, the youngest, and I order you rigorously that again you will go tomorrow to see the Bishop. Make him know for me, make him hear my wish, my will, to build, to make my temple which I ask him for. And tell him again how I, personally, the Always Virgin Holy Mary, I, who am the Mother of God, send you.[11]

Juan Diego, still sad about what had happened, said good-bye to the Lady from Heaven, assuring Her that the following day he would do Her will, even though he doubted that his word would be believed. Still, he assured Her he would obey and wait. He said good-bye to Most Holy Mary and went home to rest.

The following day, Sunday, December 10, he got ready very early and went directly to Tlaltelolco, and after listening to Mass and attending to Catechism, he headed to the house of the bishop, where, again, the bishop's household servants made him wait a long time. As he entered, Juan Diego knelt down before the bishop and with tears he told him again the will of the Lady from Heaven, assuring him that it was the Mother of God, the Always Virgin Mary, who asked for a holy little house to be built for Her at that place on the Tepeyac. The bishop listened to him with great interest, but to verify the truth of Juan Diego's message, he asked him various questions in regard to what he had affirmed, about what the Lady from Heaven looked like, about all that he had seen and heard. The bishop began to realize that what Juan Diego referred to was not possible, that it had been a dream or a fantasy, but he asked for a sign to verify the truth in the Indigenous's words. Without getting upset, Juan Diego accepted to go to the Most Holy Mary with the bishop's petition. When Juan Diego started to leave, the bishop sent two trustworthy persons to follow him, without losing sight of him, in order to see where he went and with whom he spoke. Juan Diego arrived at a wooden bridge where a river passed through, and there the servants lost sight of him; even though they looked for him desperately, they were unable to find him. The servants were very upset about what happened and when they returned they told the bishop that Juan Diego was a deceiver, a liar, and a sorcerer. They warned him not to believe Juan Diego, that he was only deceiving the bishop and that if he returned he deserved to be punished.

In the meanwhile, Juan Diego had arrived to the Tepeyac and found the Most Holy Mary waiting for him. Juan Diego knelt down before Her and told

---

[11] Antonio Valeriano, *Nican Mopohua*, pp. 38–39.

Her all that had happened in the bishop's house, how the bishop had asked all those questions in detail about what he had seen and heard, and asked him for a sign in order to be able to believe his message.

With kind words full of love, Most Holy Mary thanked Juan Diego for his diligence and the interest he had demonstrated in order to accomplish Her will, and ordered him to return to the same place the following day and there She would give him the sign which the bishop had asked for.

The following day, on December 11, Juan Diego was unable to return to the place where he saw the Lady from Heaven to take the sign to the bishop, because his uncle, named Juan Bernardino, whom he loved like a father, was seriously ill of what the Indigenous called *Cocoliztli*. He looked for a doctor to heal him but found no one. At dawn, on Tuesday, December 12, his uncle begged him to go to the convent of Santiago Tlaltelolco to ask one of the religious to come and confess him and prepare him because he was aware that he did not have long to live. Juan Diego hurried to Tlaltelolco to do the will of the dying man, and arriving close to the place where the Lady from Heaven had appeared, he naively thought that it was better if he detoured and took another road, going around the hill of Tepeyac on the east side; thus, not being held up by Her, he could get to the convent in Tlaltelolco as soon as possible, thinking that later he could return before the Lady from Heaven and keep his commitment of taking the sign to the bishop.

But Most Holy Mary went down the hill and passed a place where a salt-petrous water fountain flowed, encountering Juan Diego as he passed, and She asked him, "What is happening, the smallest of my children? Where are you going? Where are you headed?"[12] The Indigenous was surprised, confused, fearful, and embarrassed, and he answered, worried and prostrated on his knees,

> My Young One, my Daughter, the Smallest One, my Little Girl, I hope you are happy. How did you start your day? Do you feel your beloved little body well, my Lady, my Little Girl? With pain I will anguish your countenance, your heart: I let you know, my Little Maiden, that one of your servants, my uncle, is seriously ill. A terrible disease has taken him over, surely he will die soon because of it. And now I will go quickly to your house in Mexico, to ask one of the beloved of Our Lord, one of our priests, to go and confess him and prepare him for his death. So if I finish this successfully, later I will return here in order to take your word, Lady, My Little Young One. I beg you to forgive me,

---

[12] Antonio Valeriano, *Nican Mopohua*, p. 48.

have a little patience to me, because I do not deceive you, my Daughter, the Youngest One, my Little Girl, tomorrow for sure I will come quickly."[13]

Most Holy Mary listened to the Indigenous's plea with a peaceful expression. She understood perfectly the moment of great anguish, sadness, and worry that Juan Diego was going through, since his uncle, a person that was so loved, was dying. And it was precisely at that moment that the Mother of God told him some of the most beautiful words, which penetrated into the deepest part of his being: "Listen, put this in your heart, my son, the youngest one, what frightened you, what afflicted you, is nothing; your countenance, your heart, should not be upset, do not fear of that disease nor any other disease, nor any piercing, afflictive thing. Am I, who am your Mother, not here? Are you not under my shadow, and my shelter? Am I not the fountain of your joy? Are you not in the hollow of my mantle, where my arms cross? Do you need something else?"[14] And the Lady from Heaven told him, "May no other thing afflict you, upset you, the illness of your uncle should not disturb you, since he will not die from it now. Be sure that he is well already."[15]

Indeed, at that precise moment, Most Holy Mary was with the uncle Juan Bernardino giving him back his health; Juan Diego would find this out later. Juan Diego trusted completely in what Most Holy Mary, the Queen of Heaven, assured him. So, consoled and determined, he immediately implored Her to send him to see the bishop in order to take the sign of proof to him, so that he would believe the message.

The Most Holy Virgin ordered him to go to the top of the hill, where they had met before, and She told him, "You will see that there are various flowers: cut them, gather them and put them all together, then come down, bring them here to my presence."[16] Juan Diego immediately went up the hill, even though he knew that there were no flowers in that place since it was an arid area, full of large rocks, and that there were only thistles, cacti, mesquites, and thorns; what's more, it was so cold that there was ice. But when he arrived to the top he was amazed at what he had before him: a beautiful flower garden of various flowers, fresh and full of dew, of the softest scent. Putting on his *tilma*, or *ayate*, in the manner used by the Indigenous, he started to cut as many flowers as could be gathered in his *ayate*. Immediately he descended the hill, taking the beautiful load before the Lady from Heaven.

---

[13] Antonio Valeriano, *Nican Mopohua*, pp. 48–49.
[14] Antonio Valeriano, *Nican Mopohua*, p. 50.
[15] Antonio Valeriano, *Nican Mopohua*, p. 51.
[16] Antonio Valeriano, *Nican Mopohua*, p. 52.

Most Holy Mary took the flowers in Her hands and then placed them again in the hollow of Juan Diego's *tilma* and said,

> My little son, the youngest, these various flowers are the proof, the sign which you will take to the Bishop. On my behalf you will tell him to see in them my desire, so that he will fulfill my wish, my will. And you, . . . you who are my messenger, . . . in you my trust is deposited and I order you very strongly that only alone, in the presence of the Bishop, you will extend your *ayate*, and show him what you carry and you will tell him everything exactly, you will tell him that I ordered you to go up to the top of the little hill to cut the flowers, and each thing you saw and admired in order to convince the Bishop, so that then he will do his part to build my temple which I have asked him for.[17]

After saying this, the Virgin Mary said good-bye to Juan Diego. His heart was at ease, he was very happy and content with the sign because he realized that it would be a success and that his mission would have a good outcome. And carrying the roses with great care, not letting them fall, he would look at them occasionally, enjoying their fragrance and beauty.

Juan Diego arrived at the bishop's house, and implored the doorman and the other servants to tell the bishop that he wished to see him, but none of them wanted to let Juan Diego go in. They pretended not to understand, maybe because it was still dark, or because they recognized him or because they thought that he only bothered and pestered them. Juan Diego waited for a very long time, and when the servants saw that the Indigenous was still there, not doing anything, just waiting to be called, and noticing also that he was carrying something in his *tilma*, they got close to see what he was carrying. Juan Diego could not keep them from seeing what he was carrying because they might push him and even damage the flowers, so he opened his *tilma* just a little bit, and they saw that they were precious flowers that gave off a marvelous perfume. They tried to grab a few, three times they tried but they could not because when they tried they no longer could see the flowers but saw them as if they were painted, or embroidered, or sewn on the *tilma*.

Immediately they went to tell the bishop what they had seen and how the little Indigenous who had come on other occasions wanted to see him, and had been waiting for permission for a very long time. As soon as the bishop heard this, he realized that it was Juan Diego bringing the proof to convince him, in order to start what the Indigenous asked for. Right away he gave the order to let him come to see him. And Juan Diego, having entered, pros-

---

[17] Antonio Valeriano, *Nican Mopohua*, p. 54.

trated himself in his presence, as he had done other times. Again he related what he had seen and admired and Her message.

It was at that moment when Juan Diego gave Most Holy Mary's sign, extending his *tilma*, the precious flowers falling on the floor, and they saw on it, admirably impressed, the Image of Most Holy Mary, as it is seen today and is kept in Her sacred house. Bishop Zumárraga, along with his family and the servants that were around him, felt a great emotion, they could not believe what their eyes contemplated, a most beautiful Image of the Virgin, the Mother of God, the Lady from Heaven. They venerated Her as something celestial. The bishop "with tears, with sadness, begged Her, asking for Her forgiveness for not having done Her will, Her venerated word."[18]

When the bishop stood up, he untied the *tilma* from Juan Diego's neck, on which the Celestial Queen appeared. After that, he placed it in his oratory. Juan Diego spent the day in the bishop's house, and the following day the bishop told him, "let us go so that you show us where it is the will of the Queen of Heaven to have Her temple built."[19]

Juan Diego showed him the places where he had seen and talked to the Mother of God four times. Then he asked for permission to see his uncle Juan Bernardino, whom he had left seriously ill. The bishop asked some of his family members to go with Juan Diego, and ordered them to take the sick man to his presence if they found him healthy. When they arrived to the town of Tulpetlac they saw that the uncle, Juan Bernardino, was completely well, nothing hurt him. He, on the other hand, was astonished at the way his nephew was accompanied and honored by the Spaniards sent by the bishop. Juan Diego related to his uncle how his encounter with the Lady from Heaven had occurred, how She had sent him to see the bishop with the promised sign in order to have a temple built on Tepeyac, and finally, how She had assured him that he was well. Immediately Juan Bernardino confirmed that in that precise moment the Virgin had appeared to him, exactly as his nephew described Her, and that She had also asked him to go to Mexico to see the bishop, to give him the testimony of what he had seen and to tell him the marvelous manner in which She had healed him, "and that just as he had called Her, She would be named: *the perfect Virgin Saint Mary of Guadalupe*, Her Beloved Image."[20]

To fulfill this will, Juan Bernardino was taken before the bishop to relate his testimony and, along with his nephew, Juan Diego, was accommodated in

---

[18] Antonio Valeriano, *Nican Mopohua*, p. 61.
[19] Antonio Valeriano, *Nican Mopohua*, p. 62.
[20] Antonio Valeriano, *Nican Mopohua*, p. 64.

the bishop's house for a few days. In this way the bishop knew exactly what had happened, how Juan Bernardino had recovered his health, and what the Lady from Heaven looked like.

It was astonishing how the word of the miracle spread, and how the people from Mexico would visit the bishop's house to venerate the Image. When the bishop realized the great number of people who went to see up close what had occurred, he decided to take the Holy Image to the main church and he placed Her in the altar, where everyone was delighted to see Her. Here She stayed while a chapel was built in the place designated by Juan Diego. Everyone contemplated the Holy Image with astonishment. "Absolutely all the city, without exception, was touched when they came to see, to admire Her precious Image. They would come to acknowledge Her divine character. They would come to present their prayers to Her. Many admired the miraculous manner in which She had appeared because absolutely no human hand on earth painted Her beloved Image."[21]

Juan Diego's *Tilma*: A Sign, a Message, a New Life

The Image of Our Lady of Guadalupe on Juan Diego's *tilma* was the sign which the Virgin gave to the bishop of Mexico, an authentic message of new life for its consignees.

The Lady from Heaven wanted to stamp Her figure on a simple *ayate* or *tilma*,[22] made of a vegetal material, known as agave, as has been certified several times. Some of the most recent investigations have been done by Dr. Isaac Ochoterena,[23] and Alejandro Javier Molina expressed it thus: "The *tilma* is made up of a type of a maguey called *Agave Popotule*, which belongs to the family of the *Amarilidaces*,"[24] but it is not impossible that it would also have some other fibers mixed in.[25] The *tilma* is used by the Indigenous to cover themselves, as well as an instrument to work and to carry with; in the same way, in the Indigenous marriage ceremony, the men knot-

[21] Antonio Valeriano, *Nican Mopohua*, pp. 66–67.
[22] Cfr. Xavier Escalada, *Enciclopedia Guadalupana*, T. I, pp. 101–108.
[23] Dr. Isaac Ochoterena, *Análisis de unas fibras del ayate de Juan Diego o Icono de Nuestra Señora de Guadalupe*, Mexico, June 7, 1946, Instituto de Biología de la UNAM, oficio 242, file 812.2/–2, in the Archive for the Cause of the Canonization of Juan Diego, in the CCS, Holy See.
[24] Alejandro Javier Molina, *Química aplicada al manto de la Virgen de Guadalupe*, 1981, p. 3, in the Archives for the Cause of the Canonization of Juan Diego in the CCS, Holy See. Carlos Salinas says, "This is the *tilma* of Juan Diego, an *ayate* whose fabric or weave is made of a century plant, woven by hand. The Indigenous of Cuauhtitlán confirm this. Two of them, don Pablo Juárez and don Martín de San Luis call it *ichtli*." Carlos Salinas, *Juan Diego en los ojos de la Santísima Virgen de Guadalupe*, Ed. Tradición, Mexico 1974, p. 114.
[25] Friar Juan de Torquemada, *Monarquía Indígena*, p. 361.

ted their *tilma* to the *huipil* of the women. The *tilma* is therefore the symbol of protection, work, and love. Juan Diego's *tilma* measures 1.72 meters by 1.07 meters. Through time, some small pieces were cut from the *tilma* as relics, as was the custom at the time. The Indigenous used *tilmas* this size, especially in winter since they served to cover all the body, keeping it from the cold.

Friar Bernardino de Sahagún tells us about its nature and construction:

> One who sells thin maguey mantles usually knows the following: one must know how to toast the leaves of the maguey and to scrape them very well, to spread corn dough on them and wash the leaves, clean them and shake them in water. The mantles which he sells are white, prepared with dough, polished, well-fashioned and with wide, narrow, long legs, thick, stiff, or sturdy; in short, all the maguey mantles are elaborated thus. He sells some that are very thin, that seem to be headdress, woven with *nequen* fibers, and those made of twisted threads. Some are, on the contrary, thick, closed weave, and well-fashioned and other thick ones are either *pita* or maguey thread.[26]

The preservation of this Image on Juan Diego's *tilma* has always been a challenge for the human mind. There are various testimonies that point to the surprising preservation of the Image, not only because it is impressed on such a delicate fabric, made of vegetal fiber, but also because it has always been kept in a humid and saltpetrous place.

In addition, the Image has a message within itself. For those who have studied the codexes, the Image on Juan Diego's *tilma* is an elaborate document directed to the Indigenous mentality since it has a message integrated by the use of images. All of it is a comprehensible codex for the Mexicans who moved in a culture that was expressed mainly on an image basis. Even for the people who were foreign to the Indigenous culture, as were the Spaniards, the Image was not far from their perception as a manifestation of Mary, the Mother of God, as described in chapter 12 of Revelations, even if it was somewhat strange, somewhat Indigenous. For the Indigenous it was a "spoken" message, comprehensible and identifiable.

For example, while for the Spaniards the figure of the Virgin of Guadalupe is surrounded by clouds, making Her divine origin clear, for the Indigenous, apart from making this clear, it also revealed some special characteristics.

In order to understand and to examine this, it is necessary to see with the eyes of the Indigenous. A concept which can help us understand the

---

[26] Friar Bernardino de Sahagún, *Historia General*, pp. 567–68.

significance is in the way in which the Indigenous greeted those whom they thought were coming from God, with the expression "among fog and among clouds."[27] A further example of this was in 1519, when Moctezuma greeted Hernán Cortés, who he thought was Quetzalcóatl coming to take possession of his throne. He said, "Our Lord, I am neither asleep nor I am dreaming, with my eyes I see your countenance and your body. There have been days in which I expected this, days in which my heart looked at those places where you have come, you have come from among the fog and from among the clouds, a place unknown to everyone. This is what the past kings have said to us, that you would return to reign in these kingdoms and that you were to sit on your throne and on your chair. I now see that what they said is true."[28] Another example we have dates from 1524, when the noble *caciques* greeted the first Franciscans in this manner: "We know that you have come from among the fog and clouds of heaven. Your coming and your presence, your way of talking which we have heard and seen is new and marvelous to us. It all seems to us as something from Heaven, as if in our presence you had opened a trunk of divine treasures from the Lord of Heaven."[29] And one example more, also from 1524, is when the Indigenous priests talked with the Franciscan missionaries, they said, "We, so low and coarse, are not worthy to see the faces of persons as valuable as you who have brought us God, our Lord, to reign over us. We do not know from where you come and how the place from where you come is and where our lords and gods live, because you have come by sea, among the clouds and the fog (road that we never knew), sent by God among us, His eyes, ears, and mouth. He who is invisible and spiritual, in you becomes visible."[30] Without a doubt, Moctezuma's way of speaking, and that of these *caciques* and Indigenous priests, also remind us of Juan Diego's way of speaking.

This lets us understand a little better how the Indigenous could observe that the Image, which is among clouds, was something from Heaven,[31] a place unknown to all, that brought a trunk of spiritual treasures to everyone,

---

[27] *Mixtitlan Ayauhtitlan* means "Among fog and among clouds" and was synonymous with God's presence.

[28] *Códice Florentino*, edited by the government of Mexico, edition supervised by the National General Archive (Mexico) 1879, Book XII, f. 25r.

[29] *Colloquios y Doctrina Christiana conque los doze frayles de san Francisco enbiados por el Papa Adriano sesto y por el Emperador Carlo qujnto côvertierô a los indios de la Nueva España ê lêgua Mexicana y Española, 1524*, ASV, 1564, Misc. Arm. I-91, f. 34r.

[30] *Colloquios y Doctrina Christiana*, f. 35r.

[31] In addition, it coincides with the narration in *Nican Mopohua*, pp. 16–20. "And when he was before Her, he was greatly amazed how without exaggeration Her perfect grandeur surpassed. Her dress shone like the sun, as if to vibrate, and the rock on which She stood as if to radiate Her splendor as precious gems, like a jewel (everything that is beautiful) She seemed. The ground shone with the splendor of the rainbow in the fog."

that was the presence, eyes, ears, and mouth of the invisible God, made visible in Her, and so on.

In the same way, other characteristics of the Image that were understood perfectly by the Indigenous mind were the solar symbols it has, symbolized by the four-petal flower that is drawn only once on the tunic, at the height of Virgin Mary's womb, the solar rays behind Her, the combination of colors, the moon and the stars. All of this made the Indigenous perceive that She was a Virgin Maiden, Queen of the Cosmos, pregnant, and would give birth to the sun. The various gold arabesque flowers which appear on the tunic (which is made of hill flowers) show in glyphic writing that it appeared on the Tepeyac, which in fact, it all took place in the Tepeyac in Mexico.

To reinforce this, one can observe that the Virgin is standing on the center of the figure of the moon. The etymology of Mexico is: Mex(tli)=moon, Xic(tli)=center, and Co=in, or "in the center of the moon." Thus, She first appears in Mexico.

Also, the expression of Her countenance was of special importance in the Náhuatl world (*ixtli*, meaning "countenance," was synonymous of a person). Her expression, tender and loving, of a mother contemplating her child, indicates love, caresses, protection, and an intense interest for the human race. In Náhuatl the expression of looking sideways did not have a pejorative connotation, as it may have among us; on the contrary, it was equivalent to "thinking of he who is looked upon, not forgetting who is looked upon."[32] Besides, the face is dark, *mestizo*. Forming part of the Image, at the feet of the Virgin one finds an angel, which is called "the Angel of the Virgin of Guadalupe," messenger of the truth. This winged being joins Heaven and Earth (mantle and tunic). In this way he holds and shows all of the Image.

Again, if we could situate ourselves as pre-Hispanic observers of the Náhuatl culture, a synthetic reflection would be a Lady among clouds who makes the invisible visible and present, gives us the trunk of spiritual treasures, and who appears on the Tepeyac, in Mexico, among flowers which proclaim the Truth. She is all harmony and unity, as She is dressed with the stars, steps on the moon, and is transformed into Sun, because She carries in Her womb the Child Sun, the New Sun, giving us His presence. We see ourselves in the countenance of Guadalupe, we identify with Her and at the same time, we see the explicit proposition in a message of

---

[32] "To look sideways" is the meaning of the synonym verbs *Teixtlapalitta* (*Te*: person, *Ixtlapal*: transversal, *Itta*: see); *Teixtlapaltlachia* (*Te-Ixtlapal* and *Tlachia*: look); *Tenacazitta* (*Te*: person *Nacaz*: corner, ear, and *Itta*: see: "see a person over one's ear"); *Tenazcaztlachia* (*Te-Nacaz-Tlachia*: "look at a person over one's ear").

communion.[33] The angel below the Virgin's feet, is the root of this Truth and the messenger with wings of an eagle.

The Indigenous did not have angels in their mythology, but they did have gods who were only aspects of the one and true God. Because of the characteristics which one can see on this angel, they could identify it with their old religion, Quelzalcóatl, Tezcatlipoca, Huitzilopochtli, or Tláloc, which served as root and support to the New Kingdom that the Mother of the Most True God, for whom one lives, came to establish in Mexico, thus permitting what for them was essential: not an end, but a plentitude. With this, they converted instantly, as we shall see later, and Mexico became a nation. This is one of the most important reconciliations; the angel is the root, the support, the foundation of this truth, their venerated Huehuetlamanitiliztli, which means "the Elder's Tradition." That is the great message: their world is not finished, it is transformed.

But there is something more, something extremely important, pertaining to the fact that the Image was impressed on that *tilma*, precisely on the one belonging to an Indigenous called Juan Diego. As we said, for the Indigenous culture, as for many other cultures, symbols and images which sustained profound truths were very important. So it was with the *tilma* within the Indigenous society as indicative of the level and social condition of a person, as we have said; it was so important that it was present in the Indigenous marriage ceremony. During it, a knot was made with the man's *tilma* and the woman's *huipil*, symbolizing in this manner that their lives remained joined.[34] In the same manner, flowers symbolized the profound simplicity of truth, of something that was unattainable, as was the maximum Truth of God; when one cuts a flower and holds it in one's hand, the flower starts to disappear at that moment, so that man, with his limitations, is unable to retain or keep it fully. He could contemplate its beauty, could become inebri-

---

[33] P. Dr. Fidel González Fernández, the historic consultant of the Congregation for the Cause of the Saints, declared during the session of July 30, 1998, before the Image of Guadalupe that "Once when I visited the Image of the Virgin of Guadalupe I watched a young couple pass close to the Image and he said to her, "Notice that her face is like ours." Minutes from the July 30, 1998 session. *Analysis and Direct Study of Juan Diego's Ayate or the Icon of Our Lady of Guadalupe*, at the Basilica of Our Lady of Guadalupe, Mexico City, in the Archives for the Cause of the Canonization of Juan Diego, in the CCS, Holy See, p. 6.

[34] "Having done this, the matchmakers would tie the mantle of the man with the woman's *huipil* . . . and then put both of them together in a room and the matchmakers would throw them on a bed, close the door and leave them alone." Friar Bernardino de Sahagún, *Historia General*, p. 365. "Wedding . . . in front of the chimney or bonfire that was in the main part of the house, and the bride and groom sat there, tied one to the other by their clothes and tied thus, the tribe leaders arrived to wish them well and that God would give them many children." Juan Pomar and Alonso de Zorita, *Relación en Texcoco y de la Nueva España*, Ed. Chávez Hayhoe, Mexico 1941, p. 24.

ated with its aroma, but could not possess it completely, only God could: He was and is the eternal, complete, and total Truth. With these brief details we can get closer to that Indigenous symbolic reality where one is before an Image that became impressed by the contact of various flowers, miraculously blooming on the arid and frozen Tepeyac, and on a *tilma*, which is Juan Diego himself. It comes to be an Image which proclaims the same Truth printed in the heart of an Indigenous who permitted himself to be united with the Truth of God. Furthermore, he is an Indigenous who has the trust of God. He has been rescued in the unity of his own being and in his dignity. In other words, for God, Juan Diego, the Indigenous, is worthy of all credit, in order to be the messenger. The Virgin of Guadalupe retakes the seeds of the Indigenous culture and religiousness, and the renovation and conversion of the Spanish culture and religiousness so that they could have fulfillment. Juan Diego is the ambassador of this great Truth, so the Virgin of Guadalupe is the sign of unity and plenitude.

Analyzing the Image from an artistic point of view, there is no doubt that we are before a masterpiece of outstanding balance and harmony, as the great investigator Dr. Homero Hernández Illescas notes in his study on the "golden proportion" of the admirable Image of Our Lady of Guadalupe. Regardless of its supernatural origin, this Image has been studied for many centuries. Several direct studies have coincided on the extraordinary and unusual technique used in this surprising Image, as well as its incredible self-preservation in such a humid and saltpetrous place where everything gets damaged and ruined. In addition, it must be taken into account that for 116 years the Image was exposed without any type of protection. It was not until 1647 that a glass case was used. P. Miguel Sánchez declared that "Before 1647 this Most Sacred Lady was without a glass case to protect Her from the air and dust which Her church and Hermitage ordinarily had; plus the fact that it was continuously visited by great numbers of people."[35]

One of the first studies practiced on the Image of Our Lady of Guadalupe took place in March 1666. The high court and the council formulated the petition before the Viceroy Marquis de Mancera so that the Image would be studied. The most outstanding experts in New Spain were asked to practice this solemn and important assignment. By March 13, seven painters were gathered, and by March 28, three chemist physicians of the king who had the opportunity to analyze the Image directly.[36] These eminent specialists

---

[35] "Testimonio del P. Miguel Sánchez," in *Informaciones Jurídicas de 1666*, April 14, 1666, AHBG Historic Branch, f. 70v.

[36] *Informaciones Jurídicas de 1666*, ff. 177r–187v.

studied Juan Diego's *tilma* and all were surprised, not only by the technique of the Image, but also by its self-preservation.

It is important to know, at least in a synthesis, the results of these investigations. As we were saying, the study of the painters on March 13 was a very solemn event, which began between 10 and 11 that morning and was attended by the highest authorities of New Spain, such as the viceroy and the council, together with the seven specialists in the art of painting. As it is stated in the Certificate of Inspection, which is part of the *Informaciones Jurídicas de 1666*, "The greatest and best artists recognized and found in this city and kingdom, [are requested] to do in clarity, truth, and accuracy what is asked for such a great and pious matter,"[37] and they made a profound and direct study of the Image of Our Lady of Guadalupe.

It was decided, before anything else that a solemn Mass should be celebrated to ask the Virgin for Her special help. Next, the Image of Our Lady of Guadalupe was taken down

> so that the experts in art called for that purpose would see and study it. They were the lawyer Juan Salguero, clergyman priest, 58 years old and art teacher for more than 30 years; Bachelor Thomas Conrado, 28, art teacher for more than eight years; Sebastián López de Ávalos, 50, painter for more than 30 years; Nicolás de Fuenlabrada, over 50, art teacher and painter for more than 20 years; Nicolás de Angulo, 30, art teacher and painter for more than 20 years; Juan Sánchez, 30, art teacher and painter for more than 15 years; Alonso de Zárate, over 30, art teacher and painter for more than 14 years.[38]

These men inspected the Image on Juan Diego's *tilma*, front and back, before the Public and Apostolic Notary, Luis de Perea.

All the specialists unanimously declared that

> It is humanly impossible that any artist could paint and work something so beautiful, clean, and well-formed on a fabric which is as rough as is the *tilma* or *ayate* on which that divine and sovereign Image of the Most Holy Virgin, Our Lady of Guadalupe, is. These deponents have seen and acknowledged Her Image as being worked with such great skill and beauty of countenance and hands that these deponents and all who see Her admire and marvel. Also, with the inclination and the parts of Her Most Holy Body so well proportioned, and the pretty strokes and the art in Her clothes, there cannot be a painter, as skillful as he may be or as good as there have been in this New

---

[37] *Informaciones Jurídicas de 1666*, f. 137r.
[38] *Informaciones Jurídicas de 1666*, ff. 137v–138r.

Spain, who could succeed perfectly to imitate the color, nor determine if such painting is in tempera or oil, because it appears to be both, but it is not what it appears, because only Our God knows the secret of this painting, of its durability and preservation, of the permanence of its beautiful colors and the gold of its stars, the ornaments and hem of the dress, Her complexion, which seems to have been just painted, and the most beautiful incarnation of Her countenance and hands, in addition to the rest of the details which the deponents have seen so many times; at the present moment She has been seen in the presence of these deponents, with the support of Lord Viceroy Marquis of New Spain and the illustrious Council and Dean of this Holy Church, and these expert painters, who are performing all the diligence that, according to their art, they have the obligation to fulfill [the work] given and ordered to them by the Lord Council and Dean, Ecclesiastic of this Holy Church, have touched with their own hands this Most Holy Painting. They could not discover on Her anything but to be Mysterious and Miraculous, and only He, Our God, Our Lord, could have done something so beautiful and so perfect as we find in this Holy Image. They have found it impossible to prepare and paint in such *tilma* or *ayate* fabric, they have no doubts, and no problem with declaring that what is on Juan Diego's *tilma*, the Holy Image of Our Lady of Guadalupe, must be attributed and understood to be the supernatural and secret work reserved to the Divine Majesty, as is the self-preservation of the colors, the clothes consisting on a tunic and mantle which make Her stand out on a background of white clouds. We also observed that all the colors of the Holy Image are indistinctive on the front and on the back side of the *tilma*, which indicates that in fact, there was no preparation, as on a regular canvas; it is only the color that gives the *tilma* body, and the color is incorporated into the coarse threads of the fabric. What the deponents have declared, they feel is true because of their experience in their painting art; in addition, Juan Salguera swore in *Verbo Sacerdotis*, with his hand over his heart, and the other painters swore to God and to the Cross, as specified by Canon Law.[39]

On their own, the three chemist physicians, Dr. Lucas de Cárdenas Soto, Dr. Jerónimo Ortiz, and Dr. Juan Melgarejo, practiced a detailed study based on several bibliographic sources; also, they inspected the Image of Our Lady of Guadalupe stamped on Juan Diego's *tilma* directly and analyzed the area around the Hermitage. Their declaration was written on March 28, 1666. Likewise, they came to the same surprising conclusion with regard to the Image's self-preservation: because of the humidity and saltpetrousness, the *tilma* would have been destroyed a long time ago. "The Hermitage is built on

---

[39] *Informaciones Jurídicas de 1666*, ff. 138v–140r.

ground which borders the north side of a lake, thus receiving on its south side the constant humid air very closely. During the rainy season the waters reach the Hermitage, causing the ground to be very wet [this part corresponds to the main entrance of the Hermitage]. You can actually see the humidity in the sacristy and in the Hermitage, which proves that the ground where it is built is humid."[40] It is also amazing that the salt buildup caused by the humidity has not destroyed the Image. The specialists continued:

> There is no explanation for the preservation of the Image from the damage which could result from the air (which in fact, does not), or from the deposits of salt that build up and rise in the air but do not affect the Image. Instead, it surprises and amazes the human mind to see the great difference of their effect on the other things, compared to this Divine Lady, when due to experience, one knows that their effect and corrosive nature is such that the stone ornamentations where the salt builds up decompose and become powder. This can impress the greatest intelligence. Well, for over 100 years this Image has resisted this "stone cancer" [which destroys them and makes them into powder] whose audacity has not come close to this divine creation which has less resistance and hardness than the silver that adorns this Chapel. Though the silver becomes black because of its contact with the air, no doubt if it were not for the very frequent care that it receives, it too would be damaged, since it is less resistant than stone. This is proven by investigations.[41]

The chemist-physicians finished their report, declaring that the phenomenon which they saw directly on the *tilma* cannot be explained humanly. They said,

> Being one, the substance and its second qualities [judged by the touch] are different qualities, [judged by] having touched the back side, which is rough and hard, and the consistency of front side [which is equally uncorrupted] is so soft and gentle [as silk]; whoever can explain all this, do so, since our limited intelligence cannot, with regard to the type of air [humid and saltpetrous], or any accident that it had suffered, and least of all, for the place and ground. There is no explanation for the preservation of this Image until today, its incorruptibility and self-preservation; having analyzed everything, I can't affirm the contrary [that the Image was made by human hands].[42]

---

[40] *Informaciones Jurídicas de 1666*, ff. 182v–183r.
[41] *Informaciones Jurídicas de 1666*, f. 185r–185v.
[42] *Informaciones Jurídicas de 1666*, f. 187r.

Eighty-five years later, on April 30, 1751, a second inspection of this type took place. Another group of eminent artists and physicians were able to study the Image thoroughly, without the glass case that covers it. Among them the great painter, Miguel Cabrera, stood out, along with José de Ibarra, Patricio Morlete Ruiz, and Manuel Osorio, who at the time figured as the painters with greater credit. On April 15, 1752, Cabrera, with the help of José de Alcibar and José Ventura Arnaez, made three copies of the Guadalupana. Arnaez wrote that the first copy was for the Archbishop of Mexico, Manuel Rubio y Salinas,[43] the second was for Father Juan Francisco López, a Jesuit priest who was about to leave as a Procurator in Rome, where he presented it to Pope Benedict XIV, and the third copy was "for your disposal," Arnaez told Cabrera, "to keep at your house in order to make other copies from the one that came from the original."[44]

Cabrera published his report after having presented it to the other artists for their approval, with the title *Maravilla Americana*. Its chapters give us an idea of its content: 1. Marvelous duration of the Image of Our Lady of Guadalupe; 2. About the fabric on which Our Lady of Guadalupe is impressed; 3. About the lack of preparation for this painting; 4. About the marvelous drawing of Our Lady of Guadalupe; 5. About the four kinds of paints which combine marvelously in the Image of Our Lady of Guadalupe; 6. About the precious gold and the exquisite gilding in the miraculous Image of Our Lady of Guadalupe; 7. The objections which have been opposed to our most beautiful painting; 8. The design of the miraculous Image of Our Lady of Guadalupe.[45]

Moreover, also in the eighteenth century, on January 25, 1787, another group of painters made another examination and besides that, an experiment put forward by Dr. José Ignacio Bartolache was performed. When asked, "Taking into account the rules of your faculty, and without any personal passion or desire, do you consider this Holy Image as having been painted miraculously?" they responded, "Yes, in as much as what is considered substantial and primitive, in our Holy Image, but not in as much as certain touch-ups and details, which without a doubt, seem to have been done later by impudent hands."[46]

---

[43] The Archbishop of Mexico, Manuel José Rubio y Salinas (1748–1765).

[44] Abelardo Carrillo y Gariel, *El Pintor Miguel Cabrera*, INAH, Mexico 1966, pp. 21–22.

[45] Cfr. Miguel Cabrera, *Maravilla Americana y conjunto de raras maravillas observadas con la dirección de las reglas del arte de la pintura en la prodigiosa Imagen de Nuestra Señora de Guadalupe de México*, Published by the Real y más antiguo Colegio de San Ildefonso, Mexico 1756.

[46] José Ignacio Bartolache y Díaz de Posadas, *Manifesto Satisfactorio u Opúsculo Guadalupano*, in Ernesto de la Torre Villar and Ramiro Navarro de Anda, *Testimonios Históricos Guadalupanos*, Ed. FCE, Mexico 1982, p. 648.

The Image is a synthesis of incompatible Mexican and European techniques.[47] The colors, the three-dimensional, accented profiles, the "arabesque" gliding over the tunic without following the folds of the tunic, and the richness of its symbols are clearly Indigenous; the skill in the lights, shadows, volume, and perspective are typical in the European paintings. We do not find in the first half of the sixteenth century, nor in any century in the colonial period, another example of this type in Mexico. Those who have tried to copy it, or trace it, have only done it poorly.

As we said previously, not only was an inspection done of Juan Diego's *tilma* by accredited people, but also it was decided that a series of experiments be done in order to verify the self-preservation that a vegetable material such as the one of Juan Diego's *tilma* might have. Bartolache had two copies of the Image made in order to place them in the same area where the original Image was located. Right away Bartolache said of one of these copies that "It turned out very beautiful, arranged exactly in every way, though it is still a long way from the original, not in its drawing, but in the way it is painted, which is truly impossible to imitate, even if all human diligence were applied."[48] However, these copies did not last long because the humidity and the saltpetrous deposits destroyed them in a short time.

Surely, something that surprises everyone is the Image's preservation. Indeed, it is unexplainable how a fabric made of agave, which normally would not last more than 20 years, has been able to survive almost 500 years. We know that for over 100 years it was without a glass case or any other type of protection: "The Image was out in the open for 116 years, in very unfavorable conditions of humidity and temperature, exposed to the saltpeter buildup, and made with a vegetable fiber material which should have disintegrated in less than 20 years."[49]

It surprises us even more when we know of a series of events which could have destroyed it a long time ago: besides the well-known saltpetrous and humid conditions that damage the delicate vegetable fiber where is imprinted the Image of the Virgin of Gualalupe and the evident wear of the humble de-

---

[47] In the eighteenth century, the great painter D. Francisco Antonio Vallejo pointed out that "even if a talented painter wanted to make a painting with the details of the profiles and at the same time with the mysterious grace given to Our Guadalupana . . . it would be impossible because of the incompatibility that there is between one and the other extreme. Thus, for this and for the rest, the precise condition is admired in the Holy Image, lacking in preparation of the canvas, to be painted either in oil or tempera, or in a combination of different paints on one same surface. I conclude, and piously believe, it is a supernatural and miraculous work and it is formed by a superior and divine craftsman." "Report by Francisco Antonio Vallejo," in Miguel Cabrera, *Maravilla Americana*, p. 34.

[48] Juan Ignacio Bartolache, *Manifesto Satisfactorio*, p. 644.

[49] Alejandro Javier Molina, *Química aplicada*, p. 7.

votion of the people, who would touch it, caress it, place their rosaries and medallions on it, and burn candles and incense before it, other very significant facts must be mentioned.

The first of them was in 1785, when an acid called "aguafuerte" (nitric acid) was accidentally spilled over the left side of the Image; the trace of this accident still remains. In 1820, a notarized report was drawn up.[50] Manuel Ignacio Andrade declared in his testimony that it occurred

> at the moment in which one of the persons cleaning the silver was cleaning the top part of the frame. I know about it because of trustworthy people who saw it and verified that the amount of acid spilled was enough to destroy all the surface on which it fell. I also believe that they tried to hide this accident from the Abbot, D. D. José Colorado whose stern character would have moved him to give that person a very severe punishment. On occasions I myself have noticed when I get close to the Image and the case is open, that the place where the acid fell left a somewhat opaque trace but the fabric is undamaged. I also knew that the person responsible for the misfortune was so upset that it was believed that he would become seriously ill . . . because everyone knows that acid is so strong that it will even damage iron if it has the slightest contact with it. This is all I can say about this matter, assuring you that I have always believed this event is a miracle of the Most Holy Virgin, who wants the preservation of this so beloved Treasure.[51]

The second event was the bomb attack which the Image suffered on November 14, 1921, "when a bomb went off in the Basilica of Guadalupe. Luciano Pérez Carpio, employee of the Private Secretary of the Presidency, protected by soldiers disguised as civilians, placed the bomb at the feet of the Image of the Virgin of Guadalupe. The explosion was of such magnitude that it was heard within a radius of one kilometer: the Image suffered absolutely no consequences; not so to the candelabras and the bronze crucifix which were on the altar and were bent in half with the impact."[52] Today these candelabras and crucifix are exhibited for the public in the same area of the Basilica.

[50] *Instrumento Jurídico sobre el aguafuerte que se derramó casualmente, hace muchos años, sobre el Sagrado Lienzo de la Portentosa Imagen de N. Sra. de Guadalupe de México*, 1820, AHBG, Correspondence with the Supreme Government, Box 3, File 54, 24 ff.

[51] "Testimonio de Manuel Ignacio Andrade," in *Instrumento Jurídico sobre el aguafuerte que se derramó casualmente, hace muchos años, sobre el Sagrado Lienzo de la Portentosa Imagen de N. Sra. de Guadalupe de México*, 1820, AHBG, Correspondence with the Supreme Government, Box 3, File 54, ff. 19v–20v.

[52] Eduardo Chávez, *La Iglesia de México entre Dictaduras, Revoluciones y Persecuciones*, Ed. Porrúa, Mexico 1998, pp. 165–66.

Regardless of all the elements and the attempts that could have destroyed the Image of Our Lady of Guadalupe, Juan Diego's *tilma* continues there, offering Her message to us today.

Many other studies have been performed on Juan Diego's *tilma*, using the most modern techniques. Other projects still in process are nevertheless interesting roads of investigation, like that of the stars on the Virgin's mantle, which, according to Dr. Juan Homero Hernández Illescas's studies,[53] coincide surprisingly with the constellations in the sky of that year, 1531. This same Mexican scientist, as we have already mentioned, has performed profound investigations on the "golden proportion" which can be seen in the Image. In the same manner, there is the study on the Virgin's eyes, which ophthalmologists, photographers, and different people, such as Dr. José Aste Tonsmann,[54] have continued performing.

---

[53] Cfr. Juan Homero Hernández Illescas; Mario Rojas Sánchez and Enrique R. Salazar y Salazar, *La Virgen de Guadalupe y las Estrellas*, Ed. Centro de Estudios Guadalupanos, Mexico 1995. Also Juan Homero Hernández Illescas, *La Imagen de la Virgen de Guadalupe, un Codice Nahuatl*, in *Histórica* (1/2 without a date), pp. 7–20. And of the same author, in his article, *Estudio de la Imagen de la Virgen de Guadalupe, Breve Comentarios*, in *Histórica* (1/3 without date), pp. 2–21.

[54] Cfr. José Aste Tonsmann, *Los Ojos de la Virgen de Guadalupe*, Ed. Diana, Mexico 1981.

CHAPTER THREE

~

Juan Diego, Messenger and Missionary of the Love of Our Lady of Guadalupe

A little after having lived the important moment of the Apparitions of Our Lady of Guadalupe, Juan Diego surrendered himself completely to the service of God and His Mother, transmitting what he had seen and heard, and praying with great devotion, even though it grieved him very much that his house and his town were far from the Hermitage. He wanted to be close to the Sanctuary in order to look after it every day, especially by sweeping it, because it was a great honor for the Indigenous; as Friar Gerónimo de Mendieta recalled, "They have great reverence to all the temples and to all the things consecrated to God; even the principal elders take pride in sweeping the temples, maintaining the custom of their ancestors when they were pagans, that by sweeping the temples they showed their devotion (even the important people)."[1]

Juan Diego went to the bishop to beg his permission to stay any place close to the walls of the Hermitage in order to serve the Lord of Heaven all the time possible. The bishop, who was very fond of Juan Diego, accepted his petition and permitted a little house to be built near the Hermitage. Seeing that his nephew served Our Lord and His Precious Mother very well, his uncle, Juan Bernardino, wanted to be with him, "but Juan Diego did not accept.

---

[1] Friar Gerónimo de Mendieta, *Historia Eclesiástica*, p. 429.

He told his uncle that it was convenient that the uncle remained in his house in order to keep the houses and the land which their parents and grandparents had left them."[2]

Analyzing some important historical sources, such as the *Nican Motecpana*, one knows that Juan Diego and his uncle, Juan Bernardino, actually owned properties, houses, and lands, not from recent times, but inherited from their "parents and grandparents" in pre-Hispanic times. This means that they were not part of a *calpulli*, in which the land was not owned personally, but was communal, and precisely for that reason, Juan Diego and his uncle had the responsibility of maintaining it, along with maintaining the well-being of various families, workers, and employees. The same documents confirm that Juan Diego left everything in order to serve in the Hermitage, which, in the Indigenous context, was a glory, attended by the elders, even if they were very important people or if they had held jobs of high responsibility in the town. Juan Diego makes of his life what had been an honor for his ancestors.[3]

Juan Diego was a humble person whose religious strength surrounded all his life, who left his houses and lands in order to live in a poor hut next to the Hermitage, to dedicate his life completely to the service of the Hermitage of his beloved Child from Heaven, the Virgin Mary of Guadalupe, who had asked for that temple so as to offer Her consolation and Her maternal love to all men and women. He had "time for prayer in that way in which God knows how to make those who love Him understand, according to each person's capacity, when to exercise deeds of virtue and sacrifice."[4] It is also stated in the *Nican Motecpana* that

> every day he would take care of spiritual matters and sweep the temple. He would prostrate himself before the Lady from Heaven and invoke Her fervently; frequently he would go to Confession, have Communion, fast, do penance, scourge himself, wear a penance belt, and hide in the shadows in order to give himself up in prayer alone and invoke the Lady from Heaven. He was a widower: two years before the Immaculate appeared to him, his wife died; her name was María Lucía, and they both lived chastely.[5]

This they decided to do after hearing Friar Toribio Motolinia give a homily saying that chastity and virginity pleased God and His Most Holy

---

[2] Fernando de Alva Ixtlilxóchitl, *Nican Motecpana*, p. 305.
[3] Cfr. Friar Gerónimo de Mendieta, *Historia Eclesiástica*, p. 429.
[4] "Testimonio del P. Luis Becerra Tanco," in *Informaciones Jurídicas de 1666*, ff. 157v–158r.
[5] Fernando de Alva Ixtlilxóchitl, *Nican Motecpana*, p. 305.

Mother. P. Luis Becerra Tanco gave witness to this fact: "The Indigenous Juan Diego and his wife, María Lucía, practiced chastity since they received Holy Baptism after hearing one of the first evangelic ministers on purity and chastity and how God loves virgins. This reputation was known by all who were acquainted with the married couple."[6] This decision not withstanding, Juan Diego did have descendants, perhaps before the baptism, perhaps by another family member, since we know this through historic sources to be a fact. One of the principal documents which refer to this fact is kept in the Archives of the Corpus Christi Convent in Mexico City, which declares: "Sor Gertrudis del Señor San José, daughter of *caciques* [noble Indigenous], Dn. Diego de Torres Vázquez and Da. María de la Ascención from the region of Xochiatlan . . . and descendant of the blessed Juan Diego."[7]

People were edified by Juan Diego's testimony and word; in fact, they would ask him to intercede with Our Lady for them for the needs, petitions, and prayers of their people, because "whatever he pleaded for to the Lady from Heaven She would grant him."[8] He never neglected the opportunity to narrate the way in which the marvelous encounter which he had with the Virgin had occurred, and the privilege of having been the messenger of the Virgin of Guadalupe. He was a true missionary. The simple people recognized him as a true saint and venerated him. Furthermore, the Indigenous used him as a model for their children to follow and freely expressed that he was really a "Holy Man."[9] Also, in the *Nican Motecpana* one finds the wish that "Hopefully we would serve Her and turn away from all the burdensome things of this world so that we also could obtain the eternal joys of Heaven!"[10] As we know, Juan Diego died in 1548, a few years after his uncle, Juan Bernardino, who died on May 15, 1544. Both were buried in their beloved Sanctuary. The *Nican Motecpana* tells us that "After serving the Lady from Heaven there for 16 years, Juan Diego died in 1548, at the time that the Bishop died. The Lady from Heaven consoled him. He saw Her and She told him it was time to go seek and enjoy Heaven, all that She had promised. He was also buried in the Sanctuary. He was 74 years old."[11]

---

[6] "Testimonio del P. Luis Becerra Tanco," in *Informaciones Jurídicas de 1666*, f. 157v.

[7] "Gertrudis del Señor San José," in *Apuntes de algunas vidas de nuestras hermanas difuntas*, Archive of the Corpus Christi Convent for the Indies *Caciques*, Autonomous Monastery of the Clarisas of Corpus Christi, in Mexico, s.n.f.

[8] Fernando de Alva Ixtlilxóchitl, *Nican Motecpana*, p. 305.

[9] "Testimonio de Andrés Juan," in *Informaciones Jurídicas de 1666*, f. 28v.

[10] Fernando de Alva Ixtlilxóchitl, *Nican Motecpana*, p. 305.

[11] Fernando de Alva Ixtlilxóchitl, *Nican Motecpana*, p. 305.

Sworn Testimonies in *Informaciones Jurídicas de 1666*

Without a doubt, one of the key documents establishing Juan Diego's personality, since it gave concrete references to his life, his family, and his mission, is known as *Informaciones Jurídicas de 1666*, an important canonical process, approved later by the Holy See and constituted as Apostolic Process when approval was granted to celebrate the Feast of the Virgin of Guadalupe on December 12 with its own Office and Prayer.[12] These *Informaciones*, though they are from 1666, cannot be considered as a late source since they gather testimonies of old Indigenous (some of them more than 100 years old), who remembered what their families and close friends used to tell them, old testimonies of great importance, and the *Informaciones* is one of the documents which cannot be left aside, nor can anyone try to invalidate it, because it possesses official value. Miguel León-Portilla affirmed that the *Informaciones Jurídicas de 1666* "shed a certain light on Juan Diego's person. The many particular contributions about him, agreeing among themselves, are worthy of taking into account."[13]

The first part of the *Informaciones Jurídicas* took place from January 3 to April 14, 1666. The investigation was performed with seven Indigenous witnesses and one *mestizo*, neighbors in Cuauhtitlán, the town that had known Juan Diego well. Their ages ranged from 80 to 115 years old. The second part was developed from February 18 to March 11 of that same year, in Mexico City. On that occasion, official and solemn information was gathered from 12 influential people, 10 clergy and two laymen, whose ages were from 55 to 85. Also, a written testimony, called "Papel" ("Paper"), by the bachelor Luis Becerra Tanco, was taken into consideration. All this was completed with the report of the seven art teachers and the three chemist physicians who in-

---

[12] One of the most used transcripts of the *Informaciones Jurídicas de 1666* is that of 1752, required by Joseph Lizardi y Valle, priest of the Archdiocese of Mexico and Steward of the Sanctuary, and which is still kept in the Historical Archives of the Basilica of Guadalupe. It was published by Fortino Hipólito Vera as *Informaciones sobre la Milagrosa Aparición de la Santísima Virgen de Guadalupe, recibidas en 1666 y 1723*, Imprenta Católica, Amecameca, Mexico 1889, 249 pp. Primo Feliciano Vázquez, *La Aparición de Santa María de Guadalupe*, Mexico 1931, XVI, 449 pp. Lauro López Beltrán, "Almanaque Juan Diego" in *Juan Diego* (1965). Luis Medina Ascencio, *Documentario Guadalupano, 1531–1768*, Centro de Estudios Guadalupanos, A. C., Mexico 1980, 299 pp. "Las Informaciones Guadalupanas de 1666 y de 1723," in Ernesto de la Torre Villar and Ramiro Navarro de Anda, *Testimonios Históricos Guadalupanos*, pp. 1338–1377. Ana María Sada Lambretón, *Las Informaciones Jurídicas de 1666 y el Beato Juan Diego*, photographs of ms., Ed. Hijas de María Inmaculada de Guadalupe, Mexico 1991. But now we offer the notes taken from the first notarial and official transcript done on April 14, 1666, and which is found in the Historical Archives of the Basilica of Guadalupe, Ramo Histórico, 198 ff.

[13] Miguel León-Portilla, *Tonantzin Guadalupe, Pensamiento Náhuatl y Mensaje Cristiano en el "Nican Mopohua,"* Eds. El Colegio Nacional y FCE, Mexico 2000, p. 45.

spected the surroundings of the Hermitage and the self-preservation of Juan Diego's *tilma* on which the Image of Guadalupe is, and which we have already analyzed in the previous chapter. Altogether a total of 21 witnesses and specialists were consulted for the famous *Informaciones Jurídicas de 1666*.

All of the witnesses and specialists who participated in this *Informaciones* converge on what is essential in the narration of the Guadalupan Event, even though they each have their own varying logic, which shows the authenticity of their testimonies. What is more, they coincide in pointing out the essentials of the encounter of the Virgin of Guadalupe and the humble Indigenous from Cuauhtitlán, Juan Diego, as well as information about his family, especially about his wife, María Lucía, dead two years before the apparitions, the miraculous recovery of his uncle Juan Bernardino, and the attitude of Friar Juan de Zumárraga's servants, and people around him. They also talk about the extraordinary Image stamped on the *tilma* and its mysterious self-preservation in a very humid and saltpetrous place, the construction of the Hermitage as the Virgin had asked for, and Juan Diego's virtuous life. They refer to him as a model and example of holiness and talk of his mission of interceding for his people, as well as multiple miracles and his great devotion which extended prodigiously.

The first part of the *Informaciones* was entrusted to the priest Antonio de Gama, 27 years old and considered a "virtuous priest of letters and experience, who responded well and faithfully to all that was entrusted to him."[14] Gama was born in Cuauhtitlán[15] and knew the people who could best contribute to the knowledge of the Guadalupan Event.

The attitude and spirit of authenticity and truth applied in this process is apparent throughout the document. An example of this is in the oath taken by the interpreters who translated from Náhuatl into Spanish all that the Indigenous declared. In the essential part of this document we read that "They swore to God and the Cross, as required by Law, and all together they said under oath that they accepted the oath and that they would interpret the truth about all that was asked and said by those Indigenous, without adding or taking from anything, but just as they said and disclosed, and that in so doing, might God help them; if not, that God could punish them."[16]

---

[14] "Comisión de parte del Cabildo al P. Antonio de Gama," Mexico City, December 23, 1665, in *Informaciones Jurídicas de 1666*, f. 5v.

[15] Born and baptized in Cuauhtitlán on October 26, 1639, Cfr. Archives of the San Buenaventura Parish, Cuauhtitlán, *Libro de Bautizos, from April 1599 to 1711*, No. 120, f. 20r.

[16] "Juramento de los intérpretes del Náhuatl al castellano, para traducir con toda verdad el testimonio de los indígenas ancianos de Cuauhtitlán," in *Informaciones Jurídicas de 1666*, f. 20r.

All the elders of Cuauhtitlán confirmed Juan Diego's reputation as a person who led an exemplary life. Analyzing some of the statements which these witnesses gave, we can see the high regard that they had for Juan Diego. For example, one of those witnesses, Marcos Pacheco, a *mestizo* more than 80 years old, declared that since he was a child his relatives spoke to him and to his brothers about Juan Diego, especially his aunt, María Pacheco, who knew Juan Diego personally, and she told them "that when the Most Holy Virgin appeared to the Indigenous Juan Diego, he was already the widower of María Lucía, and that he was more than 55 or 56 years old."[17] It was his aunt who related the details of the Apparition because she knew it "for certain, since she had heard it directly from Juan Diego."[18] By means of his testimony Marcos Pacheco synthesized Juan Diego's personality and his reputation for holiness in the following manner: "He was an Indigenous who lived honestly and withdrawn from the world, he was a very good Christian, fearful of the Lord and of his conscience, very proper. So much so that on many occasions his aunt would tell him: 'May God make you like Juan Diego and his uncle,' because she held them as very good Indigenous and very good Christians."[19] His reputation of holiness was such that "the old painters went as far as to paint him in the convents before the Virgin."[20]

Another Indigenous witness in *Informaciones* was Gabriel Xuárez, over 110 years old. His document states that "When the prodigious miracle of the Apparition of Our Lady of Guadalupe occurred, his father, Mateo Xuárez, told him. He also told him that She had appeared to an Indigenous named Juan Diego, born in that same town and neighborhood, in Tlayacac, and that his father knew him very well. He remembered his father telling him also when he was grown up."[21] Synthesizing his testimony, he stated how Juan Diego was a true intercessor for his people. He said, "The Holy Virgin told Juan Diego the place where the Hermitage was to be built and that it was where She had appeared. This witness has seen it and he saw it being built. Like many men and women who go to see it and visit it, this witness has gone many times to ask Her for remedy, and Juan Diego as well, so that he would intercede for him."[22] Later in his testimony he declared more details of Juan Diego's personality and the great confidence that the people had in him to intercede for their needs. Gabriel Xuárez declared that

[17] "Testimonio de Marcos Pacheco," in *Informaciones Jurídicas de 1666*, f. 16r.
[18] "Testimonio de Marcos Pacheco," in *Informaciones Jurídicas de 1666*, f. 13v.
[19] "Testimonio de Marcos Pacheco," in *Informaciones Jurídicas de 1666*, f. 15r–15v.
[20] "Testimonio de Marcos Pacheco," in *Informaciones Jurídicas de 1666*, f. 16r.
[21] "Testimonio de Gabriel Xuárez," in *Informaciones Jurídicas de 1666*, ff. 19v–21r.
[22] "Testimonio de Gabriel Xuárez," in *Informaciones Jurídicas de 1666*, f. 20r–20v.

Juan Diego, being a native of Cuauhtitlán, from the neighborhood of Tlaya-cac, was a good Christian Indigenous, fearful of God and of his conscience, and people always saw that he lived quietly and honestly, without creating prob-lems or scandals but was always seen taking care of ministries at the service of God Our Lord, attending punctually to Catechism and Mass, and doing so reg-ularly and this witness saw that all the Indigenous of that time called him Holy Man, and also Pilgrim because he was always alone and would go only to Cat-echism at Tlaltelolco. After the Apparition of the Virgin of Guadalupe to Juan Diego, and his leaving his town, houses, and lands to his uncle because his wife had died, he went to live in a house made for him next to the Hermitage. There the Indigenous of Cuauhtitlán would usually go to see him and ask for his intercession before the Most Holy Virgin to give them a good crop because at that time everyone held him as a Holy Man.[23]

Another witness was Andrés Juan, an Indigenous of 112 to 115 years old, who had had important positions in the Indigenous government of Cuauhti-tlán. After having narrated all of the Apparitions of the Virgin of Guadalupe to the Indigenous Juan Diego, he declared that when Juan Diego decided to fulfill the will of the Virgin to construct the chapel She had asked for, "as was the custom of the Indigenous of that town and native of it, they would all go, by the week, to work in its construction, and the Indigenous women, to sweep and perfume it. This witness remembers it distinctively."[24] In regard to Juan Diego's personality, he said that he was "a very quiet and peaceful man, a good Christian, fearful of God and his conscience, there was no problem or scandal about him, he attended Catechism and Mass regularly in the church in Tlaltelolco, without failing to do his obligations."[25] He also declared that Juan Diego was always being sought for his intercessions. He said, "After the Apparition he was held as a Holy Man, and as such, they respected him and would go to visit him at the Hermitage, where he had his little house next to Hers. They went there so that he would intercede with the Most Holy Vir-gin so that they would have good seasons, and this witness knew that little house, where Juan Diego assisted."[26]

An Indigenous woman, Juana de la Concepción, 85 years old, testified, and according to the document,

As recorded previously by her father, a *cacique* of that town, he was the first to know the things which happened there as well as in Mexico City and all the

---

[23] "Testimonio de Gabriel Xuárez," in *Informaciones Jurídicas de 1666*, ff. 21v–22r.

[24] "Testimonio de Andrés Juan," in *Informaciones Jurídicas de 1666*, f. 26v.

[25] "Testimonio de Andrés Juan," in *Informaciones Jurídicas de 1666*, f. 28r.

[26] "Testimonio de Andrés Juan," in *Informaciones Jurídicas de 1666*, f. 28v.

surroundings. He was such a curious Indigenous that he would note down everything, and put them in what they call writings [codexes], along with many other things. And he had, if I am not mistaken, written down about the Apparition of the Most Holy Virgin of Guadalupe, for having appeared to the Indigenous Juan Diego, born in Tlayacac, in Cuauhtitlán, and whom her father knew very well, and María Lucía, his wife, and Juan Bernardino, his uncle. He had had everything written down, but on two occasions thieves had stolen everything he had in the way of money and other things, among which were the papers he kept, plus [titles to] his hacienda, lands, houses, neighborhoods, and objects which belonged to the town, as well as those [records] regarding the Apparition of the Sovereign Queen of Heaven and Mother of God of Guadalupe, as a person who also knew about it and knew Juan Diego and his wife and his uncle.[27]

And again, she confirms the opinion that all in Juan Diego's town had known of him as a holy man because he had seen the Virgin: "all the Indigenous men and women of this town would go to see him at the Hermitage, regarding him always as a holy man, and this witness not only heard her parents say it, but also many other people."[28]

Another witness we count on was the governor of the Indigenous of Cuauhtitlán, the Indigenous Pablo Xuárez, 78 years old, who said, through interpreters under oath, that "when this witness was already married and with children, his grandmother on his mother's side, Justina Cananea, would tell him how she had known the Indigenous Juan Diego, María Lucía, his wife, and Juan Bernardino, his uncle, very well. They were all neighbors, born in Tlayacac, and they had known them and talked to them, because this grandmother had died over 40 years before, being over 110 years old at the time. She would tell this witness and Isabel Cananea, his mother, all this and how the Most Holy Virgin of Guadalupe had appeared to Juan Diego."[29]

Pablo Xuárez also offers important information about Juan Diego's personality and life which confirms his reputation as a truly worthy, conscientious, and devout man, full of the presence of God. He said that "his grandmother knew the Indigenous Juan Diego very well and talked to him, and that the Indigenous men and women of that town held him as a good Christian. When the Most Holy Virgin appeared to him, he was a mature man of 56 or 58, had no type of vice, always lived honestly and in seclusion, without scandals in his way of life, a good Christian, fearful of God

---

[27] "Testimonio de Juana de la Concepción," in *Informaciones Jurídicas de 1666*, ff. 31r–34r.
[28] "Testimonio de Juana de la Concepción," in *Informaciones Jurídicas de 1666*, f. 35r.
[29] "Testimonio de Pablo Xuárez," in *Informaciones Jurídicas de 1666*, ff. 36v–38r.

and of his conscience, very fond of going to Catechism and Mass frequently and never missed this obligation in any manner, as long as she had known him,"[30] and that "his grandmother told him that a little house was immediately built for him next to the Hermitage. The witness's grandmother saw the foundation started for the Holy Hermitage, and worked there, as did all the other Indigenous men and women from Cuauhtitlán, where Juan Diego was born. They all knew him and talked to him."[31] And in the same manner, they would ask Juan Diego to intercede for the people. He declared that "after Juan Diego moved from that town to the place where the Holy Hermitage is now located, the witness's grandmother would go to see him with the other Indigenous men and women to ask him to intercede with the Most Holy Virgin, since he was so loved by Her, to favor them and give them good seasons."[32] Juan Diego was so virtuous and holy that he was truly a good example for the people to follow. The witness declared that Juan Diego was "in favor of everyone living well because, as his grandmother said, he was a holy man, and that it would please God if her children and grandchildren were like him, because he was so virtuous that he talked to the Virgin, for which reason she always had him under this opinion and so did all this town."[33]

Martín de San Luis, an Indigenous at 80 years of age, declared that

when he was 10 to 12 years old, on many occasions Diego de Torres Bullón, an Indigenous of over 80 or 90 years old, very old, born in Cuauhtitlán and sacristan in the Church for many years, very intelligent, knew about many things and knew how to read and write, told Martín that he had known the Indigenous Juan Diego very well and talked to him, as he was also born in Cuauhtitlán, in Tlayacac, and that in the same way, he knew María Lucía, his wife, and Juan Bernardino, his uncle.[34]

The witness said that this Indigenous narrated the event with precision, that

he heard Diego de Torres Bullón say how he had met and gotten to know the Indigenous Juan Diego, because, as he mentioned before, he was born in Cuauhtitlán, in the neighborhood of Tlayacac, and that when the Queen of Heaven and the Mother of God, of Guadalupe, appeared to him, he was a mature man of 56 or 58 years old, fearful of God and of his conscience, had holy

---

[30] "Testimonio de Pablo Xuárez," in *Informaciones Jurídicas de 1666*, f. 40r.
[31] "Testimonio de Pablo Xuárez," in *Informaciones Jurídicas de 1666*, f. 38r.
[32] "Testimonio de Pablo Xuárez," in *Informaciones Jurídicas de 1666*, ff. 38v.–39r.
[33] "Testimonio de Pablo Xuárez," in *Informaciones Jurídicas de 1666*, f. 40r.
[34] "Testimonio de Martín de San Luis," in *Informaciones Jurídicas de 1666*, f. 42r.

habits, never a complaint about him, very fond of going to Church and to Catechism and Mass, was a good example for all who knew him and talked with
him.[35]

Juan Diego himself had related to him how he had taken his *tilma* to the
bishop, as the Virgin had ordered him to, and what happened after that. He
declared that

> Juan Diego was obedient and he took it to the Bishop's house and he went in
> to see him after much difficulty. He went in, having announced himself to the
> doormen, gave his message, and extended his *ayate* which was tied to his shoul-
> ders; the roses and flowers fell, leaving on the *ayate* the Sovereign Queen of
> Heaven and the Mother of God, of Guadalupe, stamped on it. The Bishop, see-
> ing such a portentous prodigy, started to cry, as did all those present. Diego de
> Torres de Bullón told this witness all this, precisely and clearly, having had
> Juan Diego himself relate it to him because he talked about it.[36]

With all punctuality, Diego de Torres Bullón continued declaring that the
bishop immediately decided to construct the temple that the Virgin had
asked for,

> Which was then made. Diego de Torres Bullón was in the procession that took
> place, from Mexico City to where that Holy Image is now located. And that
> he saw how the Archbishop [Zumárraga] took part in the procession, walking
> barefooted. The best of Mexico City, the surrounding towns, and in particular,
> Juan Diego's town gathered there. It had been announced in the market and in
> the plaza of Cuauhtitlán. They all went with trumpets and drums, Diego de
> Torres Bullón with instruments, and the dances used at that time. For weeks
> the natives went to build the Hermitage, which was small and made of adobe.
> Diego de Torres Bullón also went to work in the construction, and to sweep
> and perfume it, along with the Indigenous women, with great devotion for the
> prodigious miracle and for having happened to an Indigenous who was so well-
> known, born and raised in that town. Diego de Torres Bullón told the witness
> that he would frequently go to see Juan Diego after he went to live in a little
> house, made for him next to the Hermitage. Diego de Torres Bullón told this
> witness this, but many other things he does not remember after so much time,
> all about the Most Holy Apparition.[37]

The Hermitage was constructed precisely on the spot which Juan Diego indicated, and it was Juan Diego personally who made it known. The witness

[35] "Testimonio de Martín de San Luis," in *Informaciones Jurídicas de 1666*, f. 46r–46v.
[36] "Testimonio de Martín de San Luis," in *Informaciones Jurídicas de 1666*, ff. 43v.–44r.
[37] "Testimonio de Martín de San Luis," in *Informaciones Jurídicas de 1666*, f. 43r.

declared that they were "making a church and a Hermitage in the place that Juan Diego pointed out and where he said the Holy Virgin appeared to him and gave him those messages. This is what Diego de Torres Bullón said that Juan Diego had told him."[38] Soon this place was considered sacred; many people went there on pilgrimages and to take part in novenas.[39] This witness declared that he has seen "this Holy Image many times where She is placed, having gone many times to novenas, as many people have done and still do every day, to see and visit Her, in large groups. There he has seen innumerable miracles which the Divine Majesty has worked, on behalf and through the intercession of the Holy Image of Our Lady of Guadalupe."[40] He said that Juan Diego was always considered a most holy man, "and that he would see Juan Diego doing great penances and that at that time they called him Most Holy Man."[41]

Juan Xuárez, another Indigenous witness, of more than 100 years old, declared that he had heard his father, also named Juan Xuárez, and his mother, María Jerónima, say that they knew Juan Diego and his family very well, that he was a mature man at the time of the Apparition, he was María Lucía's widower, and that he had an uncle, Juan Bernardino. After narrating the essentials of the apparitions of the Virgin of Guadalupe to Juan Diego, as did all the Indigenous, he said at the end of his account,

> Juan Diego told the father of this witness that the Archbishop [Zumárraga] and all those present were covered in tears after having seen such a prodigious miracle; and then the house and Hermitage were begun to be made in the place where everyone now goes in processions, which are organized in Mexico City, all the towns surrounding it and very particularly in Cuauhtitlán, because the prodigious miracle had been announced in the public fair. Everyone goes with many instruments and there is dancing. The father of this witness was present in all of that because Juan Diego was so well-known and was born in that town where he had his house, lands, and all his relatives. By that time he was María Lucía's widower, as she had died two years earlier. After all that was mentioned before had happened, Juan Diego returned to his house, not knowing if his uncle, Juan Bernardino, had died, but Juan Diego found him well. So he asked

---

[38] "Testimonio de Martín de San Luis," in *Informaciones Jurídicas de 1666*, f. 45r.

[39] The novenas: "A novena is a devotion consisting of praying for 9 days to the Virgin or to a Saint, asking for his/Her intercession for getting special favors." Ana Rita Valero de García Lascuráin, *Estudio Introductorio*, in Francisco de Florencia, *Las Novenas del Santuario de Nuestra Señora de Guadalupe, que se apareció en la Manta de Juan Diego* (1785), edition by Archicofradía Universal de Santa María de Guadalupe, Mexico 1999, pp. 1–2.

[40] "Testimonio de Martín de San Luis," in *Informaciones Jurídicas de 1666*, f. 45r–45v.

[41] "Testimonio de Martín de San Luis," in *Informaciones Jurídicas de 1666*, f. 46v.

him how it was that he was well, and his uncle answered that a Lady had appeared to him a short time after Juan Diego had left; when he was better, She talked to him and told him to get up. Juan Diego told him that by the description it was the same Lady he had seen three times and had told him that his uncle was well. All this the witness's father told him many times. When the witness was 15 to 18 years old he heard the story many times from many people in the town and from all of Juan Diego's relatives. This story was so well-known that every year they celebrated the Feast of the Sovereign Queen of the Angels and Mother of God of Guadalupe. The next day all the town [of Cuauhtitlán], the Governor, Mayors, and Chiefs would go to celebrate the Feast to the Virgin and Juan Diego, born in that town so that She would intercede with the Divine Majesty for good seasons. This they have practiced since the Apparition; this witness would go every year, along with everyone. Even now, it is customary to go with their candles, since all the governors have been especially careful [in keeping this practice]. Likewise, men and women would go for weeks to the construction of the first Hermitage. This witness remembers all this very well, having gone to the construction, although he was only a boy 12 to 15 years old, because he has had, and has, a great devotion of going to the Hermitage.

Also, this witness declared that "Another chapel has been constructed at Juan Diego's house [in Cuauhtitlán] by the natives of that town. This witness, born there, has had, and has, great information about what has been said, having heard it from his father and mother."[42]

Catalina Mónica, an Indigenous woman who was 100 years old, was another valuable witness who said she remembered "very well having heard her parents and her aunt Martina Salomé say that the Queen of Heaven, Mother of God, of Guadalupe, had appeared three times to an Indigenous, a neighbor born in Tlayacac, whose name was Juan Diego."[43] All of the report about the Apparition of the Virgin to Juan Diego was told to the aunt by Juan Diego personally since she had been a close acquaintance of his and his family. The witness said, "With all clarity Martina Salomé would relate it to this witness because she was a very intelligent Indigenous, and very important, and she knew and talked to Juan Diego and his wife, María Lucía, and Juan Bernardino, his uncle, and all his relatives."[44] She also testified not only about the portentous encounter between the Virgin of Guadalupe and Juan Diego, and the collaboration of the Indigenous in the construction of the

---

[42] "Testimonio de Juan Xuárez," in *Informaciones Jurídicas de 1666*, ff. 51v–52v.
[43] "Testimonio de Catalina Mónica," in *Informaciones Jurídicas de 1666*, f. 56v.
[44] "Testimonio de Catalina Mónica," in *Informaciones Jurídicas de 1666*, f. 57r.

Hermitage, as was the will of the Lady from Heaven, but also confirmed that they would ask Juan Diego to intercede for them before the Virgin:

> They would go to the Hermitage one day after the celebration of the Feast of the Most Holy Virgin, with many candles and roses, to celebrate because Juan Diego was from this town; they would all go together, to ask him to intercede with the Queen from Heaven and Mother of God. In the same manner, all the natives [from Cuauhtitlán] would go for weeks to the construction of the Hermitage, including the witness's parents and aunt to sweep and perfume the Holy Hermitage. The witness being 15 years old already, they would take her on many occasions to see the Queen from Heaven, being in the same form and manner that She is today, without changing anything.[45]

And Juan Diego was loved very much, she said: "the Indigenous was venerated very much because he was so blessed by having talked to the Most Holy Virgin of Guadalupe."[46]

Juan Diego was truly "a good and Christian Indigenous" to his people, or a "holy man." These titles would be enough to understand the magnitude of his reputation because the Indigenous were very strict about who among them they attributed a name such as "good Indigenous," and even more strict if they declared that someone was so good that they could consider him a "saint," to the extent that they would pray that God would make their own children or relatives as good and holy as Juan Diego. And not only that, but Juan Diego was so loved and venerated as a true saint that the people held him as an intercessor before the Lady from Heaven so as to hear their prayers and their needs. As the Indigenous Andrés Juan said, "They would go to see him at the Hermitage where he had a little house next to Hers, so that he would intercede with the Most Holy Virgin to have good seasons."[47] Or as the Indigenous woman, Catalina Mónica, declared, "They all went to ask Juan Diego to intercede with the Queen from Heaven and Mother of God."[48]

These *Informaciones Jurídicas de 1666* had a second part, which took place in Mexico City from February 18 to March 11, when other people testified, 10 priests and two laymen, who belonged to the highest ecclesiastic and society hierarchies. The priests were either high directors or had had very important positions in their corresponding communities; each one of them gave his testimony under solemn oath to say the truth, in *Verbo Sacerdoti*, while

---

[45] "Testimonio de Catalina Mónica," in *Informaciones Jurídicas de 1666*, ff. 58v–59r.
[46] "Testimonio de Catalina Mónica," in *Informaciones Jurídicas de 1666*, ff. 59r–60v.
[47] "Testimonio de Andrés Juan," in *Informaciones Jurídicas de 1666*, f. 28v.
[48] "Testimonio de Catalina Mónica," in *Informaciones Jurídicas de 1666*, ff. 59r–60v.

the two laymen had also held positions of great responsibility and swore by God Our Lord and by the Sign of the Cross.

The 10 priests who swore to say the truth in their testimony were: Father Miguel Sánchez, 60, living in the archdiocese of Mexico; Father Friar Pedro de Oyanguren, 80, general preacher from the Order of Preachers; Father Friar Bartholomé de Tapia, 55, from the Franciscan Order, who had been Provincial of the same; Father Friar Antonio de Mendoza, 66, Province Definitor of the Order of Saint Augustine; Father Friar Juan de Herrera, 71, Mercedarian religious and professor of Theology in the Royal University of Mexico; Father Friar Pedro de San Simón, 65, Barefoot Carmelite religious, Definitor of his Order and Prior three times in the House of Mexico under the name of San Sebastian; Father Diego de Monroy, 65, Jesuit religious, Prelate of the Casa Profesa of Mexico; Father Friar Juan de San Joseph, 76, San Franciscan religious, Provincial and Prelate of all the houses of the Order, as well as examiner of the Holy Office of the Inquisition of the New Spain; Father Friar Pedro de San Nicolás, 71, from the Order of the Hospitality of Saint John of God, Prelate of some of the communities of that Order; and Father Friar Nicolás Zerdán, 61, Provincial of the Order of Saint Hipólito of Mexico.

The two laymen who gave their testimony in these investigations were: Miguel de Cuebas y Dávalos, 81, who had the responsibility of being Ordinary Mayor of Mexico and Principal Mayor of the New Spain; and Diego Cano Moctezuma, 61, knight of the Order of Santiago and who was also Ordinary Mayor of Mexico and descendant of the Emperor Moctezuma.

In addition to those 12 witnesses, there was an additional person, Father Luis Becerra Tanco, 81, who participated. He gave a written testimony which was confirmed by the Apostolic and Public Notary who was on duty at that moment. It complements the testimony given by all the other witnesses in such a way that this "Papel" ("Paper") was totally accepted. Luis Becerra Tanco himself would polish it, giving greater accuracy to his affirmations since he later found his old notes which helped him elaborate a more perfect document, and which would be given for publication later. This was called *Felicidad de México*, which, unfortunately, he did not live to see published.

They all agree on the essential context of the Guadalupan Event. Even if Miguel Sánchez, the first witness, was the first to publish the Apparitions of Our Lady of Guadalupe in a book which he titled *Imagen de la Virgen Santísima de Guadalupe que es la que está en dicha Ermita de su Milagrosa Aparición, que está extramuros de la Ciudad*, it does not mean that it was the only source by which this Event was known. As the other witnesses declared, they knew about it from all the people who knew what had happened, as Pedro de

Oyanguren testified: "that ever since this witness can remember, having been born and raised in this City, he had a lot of information told to him by different old people and people of all ages, positions and levels, having no contact among themselves."[49] Or, as Friar Antonio de Mendoza testified, "ever since he can remember, having been born in Mexico City, and having heard it from his parents and grandparents, very old people, as was his grandfather, Don Antonio Maldonado, President of the Royal Chancellery of this city, and his father, Don Alonso de Mendoza, Captain of the Guards of the Count Coruña, Viceroy of this New Spain."[50] Or, as Pedro de San Nicolás declared, "ever since he can remember, old people and people of authority told him."[51] Or as Diego Cano Moctezuma, descendant of the Emperor Moctezuma, stated, "having heard his parents and ancestors, and having investigated himself among old people and authorities who kept the Apparition of the Most Sacred Lady a tradition."[52]

With regard to the Indigenous Juan Diego, all the witnesses coincided in exalting the exemplary and virtuous life of the visionary of the Virgin of Guadalupe. Examples begin with Father Miguel Sánchez who declared, "The Indigenous Juan Diego, to whom this Sovereign Lady appeared, was a very Christian, just man, and very fearful of God, and as such, since the Holy Image was placed in this Hermitage, he served this Most Sacred Lady in it, without missing attendance, until he died, leaving a reputation of having lived justly and virtuously, without any fault attributed."[53]

Father Friar Pedro de Oyanguren testified that the Indigenous Juan Diego was an

> extremely good man, very Catholic, fearful of God and of his conscience, and often practiced the Holy Sacraments of Penance and Eucharist, he went about things in a mature manner, even with some discretion in his conversations, he had seen a great capacity in Juan Diego, as anyone could see, because, having his own houses in which to live and lands in which to plant, in Cuauhtitlán where he was born, he had left everything, coming to live in the Hermitage of Our Lady of Guadalupe, where he lived out his life, until he died, keeping busy with those exercises, sweeping and watering it with particular care, and edifying the Christian people who saw him, who went for novenas, visits, and pilgrimages, without ever seeing nor hearing anything (nor knowing of anything

---

[49] "Testimonio de fray Pedro de Oyanguren," in *Informaciones Jurídicas de 1666*, f. 72r.
[50] "Testimonio de fray Antonio de Mendoza," in *Informaciones Jurídicas de 1666*, f. 85r–85v.
[51] "Testimonio de fray Pedro de San Nicolás," in *Informaciones Jurídicas de 1666*, f. 108r.
[52] "Testimonio de Diego Cano Moctezuma," in *Informaciones Jurídicas de 1666*, f. 125v.
[53] "Testimonio de P. Miguel Sánchez," in *Informaciones Jurídicas de 1666*, f. 69v.

said or heard) that would disprove the honesty, virtuousness, and just behavior of the Indigenous Juan Diego, who was mature in age.[54]

Father Friar Antonio de Mendoza declared that "The Indigenous Juan Diego, to whom the Most Sacred Virgin appeared, was a man of mature age who had always lived honestly and withdrawn, a good Christian, fearful of God Our Lord and of his conscience, without disproving his good habits and manners in any way that could be seen, and causing with his just behavior a great example to all who met him and talked to him. Under this good life and habits he had died, serving this Most Sacred Lady in Her sanctuary and Church since the day She was placed in it."[55]

Father Diego de Monroy declared about Juan Diego that "According to what he has heard from many old Christian people and others, since it is a permanent tradition that the Indigenous Juan Diego, to whom the Most Sacred Lady talked to and gave the mentioned messages to His Majesty, was a mature man, who had always lived honestly and withdrawn like a good Christian, fearful of God Our Lord and of his conscience, without fault in his good habits and manners in any way that could be seen, causing with his way of life and just manners a great example to all who met him and talked to him. He was always in that Church and Sanctuary, serving that Lady until he died."[56]

Miguel de Cuebas, a layman, added that "Giving with his just manner a great example for all who met him and talked to him, his life ended virtuously and most holy, serving that Lady, until he died."[57]

A lot of the information given to us in Informaciones Jurídicas de 1666 converges not only with the publication which Father Miguel Sánchez did in 1648, which in fact he mentioned in his testimony that he wrote with diligence, looking for the most sure news of this tradition and Apparition, and he started a book, which he truly made and titled Imagen de la Santísima Virgen de Guadalupe que es la que está en dicha Hermita de su milagrosa Aparición que está extramuros de la ciudad [Image of the Holy Virgin of Guadalupe which is in such Hermitage of her miraculous Apparition that is out of the walls of the City], which is the one given to the editor, but also with several other publications; thus, it was a true history, known by many through different sources, as well as by oral tradition.

---

[54] "Testimonio de fray Pedro de Oyanguren," in Informaciones Jurídicas de 1666, ff. 75r–77r.
[55] "Testimonio de fray Antonio de Mendoza," in Informaciones Jurídicas de 1666, f. 88r–88v.
[56] "Testimonio de fray Pedro de Monroy," in Informaciones Jurídicas de 1666, f. 101v.
[57] "Testimonio de Miguel de Cuebas," in Informaciones Jurídicas de 1666, f. 123r.

Some of the Sources That Converge with *Informaciones Jurídicas de 1666*

Some of the old sources that converge with the information given by the witnesses in these *Informaciones Jurídicas de 1666* were, for example, *Nican Mopohua* by Antonio Valeriano, written between 1545 and 1548, a narration which we saw as essential. Likewise, it converges with a narration written before *Nican Mopohua* which has been called *Relación Primitiva*, known also as *Ininhueytlamahuizoltzin* and included in the *Sermonario* of 1600 by Father Juan de Tovar, S.J., written approximately between 1541 and 1548 and in which Juan Diego is described in a peculiar way, when exalting his great humility, as "a poor man from the common people, a *macehual*, of truly great piety. This peasant, *mecapal*, was walking around on the summit of the Tepeyac (to see if by chance he could find a little root to dig up) trying to make a living."[58] The Event is narrated in a synthetic manner, essentially, emphasizing some important moments, such as when the Virgin asked Juan Diego to go cut the flowers: "'Do not be sad,' the Virgin said, 'my young boy. Go gather, go cut some flowers there where they bloom.' These flowers bloomed there only by a miracle because in that area the soil is very dry. The flowers would not bloom in any part. When our little man cut them, he placed them in the hollow of his *tilma*."[59] And further on said, "And when he extended his *tilma* to show the flowers to the Archbishop, he also saw, there on our little man's *tilma*, impressed there, The Little Girl Queen; She was in a sign-portrait, in a prodigious manner."[60] About this so-called *Relación Primitiva*, the historians Ernesto de la Torre and Ramiro Navarro de Anda said, "It was studied by Father Ángel María Garibay, who, because of its style, estimated it to be written before *Nican Mopohua*, by Antonio Valeriano. Both accounts coincide in what is essential, but this one is briefer, plain, and appears to have been written, not by Indigenous, but by a person of Spanish origin, although an excellent connoisseur of Náhuatl. . . . We have published here this text, considering it to be the most ancient one among the historical narrations, due to its doubtless value."[61]

---

[58] *Relación Primitiva*, 1541–1548, in Ernesto de la Torre Villar and Ramiro Navarro de Anda, *Testimonios Históricos Guadalupanos*, p. 24.

[59] *Relación Primitiva*, p. 25.

[60] *Relación Primitiva*, p. 25.

[61] Introduction to *Relación Primitiva*, p. 25.

The testimony of the pirate Miles Philips[62] also converges. It is the only case known until now about the Guadalupan devotion in the sixteenth century resulting from a non-Hispanic European source. But let's see about his history. On October 8, 1568, the pirate John Hawkins had a surprising encounter with the fleet of the new viceroy, Enríquez de Almanza, who was arriving to govern New Spain, and which obligated him to leave some members of his crew on the coast of the Panuco [River, Mexico]. Miles Philips was one of those Englishmen left on land, making it easy for the Spaniards to capture him and send him to Mexico City. Philips had the custom of writing down everything that happened to him. Thanks to this we have his fresh and spontaneous narration of what most called his attention. What he saw when he arrived at the Tepeyac is of revealing importance and he contributes information which helps us understand how people lived at that time. Obviously the participants of the *Informaciones Jurídicas de 1666* did not know about all this; however, what he exposes converges in many aspects with their testimonies. Philips said,

> The following day, in the morning, we walked to Mexico until we got within two leagues from the city, to a place where the Spaniards have built a magnificent church dedicated to the Virgin. There they have an image of Hers in gold-covered silver, as big as a tall woman,[63] and in front of Her, and the rest of the church, there are as many silver lamps as there are days in a year, all of them lit on solemn festivities. Always if the Spaniards pass by that church, even if it is on horseback, they get off, go into the church, kneel down before the Image and pray to Our Lady to keep them from all evil. So, whether they are walking or on horseback, they do not go past without entering the church to pray, as I mentioned, because they think that if they did not do so, nothing would turn out right. This Image is called in Spanish *Nuestra Señora de*

[62] Source: Ms. of 1568, in the AGN, Mexico, published in the *Boletín del Archivo General de la Nación*, T. XIV, 2, Mexico 1943. Also in Juan Suárez de Peralta, *Tratado del descubrimiento de las Indias*, Chapter XLI (1589). After his return to England, Miles Philips gave information in 1582 for a brief chronicle which was published for the first time in 1600, and it has now a new edition in Richard Hakluyt, *Voyages and Discoveries: The Principal Navigations, Voyages, Traffiques and Discoveries of the English Nation*, Ed. Penguin Group (Col.=Penguin Classics), London 1985.

[63] He is referring to an image of gilded silver, donated in 1566 by the wealthiest man in New Spain, Alonso de Villaseca. Cfr. *Anales de Juan Bautista*, Historical Archives of the Basilica of Guadalupe, f. 21. Also in Francisco Javier Alegre, S.J., *Historia de la Provincia de la Compañía de Jesús de Nueva España*, Ed. Institutum Historicum, Rome, 1959, T. I., p. 175: "On Sunday, September 15, 1566, they celebrated the octave of Our Mother Holy Mary of the Nativity, and the festivity was celebrated then, in the Tepeyac, of Holy Mary of Guadalupe. Villaseca was present there, and he showed an image of Our Mother, which is all in silver. . . . And to him we owe it, as well as the house where the sick rest [the hospital]. The authorities were present: the auditors and also the Archbishop and all us Indigenous. Villaseca offered a meal for the auditors and the authorities and he reported how the church in the Tepeyac was built."

Guadalupe. Here they have two cold baths; water here is somewhat salty to the taste, but very good for those who have wounds or sores, because it is said that many have been healed. Every year, on the day of Our Lady's feast, the people are used to coming to offer and pray in the church before the Image, and they say that Our Lady of Guadalupe does many miracles.[64]

Another interesting source which converges is offered by Juan Suárez de Peralta, Creole from New Spain, who was magistrate and mayor of Cuauhtitlán. He moved to Spain in 1579, and died after 1589 in Trujillo, Extremadura. Peralta mentioned the Apparitions in a brief but substantial manner in his book, *Tratado del Descubrimiento de las Indias*, written in 1589, which was not published until 1878, in Madrid, under the title *Noticias Históricas de la Nueva España*, and later, Federico Gómez de Orozco published it in Mexico in 1949. As we can see, the book was unpublished for a long time, since the manuscript was finished in Seville in 1589. After presenting a report at the arrival of the Viceroy Martín Enríquez de Almanza, going through the Tepeyac, on November 5, 1568,[65] Juan Suárez de Peralta informs us that "In every town we arrived in they made many receptions, as is customary for all the Viceroys who come here. Thus, he arrived at Our Lady of Huadalupe [Guadalupe], which is a most venerated image and who has performed many miracles (She appeared among some cliffs and all the people go to this devotion). This is two leagues from Mexico City. From there he entered Mexico City and on that day a great party was given for him, with servants dressed in silk; a skirmish of many on horseback, very costly."[66]

Another source that also gives interesting details and that is in agreement with the testimonies of *Informaciones Jurídicas de 1666* but whose witnesses did not know anything about it either, was that offered by the Clare nun Ana de Cristo, who accompanied Mother Jerónima de la Asunción as her secretary. These nuns would travel to the Philippines to establish a new monastery. They were obligated to pass through Mexico, where they stayed from September 1620 to April 1, 1621. Ana de Cristo would take notes on the most important moments of their trip and thanks to this, we are offered

---

[64] "A Discourse Written by Miles Philips, Englishman, Put on Shore in the West Indies by Mr. John Hawkins" 1568, in Richard Hakluyt, *Voyages and Discoveries*, p. 143.

[65] Cfr. Niceto de Zamacois, *Historia de México desde sus tiempos mas remotos hasta nuestros días*, Ed. J. F. Parres y Compañía, Barcelona-Madrid [date of the introdution: 1876]. T.V., p. 149.

[66] Juan Suárez de Peralta, *Tratado del Descubrimiento de las Indias*, Biblioteca Pública de Madrid, manuscript no. 302, f. 163v. Also in *Noticias Históricas de Nueva España. Tratado del Descubrimiento de las Indias*, Madrid 1878, cap. 41. Also in Fortino Hipólito Vera, *Tesoro Guadalupano*, Imp. del Colegio Católico, Amecameca 1889, T. I, p. 68. It has also come out in the edition of the Secretary of Public Education: Juan Suárez de Peralta, *Tratado del Descubrimiento de las Indias*, Ed. SEP, Mexico 1949.

also a narration about the moment in which they passed through the Tepeyac and they heard the people narrate what happened. Ana de Cristo captured the essential part when they talked about Juan Diego, obviously when
they mentioned, "She appeared to an Indigenous"; the Clare nun informs us
in her report that

> The last journey to New Spain was to a hermitage which they call "of Our Lady
> of Guadalupe." We were there one night, it is a paradise, and the image of great
> devotion. They saw Her when Mexico was beaten, when She was throwing dirt
> into the eyes of the enemy; She appeared to an Indigenous in that place where
> She is, which is among some rocks, and She told him to make a house and where
> She stood She poured forth a little clear water that we passed by and saw and it
> is boiling as though it were over a great fire; they gave us a cup to drink and it is
> salty. Some pious women who cared for the hermitage told us the Virgin Herself
> had asked the Indigenous for his mantle and measured it from head to foot.[67]

As we can see, the nun Ana de Cristo captured the essential part of the narration about the Apparitions of the Virgin of Guadalupe, and with great
naivete she transmits a version which is somewhat distant from the traditional one, from the *Nican Mopohua*. However, she is explicit in her attention to point out that the information about the Apparitions, about Juan
Diego and of the Image on the *tilma*, and so on, was common knowledge, ver-
ifying that reality which the *Informaciones Jurídicas de 1666* upholds.

There is also convergence in another important source which is that of
Luis Lasso de la Vega, *Huei Tlamahuizoltica* or *The Great Event*, which in 1649
he had published in regard to the matter and, as it is known, it is part of the
Nican Mopohua and the *Nican Motecpana*, of whose context we have mentioned before and that point out the most important parts that describe Juan
Diego's personality and his virtues, as well as his family. What Father Baltasar
González pointed out is important. On January 9, 1649, he granted the license so that this publication could be written and he noted that there were
annals and tradition about this Event. He said, "I find this is in step with
what is known by tradition and in annals about the facts, because it will be
very useful to liven up the devotion of those who are lukewarm, and it will
generate it in those who live in ignorance of the mysterious origin of this celestial portrait of the Queen of Heaven, and because there is nothing that op-
poses the truth and mysteries of our holy faith."[68]

---

[67] Congregatio pro Causis Sanctorum, Prot. 1720, Manilen. Beatificationis . . . Hieronymae ab Assumptione (in saec. H. Yáñez) . . . *Positio super vita et virtutibus*, Rome MCMXCI, pp. 648–56, 726.
[68] Luis Lasso de la Vega, *Huei Tlamahuizoltica o El Gran Acontecimiento*, 1649, in Ernesto de la Torre
and Ramiro Navarro de Anda, *Testimonios Históricos Guadalupanos*, p. 288.

Also, the substantial information converges with the publication that was written in 1668 by Carlos de Sigüenza y Góngora, titled *Primavera Indiana. Poema Sacro-histórico. Idea de María Santísima de Guadalupe de México, copiada de flores*,[69] in which he describes the Great Guadalupan Event in a poetic, baroque style.

The *Informaciones* also converge with some works of art, such as the Virgin of Guadalupe by the great painter Baltasar de Echave,[70] signed and dated in 1606.[71] Surely there are many images of Our Lady of Guadalupe, copies of the original, painted before Echave's. But the importance of this work is that this one is the oldest signed and dated copy known, and besides it has the particularity that the *tilma's* details are painted also, which obviously reminds us of Juan Diego himself. With regard to this painting, Elisa Vargas Lugo comments, "Baltasar de Echave Orio's painting, in contrast with the majority of the Guadalupan reproductions found throughout the country, offers a reproduction of the Virgin painted on a large *tilma*, whose folds fall abundantly on each side of the composition, clearly showing the artist's intention that the particular quality of the fabric on which the original Image is created not be lost."[72] As one can see, the intention of the artist to re-create not only the Virgin, but also Juan Diego's *tilma*, where the prodigy manifested itself, is important for Elisa Vargas too. Likewise, the specialist and art critic Jaime Genaro Cuadriello, in his *Maravilla Americana. Variantes de la Iconografía Guadalupana, siglos XVII–XIX*, expresses it emphatically:

Recently, to the wonder of all, Mr. Manuel Ortiz Vaquero revealed an [Image] which he considers "the best reproduction, oldest and without a doubt of the greatest skill," and it is, in effect. It is signed and dated by Baltasar Echave Orio (the old one) in 1606. It is indisputably, as all of his paintings, of great artistic quality and rich documental interest: on the figuration of a mantle which has

[69] Carlos de Sigüenza y Góngora, *Primavera Indiana*, 1668, in Ernesto de la Torre and Ramiro Navarro de Anda, *Testimonios Históricos Guadalupanos*, pp. 350–351, 352, and 355.

[70] Baltasar de Echave y Orio, called "the Old One" because he was the father of two other painters with the same last name, Baltasar and Manuel Echave Ibia, and the grandfather of another, Baltasar Echave Rioja. Born in Zumaya, Guipuzcuoa, in 1558, he lived in Seville, where he received the influence of the Flamincan and Italian schools. He arrived in Mexico in 1580 and was married in the Cathedral to Isabel de Ibia, daughter of another painter, Francisco de Zumaya. He was a Renaissance painter of great color, and we still have many of his beautiful artworks. He created a workshop from which his two sons and other disciples emerged. He died in Mexico in 1660. Cfr. Manuel Toussaint, *Pintura Colonial en México*, UNAM, Instituto de Investigaciones Estéticas, Mexico 1965, pp. 84–97.

[71] This painting belongs to a private collection and was exhibited in the exposition called *Imágenes Guadalupanas Cuatro Siglos*, in the Centro Cultural de Arte Contemporaneo, in Mexico City, 1988, and it was published in the commemoratory book of that exposition.

[72] Elisa Vargas Lugo, "Algunas notas más sobre Iconografía Guadalupana," in *Anales de Insituto de Investigaciones Estéticas*, UNAM, Mexico 1989, p. 60.

been set on the top angles and falls, forming soft pleats, the Virgin appears in perfect proportion and just as She looked in 1895 when Her crown disappeared. Attached to its support [signifying reproduction of the *tilma*], it obtains a true naturalness of painting and, of course, manifests that it pertains to a miraculous stamping, in the same fashion as those reproductions of the original "Veronica's veil" or of the "Divine Countenance." Surely familiar with this artistic concept, Echave must have undertaken this copy at the request of some high church dignitary [maybe the Archbishop Friar García Guerra?] who was known for protecting the hermitage. Four decades before the first historic presses existed, this painting proves without a doubt, by its own method of representation, that the details of the Apparition were of common knowledge.[73]

These and many other documents coming from diverse historical sources converge with the essential and substantial information of the Guadalupan Event, especially in the testimony and inspection of the participating witnesses in the *Informaciones Jurídicas de 1666*.

---

[73] Jaime Genaro Cuadriello, *Maravilla Americana. Variantes de la Iconografía Guadalupana, siglos XVII–XIX*, Ed. Patrimonio Cultural de Occidente, Guadalajara 1989, p. 33.

CHAPTER FOUR

∼

Some Characteristics of the Indigenous Education which Draw Us Closer to Juan Diego

It is certain that Juan Diego was a virtuous man, who tried to direct his life along the road of righteousness, of honesty, of virtue, and to make all that pleased God bloom, who was chosen by the Mother of God Herself to be Her messenger. He came to be considered a model of holiness, a fact that was more than evident to the people, as Justina Cananea expressed, "That he was a holy man and that he should pray to God that their children and grandchildren would be like him, since he was so virtuous that he spoke to the Virgin, the reason for which she and all the people held him in this opinion."[1] It is also true that the education which he received as a child, as well as the religiousness he lived, contributed, in certain aspects, to make this man someone who could be the fertile ground where the seed of the Word of the Lord fell and bore fruit, and let us not forget that Juan Diego had been converted and was baptized before the occurrence of the Apparitions.

For this reason, it is important to see some sketches of the education that an Indigenous as himself would receive, in the pre-Hispanic atmosphere, so that in this manner we may understand a little better all that surrounded a person such as Juan Diego, who walked on the road to holiness.

Even before the arrival of the first missionaries, the Indigenous lived very closely in accordance with the "Evangelic requirements." One of the men

---

[1] "Testimonio de Pablo Xuárez," in *Informaciones Jurídicas de 1666*, f. 40r.

who knew the Indigenous culture more profoundly was Friar Bernardino de Sahagún, who helps us precisely to enter that world of the Indigenous education. From book six of his important work, we can see how he had the opportunity to appreciate not only their education but also the good manners and the values within the Indigenous society as well. Precisely for having exalted these values he was severely criticized by his "opponents," those Spaniards who thought that a pagan culture had nothing good to offer. He was even accused of inventing virtues and merits which the Indigenous, being Indigenous and pagans, could not have ever had. What is more, for implying that they were better off in their paganism than in the situation in which the Christians had placed them, the Franciscan said, "because, now they have lost everything, as anyone could see if one compared what this book contains with the life they now have."[2] For this he would argue polemically: "In this book one can clearly see that some opponents have stated that all which is written in these books, before this one and after this one, is fictional and lies. They speak as passionate people, liars, because what is written in this book, the reasoning of human men cannot accept, pretending it is not so, such as a live man can pretend it is not in the language in which it is written. And all the educated Indigenous, if they were asked, would state that this manner of speaking is that of their ancestors, and the traditions that they used to have."[3]

Sahagún's amazement is clear in the very qualifiers that he uses to convey characteristics of the Indigenous culture, for example, "very beautiful metaphors and manners of speaking," "very delicate sentences," "many delicacies in sentences and in language," "very fine language and very delicate metaphors," "has marvelous language and very delicate metaphors and admirable advice," "uses in it many colorful rhetorics," "rebuking vice with anger," "marvelous manners of speaking and delicate metaphors and the most proper terms," "many appetizing things to read and learn and a very good feminine language and very delicate metaphors," "very tasty things to read," "very tender and loving language, full of a thousand charms." But it is in chapter 19 where his commentary turns even aggressive toward his friar colleagues, because he does not fear assuring them that "they would learn more from these two talks given in the pulpit to the boys and girls, because of the language and the style in which they are [mutatis mutandis] than from many other sermons."[4] It is then interesting and enlightening to know these "very

---

[2] Friar Bernardino de Sahagún, *Historia General*, p. 297.
[3] Friar Bernardino de Sahagún, *Historia General*, p. 297.
[4] Friar Bernardino de Sahagún, *Historia General*, p. 349.

tasty things to read" in order to have a closer idea of the education of the Indigenous, and therefore, of Juan Diego.

One can say that their education began before they were born since the grandfather or one of the oldest members of the family would have the task of directing solemn lectures to the future mother when it was certain that she was pregnant, a lecture which valued fertility as a gift that came directly from God, and not by the parent's merit but by the benevolence of God Himself: "My very beloved and precious granddaughter . . . it is clear that you are pregnant and that Our Lord wants to give you offspring . . . see that you do not attribute this mercy to your deserving . . . fortunately the generation of your great-grandparents and your great-great-grandparents already wants to blossom, and of your parents who drew you over here, and Our Lord wants the maguey that they planted to conceive and produce an offspring . . . see that you take very good care of God's creature that is inside of you."[5] The grandfather adds advice and assures the child's health:

> see that you keep from taking heavy things in your arms or picking them up so as not to hurt your creature. . . . I advise you about something else, and this I want our son, your husband who is here, to hear and take note, and it is this: because we are old and we know what is fitting, both of you see that you do not upset each other so you do not hurt your creature; see that you do not use the carnal act too much because you could harm the creature with which Our Lord had adorned you. . . . Oh my Daughter, tiny dove! These words I have said to strengthen and encourage you, and they are words from the elders, your ancestors, and of the old women who are present here, with which they teach you all that is necessary for you to know, and see that they love you very much. . . . Be, Daughter, very fortunate and prosperous, and live in good health and contentment, and be alive with holiness and with health for the child you have in your womb.[6]

All along the process of pregnancy and childbirth itself, these beautiful lectures, prayers, and advice were given, and "as soon as the child was born, the midwife would yell as do those who are fighting in battle, and this meant that the patient had won as a man and had captured a child,"[7] and the child was received with the warning that it was born into a world that was not really his and that his true birth would depend on having the good fortune of deserving a flowered death, which means to die in war or in sacrifice: "My

---

[5] Friar Bernardino de Sahagún, *Historia General*, p. 369.
[6] Friar Bernardino de Sahagún, *Historia General*, pp. 369–370.
[7] Friar Bernardino de Sahagún, *Historia General*, p. 383.

very beloved child, very tender . . . this house where you have been born is just a nest, a shelter . . . your own land is another, it is promised elsewhere, which is the field where wars are made, where battles are engaged: you are sent for it. Your role and job is war, your role is to give the sun the blood of your enemy to drink and to give the earth . . . the bodies of your enemies to eat. Your own land, your inheritance, and your father are the house of the Sun. . . . Hopefully you will deserve and be worthy of dying in this place and receiving in it a flowered death."[8]

War and Death set the tone for every lecture and ceremony that would accompany the Indigenous all his life. We can be aware of the great love that was in the Indigenous education, but it must be emphasized that at the same time it was most rigorous and that it contemplated tremendous punishments for those who wandered off, punishments that included a whole series of treatments which bordered on cruelty, such as whipping the children with nettles, nailing maguey thorns in them, or making them breathe smoke with chili.

In their polygamous family scheme, the mother figure was extremely important and crucial; the father was more of an absent figure, who, without leaving his social predominance, was substituted for on occasions by an older brother, uncle, or another close relative, to whom the family was entrusted while the father went off to war. "It was customary to leave this uncle as caretaker or tutor of his children, his property, his wife, and all the house. The loyal uncle would take charge of his brother's house and his wife as though it were his own."[9] Even so, as we have said, the father was always predominant in the family and his return home from foreign missions was a great event, celebrated in a solemn manner: "When the father wanted to see his children, they would be taken in procession, guided by an honorable midwife, and now, if they all went or if only one in particular wanted to see his father, they always asked permission and they knew from the beginning they were at peace about it . . . they were to be quiet and withdrawn, especially the girls, as if they were very mature and intelligent people."[10]

The father would remain serious and stern with his children, and in the few moments that he had to relate to them, he would address severe lectures to them. The synopsis which Sahagún did of one of the lectures helps us understand the integrity with which the Indigenous faced the initial chaos of

---

[8] Friar Bernardino de Sahagún, *Historia General*, pp. 384–385.
[9] Friar Bernardino de Sahagún, *Historia General*, p. 546.
[10] Friar Toribio Motolinia, *Memoriales*, pp. 309–312.

their contact with the Spaniards, as well as the self-composure they kept during those moments, in unconditional disposability and humility:

> My children, listen to what I want to tell you, because I am your father, and I take good care and rule this home. . . . Know that I am sad and afflicted because I think one of you is to be useless and worthless. . . . Listen, then, now, I want to say how you will know how to be appreciated in this world, how you are to get to God in order to become worthy, and for this I tell you that those who cry and grieve . . . those who volunteer with all their heart to stay up at night and at dawn in order to sweep . . . and straighten up places where God is to be served. . . . One enters the presence of God and becomes His friend. . . . I have no dignity of my own, neither for my deserving or for my wanting—only God can give what He wants, to whom He wants, and He needs no advice from anyone, only His will. . . . I want to tell you what you have to do, hear and take notice: be careful of not wasting your time . . . try to learn some honest trade, such as working with feathers or other mechanical trade, because these things can be accomplished to earn a living in time of need, especially be careful of agricultural aspects. . . . Your ancestors tried to know and do all these things because, even though they were of noble birth, they were always careful to keep their lands and inheritance sown and cultivated, and they said to tell us that it is what their ancestors did. . . . I have never seen in any place that one made a living only by his nobility. . . . There is no man on earth who does not need to eat and drink. . . . See, children, be careful to sow the corn fields and plant magueys and prickly pears [cacti] and fruits. . . . I would have to say many things, but I would never finish. . . . First is to be sure to make yourselves friends of God . . . do not become proud or lose hope, or let fear enter your heart, but be humble in your heart and trust in God. . . . The second thing you have to make sure is to be in peace with everyone, with no one to earn you shame or be disrespectful, respect everyone, have reverence for everyone, do not dare anyone, never confront anyone under any condition, do not let anyone know all you know, humiliate yourself before others even if they say what they want; keep quiet and even if they strike you, do not answer . . . because God sees you very well and He will answer for you, and avenge you; be humble with everyone and with this, God will make you worthy and honor you. The third thing is that you must never waste the time that God has given you on this earth . . . keep yourself busy with worthwhile things every day and every night, do not rob yourself of your time nor lose it. Suffice yourself with this, and with this I have done my duty.[11]

It is inevitable to contemplate and compare many of the Indigenous concepts with the Christian ones and find the astonishing affinity that exists

---

[11] Friar Bernardino de Sahagún, *Historia General*, pp. 343–345.

within them. Let's see another example of those lectures that a father gave his children, since they draw us even closer to that world full of human and "pre-Christian" characteristics which drenched every Indigenous soul, spirit, and mind:

"Come, my children, listen to me, you are my children; your mother and your father am I, who for some days, for a short time, is making mistakes and foolishness in the city, governing your neighbors with ridiculous ineptitude, destroying 'mat and chair,'[12] the place of the glory of *Tloque Nahuaque*.[13]

"You are here, the oldest, the firstborn; you the second one, you who are next, and you, finally, the youngest. I cry, I worry, I grow sad when I think which of you will be 'my dead hand, my dry mouth,'[14] who will prosper, of whom shall Our Lord have mercy.

"Perhaps one of you will be worthy of the mat and the chair, of the care of the people, perhaps not. Maybe I am the last one, and that is all, so it ends; maybe Our Lord, *Tloque Nahuaque*, has decided for it to be so.

"Will it perhaps fall, will the construction with a cane fence that I built be ruined, where I await the word of Our Lord, and that ended with difficulties and misery? Will it turn to dust, to a dunghill? Will my fame and my name end here? Will nothing of my tradition remain? Will nothing live from my memory in the world? Will I totally perish?

"Listen to how one lives on earth, how one obtains the mercy of *Tloque Nahuaque*. There are only tears, pain, sighs, and worry. The devout dedicates himself to sweep, clean, pick up; he accepts it, it is imposed on him as an obligation, he stays up to do so, in order to please Our Lord, he gets up in order to fulfill his duties, to take care of the incensory, of the offerings of *copal* [incense].

"Thus one enters in the presence of *Tloque Nahuaque*, the eagle's mat, the tiger's mat[15]; in his hands He places the eagle's glass, the eagle's tube.[16] Thus He converts Himself into mother, into father of the Sun, He nourishes with food and drink, the Heaven, and the region of the dead. The eagles and the

---

[12] "Mat and chair" is *in petatl in icpalli*, an expression meaning the government, the authority.

[13] "In all these cases the only god is named *Tloque Nahuaque*, Owner of near and close." Miguel León-Portilla, *Los Antiguos Mexicanos a través de sus Crónicas y Cantares*, Ed. FCE, Mexico 1995, p. 183.

[14] "Dead hand, dry mouth" means to be unable to act and to talk.

[15] "Eagles and tigers [jaguars]" were the symbols of the sun and the stars, because of the jaguar's spotted fur; in other words, day and night, therefore symbolic of the cosmic conflict in which it was man's mission and honor to help and to keep assisting and nourishing the sun with his blood.

[16] The *cuauhxicalli* was the bowl that received the hearts of the sacrificed; the *cuahpiaztli* was supposed to be the straw with which the sun drank the blood to nourish himself; "the glass of the eagle," "tube of the eagle" is the man who reaches complete dignity when he assists God in maintaining the universe with life.

tigers see Him with veneration, they see Him as mother, as father, *Tloque Nahuaque* said so, He ordered it; He did not create Himself, He was not made by Himself.

"So he does grant him the mat and the chair, responsibility of the government, as something he deserves and as a gift. . . . Perhaps He makes him lord of men, lord of arms, perhaps He makes him worthy of some little mat, of some little stool to bring order, makes him mother, father of the people, obedient and respected, or maybe, only because of His goodness He makes him worthy of the kingdom, of the power that I now have, as in a dream, without deserving it. Perhaps Our Lord only simply confused me. Did I alone make myself, did I create me by myself? Did I say, 'be I this'? It was the word of Our Lord, it was His mercy, His goodness. Property and possession are from Our Lord, they come from Him, because no one says, 'be I this'; no one takes charge of the government by himself, it is Our Lord who does things for us, He puts them in order and disposes of them according to His will.

"Listen still, I cry, suffer, become sad, I worry at night, wherever my heart goes, if it goes down, if it goes up, because I do not see any of you as good, no one has me at peace. You, the oldest, in vain you are the oldest, in vain you are the firstborn. Why are you the first? There is nothing in you but childishness and immaturity. And you, the next one, and you the youngest, just because you are the second one or the youngest one, do you have to lose or do you have to despair? Our Lord sent you in second place; and you in the last, do you have to get lost because of that?

"Please listen to me. What will you do on earth? You have not been born noble in vain, you descend from our lords, who have gone already to stay on the other side, the Lord Kings, you were not born in, did not come to the world in, an orchard, in the woods. What are you to do then? Will you take care of the cane and of the panniers?[17] Will you care for the furrow and the irrigation?[18] Will you dedicate yourself to the crops and wood? Listen. This is your job: to take charge of the drum and the rattle,[19] to awaken the city and

---

[17] "Cane and panniers" refer to the businessman who carried a cane. If it said *in mecapal in cacaxtl*, it would mean a simple loader.

[18] "Furrow and the irrigation," expression referring to agriculture.

[19] "The drum and the rattle" meant the dance, which represented for the Indigenous *total prayer*. Not only did they call and honor and praise their gods with their songs, but also with their heart and of the senses of their body for which, in order to do this well, they had and used many memorized signals, thus, in the swaying of their head, of their arms and of their feet as well as all of their body, they tried to call and serve their gods. For that reason they took laborious care to lift their heart and their senses to their demons and to serve them with all the parts of their body, and *macehualiztli* which was their effort of persevering in penance and deserving during one day and most of the night. Friar Toribio Motolinia, *Memoriales*, p. 386.

bring joy to *Tloque Nahuaque*. With this you will seek His word, you will launch yourself into Him again and again. This is how one prays for, how one seeks, the word of Our Lord.

"Take care of the arts, of the work with feathers, and of the apprentice-ship, which in hard times, when there is misery in the courts, is a wall and protection, one can eat and drink.

"Above all, you shall take care of the furrow and irrigation, plant and sow the field. Does it not belong to you? Is it not you who has to make it grow, who has to water the corn? Those who went before left it for you, those from whom you descended, the lords, the kings, they took care of it, they talked about the furrow and the irrigation, they sowed, they planted. They used to say, according to a tradition they left us, that they made us keep, 'If you only see to the nobility, if you do not put in order that which has to do with the furrow and irrigation, what will you give the people to eat? What will you eat,? What will you drink? Where have I seen that one eats nobility for breakfast or dinner?'[20]

"Listen: sustenance deserves all our care. Someone has said, someone has called it our bones and our flesh; it is our life, it makes us walk, move, rejoice, live, it revives us. There is a lot of truth in that it is who governs us, who reigns, who conquers. Where have you seen someone reign, govern, on an empty stomach, who does not eat? Where have I seen a conqueror without abundance of food? Earth exists because of sustenance, the world which we all fill, lives because of it; we are all waiting for sustenance.[21]

"In the fields you shall plant the little maguey, the little cacti, the little tree, they will give rest to the little ones, the elders used to say. And you, young man, would you not like some fruit? And how is there going to be any if you do not plant your land?

"My lecture will end with this, you shall place it in your heart, keep it and put it in the house of your heart, paint it in your heart. It is not much, the lecture is not long, it will not last long, until then I want to have my say. So there, then, there are two things that must be kept, that must be placed in the heart, those which were left for us, were given to us, they made us keep, they who abandoned us when they left.

---

[20] "According to a tradition that they left us, that they made us keep." This shows that the Indigenous always knew how to provide for and face stoically and serenely the worst difficulties, as well as not to attach themselves in excess to wealth and privileges, which explains to us Juan Diego and his uncle's noble attitude.

[21] "Our sustenance" is *in tonacayotl*. Take into account this emphasis in order to understand that Juan Diego called Heaven *in tonacatlapan*, or "the land of our sustenance."

"The first one is to enter into the presence of Our Lord *Tloque Nahuaque*, the Lord Who is Night and Wind: give Him all your heart and all your body, do not turn away. Do not talk to yourself, nor say anything to yourself, do not blaspheme in your exasperation, Our Lord the prudent one, the provider, sees and hears even inside the tree, the stone. He will dispose something for you.

"The second one is that you live in peace among the people, give respect and reverence to all; do not offend them in any way, do not turn against them in any way, do not stop being in peace, let them say what they want to say and even if you end up as you may, do not look for vengeance. Do not rise like a serpent and shoot out in anger against the people, instead receive them with love, because Our Lord sees you and He will get angry and take vengeance on you. Live, then, in a simple manner, since you have been guided, you have been prepared.

"The third one is to avoid vain science, do not presume about your vain science in the world; do not waste night nor day, what matters most to us are our bones and our flesh, what strengthens us, sustenance. Ask Our Lord for life, ask Him also for that which we hang on our neck and our hips.[22] Think about this day and night instead of paying attention to vanities.

"This is all, with this I fulfill my duties with you. Perhaps you will throw it out somewhere, perhaps you will not pay attention to it; in any case, now you know it, and I have fulfilled my duty."[23]

A great majority of the Indigenous children were educated in the *Calmecac*, or in the *Tepochcalli*, extremely severe schools, whose primary objective was that their alumni become as virtuous and generous as possible, where they were guided in the manner of doing penance, serving the gods, living in cleanliness, in humility, as well as chastity:[24] "where nobility is bounded and shaped, sprouts and blossoms, where like necklaces and fine feathers Our Lord *Tloque Nahuaque* disposes of them and orders them, where *Ipalnemohuani* has mercy on them and chooses them . . . Our Lord *Tloque Nahuaque* chooses them, they are in the mat of the eagles, in the mat of the tigers, in His hand is the glass and the tube of the eagle."[25]

---

[22] Allusion to the expression *In Maxtlatl in Tilmatli*, "loincloth and mantle," a form of referring to the man and to virility, not only in the sexual sense, but also integral. The sentence could be interpreted as "Ask Him that you be a man!" It also can be taken into account this identity of the *tilma* with the person in order to understand the fact that the Queen of Heaven left Her Image (also a symbol of a person) specifically on Juan Diego's *tilma*.

[23] *Huehuetlatolli. Sexto Libro del Códice Florentino*, paleography, version, notes, and index by Salvador Díaz Cíntora, UNAM, Coordinación de Humanidades, Mexico 1995, pp. 25–31.

[24] Friar Bernardino de Sahagún, *Historia General*, p. 401.

[25] *Huehuetlatolli. Sexto Libro del Códice Florentino*, pp. 126–128.

The parents and relatives, as well as those in charge of these schools, gave the student a clear line of study:

> This is what you are going to do: you are going to sweep, to pick up, fix, stay up, spend the night awake. When its time to run, you will run, you will hurry, you will not be lazy nor idle. All you will need is to hear it once, having heard it once you will stand up quickly, in a jump, you will not be called twice; and even if you are not called, stand, run, get what you have to bring, do what is required of you.[26]
>
> Listen, my child, where you are going you are not going to be honored, obeyed, respected; instead you are going to humiliate yourself, obey, and live in poverty. When you become mature, if you sweat and your body becomes restless, reform and submit; do not remember, do not wish for dirt or trash. You will be wretched if you want to accept what is evil, dirt, and trash inside, if you abandon your merit, your destiny. Try as much as you can to put aside sexual uneasiness. What you have to do is cut spruce thorns and branches and offer them, and get into water.[27] Do not eat until you are stuffed, know and love abstinence: the one who suffers hunger, the one who looks like a skeleton, his flesh and his bones will not get too hot; only once in a while, like a fever, will he experience anxiety. Do not use too many clothes, may your body not tremble with the cold. The truth is that you have gone to become worthy, you have gone to ask *Tloque Nahuaque* for something, you have gone to throw yourself into His bosom, into the innermost of Our Lord. In time of fasting, when your lips get dry, do not hurt them, everything is so that there will be life. Do not consider it painful, make yourself part of it.
>
> You shall take care of the black and the red, the book and the scripture,[28] go to the prudence of the prudent, of the wise. My child, my little boy, you are no longer like a little bird, you can see and hear by yourself. Here is the brief word, the duty of the elder men and women: take it with you where you go, do not throw it away, you will be wretched if you laugh at it. They will say more to you, they will offer you more there, well you are going to the house of instruction; [this word] will not be with you there, you will not find the word of the elder there; and if you hear something that seems mistaken, do not laugh. Go then, my beloved son, my little one, go, enter to sweep and to offer incense.[29]

Professors and teachers in the schools assumed responsibility, thinking that they were dealing with a divine mission. The teachers said that the child's parents were offering their child to God,

---

[26] We see Juan Diego's behavior here, obeying in an instant when the Lady from Heaven indicated something. It came from a tradition which was received and assimilated as a child.

[27] "Getting into water" means cold water, as a mortification.

[28] It refers to science, the wisdom consigned in the written tradition.

[29] *Huehuetlatolli. Libro Sexto del Códice Florentino*, pp. 126–128.

and we, in His name receive him, He knows what He should do with him. We indignant caducous [limited] servants, with doubtful hope, wait for the outcome and what pleases Him to do with your child, according to what He already has planned in His mercy, according to His disposition and determination, since before the beginning of the world. True, we ignore the talents that were given to him and the property and condition that were given to him. . . . We wish and pray that the riches of Our Lord be given to him; we hope that those talents and mercies with which Our Lord adorned and beautified him will be manifested and brought to light in this school.[30]

These are some of the characteristics of the philosophical and religious planning of education, which not only evolved around the purpose of transmitting an accumulation of knowledge, but also consisted in a true integral formation of the children and youth, who were not exempt of ability and intelligence to understand, memorize, and analyze their message. As the first missionaries had the opportunity to prove, Friar Toribio Motolinia said, "Who teaches man science, is the same Who provided and gave these Indigenous great intelligence and ability to learn all the sciences, arts, and trades that they were taught."[31] Also, Friar Gerónimo de Mendieta pointed out that "They had such a memory that after having heard a sermon or a story of a saint once or twice, they had it memorized and would retell it with charm, audacity, and effectiveness."[32] In the same manner, the Jesuits manifested admiration for these virtues in the Indigenous in a report or narration at the end of the sixteenth century or the beginning of the seventeenth, saying, "and what are more valuable are their great intelligence and happy attitudes, so that all this leads to hope for a great harvest for God."[33] In folios further ahead in this same report, after narrating some concrete examples of the Indigenous fidelity and nobleness, he pointed out, "This is how all the rest are, healthy, loyal, and sincere."[34]

The mind of the Indigenous was well trained, as the Jesuit P. Juan de Tovar wrote in a letter to P. Joseph de Acosta, S.J.:

In order to memorize all the words and the scheme of the speeches made by orators and poets, the many songs they had, which were composed by the same orators and which everyone knew without changing a word (although they

---

[30] Friar Bernardino de Sahagún, *Historia General*, p. 209.
[31] Friar Toribio Motolinia, *Historia de los Indios*, p. 163.
[32] Friar Gerónimo de Mendieta, *Historia Eclesiástica Indiana*, pp. 225–226.
[33] *Narración sobre la misión de los indios acaxes en la Sierra de San Andrés*, sixteenth or seventeenth century, AHSI, Rome, Mexican, *Annuae* 1574–1614 (Mexico 14), Volume I, f. 32r.
[34] *Narración sobre la misión de los indios acaxes en la Sierra de San Andrés*, p. 34v.

were drawn), there was an exercise in this memorization every day in the schools for the best students, who were to be their successors, and with continuous repetition they memorized them without changing a word. They took the most famous rhetoric that was given at the time as a method to train the boys who were to be speakers. In that way, many speeches were preserved, without losing a word, from person to person, until the Spaniards came, who in our writing wrote down many of their speeches and songs, which I saw, and that have been preserved.[35]

As we can understand, in many of the characteristics presented by the Indigenous education, the attitudes and the concepts clearly harmonized with Juan Diego's life. There are various aspects where the light of the virtues with which God adorned Holy Mary of Guadalupe's faithful messenger are manifested. There is no doubt that Juan Diego was a humble and obedient person, who had a profound education, with a religious strength that evolved through all this life and that manifested itself in the way he acted, especially in the encounter with the Virgin of Guadalupe. He was a virtuous man "who performed great penance and at the time was called a 'Most Holy Man.'"[36]

---

[35] "Carta del P. Juan de Tovar, S.J., al P. Joseph de Acosta, S.J.," in Ángel María Garibay K., *Fray Juan de Zumárraga y Juan Diego—Elogio Fúnebre*, Ed. Bajo el signo de "Ábside," Mexico 1949, pp. 11–14.
[36] "Testimonio de Martín de San Luis," in *Informaciones Jurídicas de 1666*, f. 46v.

CHAPTER FIVE

~

A Conversion from the Bottom of the Heart

The light from the Star of Evangelization revealed itself as a moment of God's intervention in the history of humanity. Even if man, regardless of the divine intervention, continues having limitations, infidelities, and treasons, there is no doubt that immediately after the date of the Apparitions an impressive change was noticed in regard to the conversions of the Indigenous, as well as in the attitude of the Spaniards themselves: a change in the soul of Mexico's population.

Friar Juan de Zumárraga, the Bishop of Mexico, was the first to manifest a radical change in spirit. As we saw previously, in 1529, Zumárraga showed great anguish, impotence, and worries, not only because the Indigenous were going back to their idolatrous rituals, but also because of the disasters committed by his own Spanish brothers, who cared very little about going against the Friars and the most basic principles of their mission. After 1531 Zumárraga showed a totally different spirit. He wrote a note to Hernán Cortés, saying,

> Now I understand in my procession and in my writing to the Veracruz, the joy in everyone cannot be described. One cannot write with Salamanca. I sent the Custodian to Cuernavaca as messenger. There is an Indigenous already going to Friar Toribio, and may everything be for the praise of God, *Laudent nomen domini*, with Indigenous praises. Eve of the Feast of feasts.
>
> Your Majesty, tell the Marchioness that I want to name the main Church the 'Conception of the Mother of God,' because on that day God and His

Mother wanted to perform this mercy for this land which you won. No more
for now.

From Y. L. Chaplain [Zumárraga]

Signed "The rejoicing elect"[1]

Mariano Cuevas, who published this document, comments, "The Bishop,
leaving his habitual grave character, his seriousness and serenity, . . . gave
Cortés such notice, or better said, a notice that was given or known, for
which 'One cannot describe the joy of everyone and all *Laudent nomen domini.*' He supposed there would be a great rejoicing of the people, which had
to be celebrated with religious festivities and clearly expressed a favor granted
by the Most Holy Virgin, around the Day of the Immaculate Conception, an
extraordinarily great favor, performed for all of the land conquered by Hernán
Cortés and related very closely to the Immaculate Conception."[2] Cuevas, after making a thorough examination in order to clarify the date, concluded
that this document corresponded to the end of December 1531. Surely, the
bishop-elect, Friar Juan de Zumárraga, manifested a great difference in spirit
between the letter of 1529, sent to the king, which he could have signed "the
overwhelmed elect," and this one from 1531 to Cortés where he exclaims
that he is "the rejoicing elect."

But this letter is not the only manifestation of the important change
brought about at the end of 1531; there is another concrete sign, clear and
objective, that this joy penetrated completely: the conversions of the Indigenous, which after that moment counted in thousands. And this is proven
by historical records. For example, just as Friar Toribio Motolinia pointed out
to us that the great work of the Franciscans had had a certain amount of baptisms of Indigenous as a result, he could not deny that during the first years
the Indigenous remained reluctant to convert to Catholicism. The missionary declared that "The Mexicans remained very cold for five years."[3] What is
more, he was aware of the insignificance of their resources for this enormous
task, their terrible problems, and the uncertainty that their conversion would
be sincere.[4] The fear that the piety of the Indigenous was disguised idolatry

---

[1] Friar Juan de Zumárraga, *Recado urgente a Hernán Cortés*, ACI, Stand 51, box 6, file 3, in Mariano Cuevas, *Notable Documento Guadalupano. Informe leído en la Real Academia de la Historia, en sesión
del 27 de junio de 1919*, Ed. Comité General de la ACJM, Mexico 1919, p. 9.

[2] Friar Juan de Zumárraga, *Recado urgente a Hernán Cortés*, pp. 9–10.

[3] Friar Toribio Motolinia, *Historia de los Indios*, p. 78.

[4] In fact, some of the missionaries, like Sahagún and Durán, took it upon themselves to investigate, meticulously, the Indigenous culture, in order to better combat any kind of idolatry, which could
jeopardize their recently converted flock: "The doctor cannot apply the medicine correctly to the patient if first he does not know what causes the illness. . . . In order to preach against these things, and

subsisted for a long time among all the missionaries and it got to be an obsession for some of them, as it did for Friar Diego de Durán.[5]

However, after those first years, Motolinia wrote of the great number of Indigenous who asked for baptism, and that at that moment, unexplainably, they counted in the thousands. He confirmed that "Friar Juan de Perfiñán and Friar Francisco de Valencia, baptized more than 100,000 each from the 60 that are in this year 1536."[6] Motolinia continued counting by thousands the ones who had been baptized and came to the conclusion that the total in 1536 "would be close to 5 million baptized until today."[7] On his part, Friar Juan de Torquemada informs us in his manuscript *Monarquía Indiana* that "Many thousands were baptized in one day."[8]

Even the friars were surprised by this massive conversion. Mendieta pointed out that "In the beginning, they started going 200 at a time, then 300 at a time, always growing and multiplying, until they reached the thousands; some from two days journey, others from three, others from four, and some farther away. This caused great admiration to those who saw it. Grown people and young, men and women, healthy and ill went. The old baptized people brought their children to be baptized, and the young baptized brought their parents; the husband brought his wife, and the wife, her husband."[9] The Indigenous would stay in the monasteries in order to learn the catechism; they would repeat it many times in order to memorize the prayers in Latin. "At the time of their baptism, many received that sacrament with tears in their eyes. Who would dare to say that they came without faith: they came from so far away, with so many problems, no one forced them, in their search of the sacrament of baptism?"[10]

Some Indigenous, as Mendieta said, made great efforts to get to the monastery where the sacrament of baptism could be administered to them. For example, in order to get to the monastery of Guacachula, the Indigenous

---

even to know if they exist, it is necessary to know how they were used." Friar Bernardino de Sahagún, *Historia General*, p. 17. This was the general attitude. However, there were exceptions, such as Friar Jacobo de Testera, who wrote: "Their idolatry did not frighten us religious when we entered this land, and by having compassion for their blindness, we had great confidence that all that and much more would be in the service of Our God, when they get to know him." *Carta de fray Jacobo de Testera*, Huejotzingo, May 6, 1533, in *Cartas de Indias*, Madrid 1877, p. 66.

[5] Cfr. Friar Diego de Durán, *Historia de las Indias de Nueva España e Islas de Tierra Firme*, finished in 1591, Ed. Porrúa (=Col. Biblioteca Porrúa, no. 36 and 37), Mexico 1967.

[6] Friar Toribio Motolinia, *Historia de los Indios*, p. 85.

[7] Friar Toribio Motolinia, *Historia de los Indios*, p. 85.

[8] Friar Juan de Torquemada, *Monarquía Indiana*, Ed. Porrúa (=Col. Biblioteca Porrúa, no. 43), introduction by Miguel León-Portilla, Mexico 1986, T. III, p. 140.

[9] Friar Gerónimo de Mendieta, *Historia Eclesiástica*, p. 276.

[10] Friar Gerónimo de Mendieta, *Historia Eclesiástica*, p. 276.

had to cross mountains and gorges, almost without food. This flow of Indigenous was not a passing phenomenon; they continued arriving from far-off lands and with all those difficulties, for months. Mendieta added that

> A religious servant of God, who was there as a guest, said that in five days that he was baptizing there, and he and another priest counted more than 14,200. Even though there was a lot of work (because he placed oil and chrism on each one) he said he felt in his heart something more joyful in baptizing them than others. Their devotion and their fervor placed spirit and strength in the minister so he could console all of them, so that no one would leave without consolation. To see the fervent desire which these new converts brought to their baptism was truly something to notice and marvel at; one does not read about greater things in the primitive Church. One does not know what to marvel at most, seeing these new people coming or seeing how God brought them. Though it would be better to say to see how God brought them and how His Holy Church received them. After being baptized, it was remarkable to see them so consoled, rejoicing, and happy, with their young children on their back, that they seemed not able to contain in themselves all the joy.[11]

When this conversion acquired massive dimensions, they questioned themselves about the best way of administering baptism and they sought a sure guide, writing to the pope in order to know the solutions which could be given to this situation. While the answer arrived from Rome, the friars had to suspend the baptisms in big masses. This caused a situation that broke the friars' hearts, as the people were anxious to receive the sacrament, with attitudes that moved and surprised the missionaries. For example, Mendieta himself tells us about these Indigenous, who did not care about distances, weather, hunger, and so on, just to have their baptism; and of course, they did not mind waiting. In the convent of Guacachula, as well as in that of Tlaxcala, 2,000 Indigenous were counted waiting patiently in the courtyards and they would beg any missionary they saw to baptize them. The missionaries witnessed how, when sent off without being baptized, the Indigenous went home, "crying and complaining, with many regrets, which broke their hearts, even if they were made out of stone."[12]

There is no doubt that it was a surprise, this massive conversion of the Indigenous, "something to notice and to marvel at," and the same may be said of the Indigenous who tried to go to confession. Mendieta said

---

[11] Friar Gerónimo de Mendieta, *Historia Eclesiástica*, p. 277.
[12] Friar Gerónimo de Mendieta, *Historia Eclesiástica*, p. 278.

It happened that on the roads, hills and wilderness, 1,000, 2,000 Indigenous men and women would follow the religious, only to confess, leaving their homes and lands alone; many of them were pregnant women, some giving birth on the way, and almost all of them with their children on their back. Other old men and women who could hardly stand, with their canes and even blind, were taken 15 or 20 leagues at a time, to look for a confessor. Among the healthy, many came from 30 leagues, and others would walk from one monastery to another, more than 80 leagues, looking for someone who would confess them. Because there was so much to do everywhere, they were not accepted. Many would take their wife and children and their food as if they were moving to another place. They might stay one or two months waiting for a confessor, or some place to confess.[13]

One of the most difficult sacraments to be accepted by the Indigenous was that of matrimony, because leaving their wives and having only one was not easy, a family scheme which even in some parts of Mexico is still the norm today. The Indigenous, people who submitted to wars and human sacrifices as part of cosmic harmony, could not conceive not having many children, a fundamental part of this sacred harmony. For this reason, even if the massive conversion that took place after the Guadalupan Event was surprising, the missionaries knew that the Indigenous rejected the sacrament of matrimony with only one woman, so it is even more admirable that just after the Guadalupan Event they would fervently ask for the Christian matrimony.

Friar Toribio Motolinia tells us about this process of change. After much effort and fatigue, the first Christian marriage took place on October 14, 1526, when eight couples were married, among whom was don Hernando, brother of the lord of Texcoco; Motolinia mentions this first matrimony in the land of Anáhuac, pointing out this date as a reference due to the fact that matrimonies were very scarce, and he tells us the reason for this: "Men have many women, they do not want to let go of them, not even the missionaries can make them let go; no persuasions, no sermons, nor anything they did was enough for them to leave all but one, to marry by the Church. They would answer that the Spaniards also had many women; and if they were told that they had them at their service, they would say that they also had them for the same. So, even though the Indigenous had many wives whom they married according to their customs, they also had them for profits, because they made them all weave and make cloths and other trades."[14] Motolinia proves

---

[13] Friar Gerónimo de Mendieta, *Historia Eclesiástica*, pp. 282–83. One league is 3 miles or 5 kilometers.

[14] Friar Toribio Motolinia, *Historia de los Indios*, p. 98.

and was a witness that after 1531 things changed radically, and he continued, "It has pleased Our Lord that through His will some have left that multitude of women which they had and are content with only one, marrying her, as the Church demands. The young men that marry for the first time are so many now that the churches have grown, because on some days 100 couples marry, some days 200, 300, and some days 500."[15]

Mendieta, on his part, said, "There was much to admire about the faith of the Indigenous. Many left their legitimate wife because they did not love her, and got involved with the concubines whom they were fond of, had three or four children with them; but then, in order to do what was ordered, they would leave these ones for whom they felt a great passion, and they would go look for the first one, 15 or 20 leagues away, so that their baptism would not be denied."[16]

The missionaries were confused with this radical change, of so very many conversions, and they would try to reason this phenomenon, saying that, in part, it had been the result of their preaching and testimony. As we have said, there is no doubt that this certainly influenced the first conversions. However, the massive conversion left the seraphic missionaries admiring and astonished; as Mendieta said, "it was something to notice and marvel" and "very admirable," and he confirmed that this had overreached the missionary intervention: "Who could dare to say that they came with no faith, since they came with so much sacrifice and by themselves?"

The *Nican Motecpana* also verifies and confirms this change within the Indigenous heart, which manifested itself in the acceptance of the faith. In its own manner and style, through this important source we are told that the Indigenous, "submerged in profound darkness, still loved and served false little gods, clay figurines and images of our enemy the devil, in spite of having heard about the faith. But when they heard that the Holy Mother of Our Lord Jesus Christ had appeared, and since they saw and admired Her most perfect Image, which has no human art; their eyes were opened as if suddenly day had dawned for them."[17] The conversion was such that many of them threw away their idols, "and then (according to what the elder left painted) some noblemen, as well as their plebeian servants, willingly threw their images of the devil out from their houses and scattered them, and they started to believe in and venerate Our Lord Jesus Christ and His precious Mother."[18]

[15] Friar Toribio Motolinia, *Historia de los Indios*, p. 98.
[16] Friar Gerónimo de Mendieta, *Historia Eclesiástica*, p. 300.
[17] Fernando de Alva Ixtlilxóchitl, *Nican Motecpana*, p. 3.
[18] Fernando de Alva Ixtlilxóchitl, *Nican Motecpana*, p. 307.

One of the key aspects of this conversion is that Mary came to bring us Her Son, Jesus Christ; which is to say that the Image of Our Lady of Guadalupe is Christ-centered, because She places Her Son in the place that corresponds to Him, in the center of the Image, in the flower with the four petals, which for the Indigenous represented movement, life, the Only True God Who is life and gives life: *Ometeotl*. The pregnant Maiden-Mother is expecting Jesus Christ, carries Him in Her womb, as a treasure offered to us. This is also confirmed in the *Nican Motecpana*: "In what was realized, She not only came to show Herself as the Queen of Heaven, our precious Mother of Guadalupe, in order to help the natives in their mundane miseries, but actually, because She wanted to give them Her light and Her help, so that finally they would know the True and Only God and through Him see and know life in Heaven."[19] In the same manner, She does not dislike the work of the missionaries but adds it to the evangelizing work, as is expressed in the *Nican Motecpana*: "In order to do this, She came Herself to introduce and strengthen faith, which the reverent sons of San Francis had started to share."[20]

Truly, this change, which had its origin in the depth of hearts, is surprising, and this new attitude, which reveals a light of hope, that permits Evangelization to take place in a people, who were like earth which is well prepared, to receive the message of Salvation. In fact, a devotion that no one can hold back is initiated, and what is more, it went deeper and it spread out during the diverse historical periods which took place in Mexico. This is a fascinating story that transcends frontiers, cultures, ethnicity, and time; and in which the humble Indigenous Juan Diego had an important participation, being the ambassador of this message, a message that gets precisely to the heart of all men in order to free him, an enculturated message of Mary of Guadalupe, Star of Evangelization.

---

[19] Fernando de Alva Ixtlilxóchitl, *Nican Motecpana*, p. 307.
[20] Fernando de Alva Ixtlilxóchitl, *Nican Motecpana*, p. 307.

CHAPTER SIX

~

A Report Which Sheds Light on the Truth about the Great Devotion to Our Lady of Guadalupe

The fame of the miracles performed by Our Lady of Guadalupe made Her devotion spread quickly, from the very beginning; and, as we have pointed out, it was clear that a mentality based on the medieval theology of the Franciscans resisted trusting the devotion coming forth from the Tepeyac, fearing idolatry. Some Franciscans kept a prudent silence about this devotion and some spoke against it, such as Friar Bernardino de Sahagún, who could not hide his anger and called it "a satanic invention," fearing that the Indigenous would return to their old idols. But it is also true that there were other reasons that were not within this paternal protection, and they originated with the inconvenience that the Provincial of the Franciscans, Friar Francisco de Bustamante, experienced when the Dominican Archbishop, Alonso de Montúfar, started to install a more diocesan church, which meant taking pastoral territories from the Franciscans and turning them over to the secular clergy, or to the friars of other religious orders, such as the Dominicans; since Montúfar had admired the devotion to Our Lady of Guadalupe, he found himself firmly rejected by Bustamante.

This silence and rejection, direct from the first missionaries, was apparently somewhat contrary to the devotion, but in fact, it helps to confirm that the *Guadalupana* from Mexico was not a devotion brought over by the Spaniards in order to subdue the Indigenous because then it would have appeared contradictory to the devotion, even a direct attack against it. Our Lady of Guadalupe from Mexico is a devotion originating in the Tepeyac, and has only the same name as the Virgin of Guadalupe in Extremadura, Spain. In fact, the Franciscan Friar Alonso de Santiago wanted Saint Mary of Guadalupe in Tepeyac "not to be named Our Lady of Guadalupe, but of Tepeaca or Tepeaquilla."[1]

But let us see how events developed. After the death of Archbishop Friar Juan de Zumárraga, in 1548, the archdiocese remained vacant for a long time; and if the archbishopric was offered to the Franciscans, they did not accept, basically because they wanted to be completely dedicated to their mission. In 1551 the Dominican Alonso de Montúfar was elected, who arrived in Mexico on June 23, 1554, and took possession of his see on July 7, 1554; he was a religious from the Order of the Preachers, a sincere, honest man, and a great religious who had worked in the Holy Office in Spain; an "enemy of abuses and disorders, he had a clear intelligence for knowing the cause that originated them, and did not lack the energy to oppose them either."[2] Montúfar realized that a reform was necessary at different levels: the administration of the Church, the mission that was being developed, beginning with the teaching of catechism, and the administration of the sacraments, because the archdiocese had remained without a pastor a long time.

Five months after arriving in Mexico, on November 30, 1554, Archbishop Montúfar wrote to the Council of the Indies about the mishaps of his arrival in Mexico, showing how he had found his archdiocese. Already different ways of thinking were being outlined about the mission that had to be developed in the New World and a local Church which had to be established. The direct confrontation was with the Franciscans.

Anger made pastoral life more problematic. The historian Joaquín García Icazbalceta tells us that "They asked the Archbishop for a report about all of his diocese, but as the majority of the administration was still in the hands of the [Franciscan] Friars, the Archbishop turned to them to give him the pertinent information that they had charge of. The Friars refused to give it to him, saying that the King had asked for that information and that they corresponded directly to the King. For this reason he was only able to report on that which referred to his clergy."[3]

---

[1] "Testimonio de Gonzalo de Alarcón," in *Información de 1556 ordenada realizar por Alonso de Montúfar, Arzobispo de México,* in Ernesto de la Torre Villar and Ramiro Navarro de Anda, *Testimonios Históricos Guadalupanos,* pp. 61–62.

[2] Vicente Riva Palacio, *México a traves de los siglos,* Ed. Cumbre, Mexico 1891, T. III, p. 366.

[3] *Códice Franciscano,* siglo XVI, gathered by Joaquín García Icazbalceta, Ed. Salvador Chávez-Haynoe, Mexico 1941, p. VIII.

Tensions were obvious; "as the secular clergy organized itself, it rivaled with the orders. There were also conflicts among them and with the civil population. This resulted in the continuation of passionate reports about the Church life."[4]

In fact, problems not only arose between the archbishop and the Franciscans, but also between them and the Dominicans. Discussions reached such a point that the Holy See itself had to intervene in order to reestablish peace. "At that time, there were many problems that kept the two religious orders in Mexico separated, beginning with the issue related to the opportunity and the legality of the baptisms given to the Indigenous, at a mad pace, surely, by the seraphic missionaries, without great ceremony, and with the simplest liturgical elements. Disputes became so serious that it was necessary to submit them to the pontific authority."[5]

On November 20, 1555, the Provincial Friar Francisco de Bustamante, along with other Franciscans, among whom Friar Toribio de Motolinia and Friar Juan de Gaona, stood out and wrote a long letter to the king, complaining about Archbishop Montúfar and of the bishops who at that moment were celebrating the First Mexican Provincial Council.[6] The trigger had been, specifically, the tithe and the pastoral places which were taken away from them. It must be mentioned that the bishops were united in the regal petition of June 23, 1543, where it was determined that a tithe should be charged to the Indigenous in order to maintain the local Church. In fact, the tithe was one more of the installments of a diocesan Church.

In the letter that the Franciscans wrote to the king, in addition to the disagreement over the charging of the tithe, their anger was obvious because some of their pastoral territories had been taken from them in order to install the diocesan Church. The attacks against Archbishop Montúfar were clear and direct. Bustamante said "[Archbishop Alonso de Montúfar] has taken from us some places that we had taken with permission from your Viceroy

---

[4] Silvio Zavala, *El servicio personal de los indios en la Nueva España 1521–1550*, Eds. El Colegio de México y El Colegio Nacional, Mexico 1984 [republished, Mexico 1991], T.I., p. 485.

[5] Georges Baudot, *La pugna franciscana por México*, Eds. Alianza Editorial Mexicana y Consejo Nacional para la Cultura y las Artes (=Col. Los Noventa, no. 36), Mexico 1990, p. 49.

[6] In fact, the Audience of the New Spain had already written to the king, on September 14, 1555, when all of the priests were still in the council, giving a report about the mistreatments that the Indigenous received when they continued asking them for the tithe which the king had ordered in his disposition of June 23, 1543. The princess wrote to the Audience of New Spain, ordering that they continue charging the tithe, but that they talk to the archbishop and the provincials from each order to reach a determination. Cfr. Genaro García, *Documentos inéditos o muy raros para la historia de México*, Ed. Porrúa (= Col. Biblioteca Porrúa, no. 58), Mexico 1974, pp. 448–449. About this issue of the tithe, its antecedents, and the confirmation of its end, Cfr. Silvio Zavala, *El servicio personal*, T. I. pp. 485–509.

and the previous Archbishop; and also he has given our monasteries to clergy monasteries where, by chapter, religious and guardians have been named . . . thus he [the Archbishop] does not want help and he says one thing but does another. He has taken the towns where we have been catechizing for 20 or 30 years and regard them as our children and has given them to clergies and religious of other orders. We offer to take care of them ourselves and place Friars there, but he does not think it is appropriate and he responds that it is fair that the clergies be where they can provide."[7] Friar Bustamante got to the point of preferring to obey the viceroy rather than the pastor of the archdiocese. The Franciscan added that "It would be necessary that your Highness deal with the Pope so that we would not be obligated to ask the consent of the Bishops of both assemblies, as we do outside of them, and that we would not be obligated to ask for approval in the locations which we are to take, but that the license from your Viceroy be enough, because, once they are notified of a good location they try to place a clergy there . . . where the Indigenous receive great damage."[8] In some way, Bustamante's harsh words help us understand a little better the feeling of vexation which the Franciscans experienced, seeing the archbishop as a real enemy, and taking an attitude contrary to any initiative from the prelate.

Archbishop Montúfar had made several efforts to install this diocesan Church, a local church, according to the demands of the moment within all of his pastoral province. The prelate as well had fixed his eyes on the Image of Our Lady of Guadalupe and wanted to continue fortifying Her veneration, because he could see the miracles done, especially the massive conversion. For Bustamante, any pretext was enough for him to manifest his opposition to the prelate, and one of those circumstances was when the archbishop preached in the Metropolitan Cathedral on Sunday, September 6, 1556, supporting and motivating the veneration of Our Lady of Guadalupe.

Montúfar, in his homily, spoke in favor of continuing the devotion to the Virgin of Guadalupe, using the Biblical quotation "*Beati oculi qui vident que*

---

[7] *Carta del provincial franciscano, fray Francisco de Bustamante y comunidad al rey Felipe II*, Mexico, November 20, 1555, AGI, S. Indiferente General, 2978.

[8] *Carta del provincial franciscano, fray Francisco de Bustamante y comunidad al rey Felipe II*. Actually, in times of Friar Juan de Zumárraga, on June 23, 1543, the king had given orders that the Indigenous were to pay the tithe; however, this was not imposed rigorously. But because of the letter written by Friar Francisco de Bustamante, sent to Spain in 1555, on April 10, 1557, almost two years later, the Spanish Crown decided that the Indigenous would not be obligated to pay the tithe: "That the chapter which refers to the Indigenous of this land paying the tithe not be kept . . . do not bother them nor humiliate them in any way, until you have received instructions from here of what we advise." "Cédula Real a la audiencia de México," Valladolid, April 10, 1557, in *Cedulario Indiano*, facsimile reproduction, gathered by Diego de Encinas, Ed. Cultura Hispánica, Madrid 1945, ff. 191–92.

vos videtis" ("Beatified the eyes that see what you see") (Lk 10:23; Mt 13:16) and one listener, Friar Alonso de Santiago, later declared, "Then I saw that he was referring to Our Lady of Guadalupe."[9] In his sermon, the archbishop "tried to persuade all the people of the devotion to Our Lady, saying how Her precious Son granted the devotion to the Image of His precious Mother in many places."[10] Indeed, "He granted a great devotion to all the people, and so, all the greater part of this city . . . follows and continues this devotion."[11]

On September 8, only two days after the archbishop's preaching, on the feast of Mary's Nativity, in the chapel of San Francisco's Convent, Friar Francisco de Bustamante preached a sermon before the Viceroy Luis de Velasco, and the Audiencia de México [civil council], and if he basically did not give the Virgin of Guadalupe any importance, at the end he could not refrain from ending his Marian sermon attacking Archbishop Montúfar, "with a very arid countenance, showing his great anger against what in this case [the Archbishop] had preached and sustained."[12] In addition, he did not limit himself to making his disagreement public, but accused Montúfar directly of nothing less than fomenting the idolatry in his support of the devotion to the Virgin of Guadalupe Image which, according to him, had been painted by an Indigenous, "the Indigenous Marcos," pointing out that it was false that She performed miracles, or at least, it was not proven, thus promoting idolatry[13] and also accusing him, indirectly, of embezzlement, insinuating that he disposed of alms improperly,[14] "and that it would be a good idea to lash the first one who claimed that She performed miracles 100 times, and that whoever said it from then on, be lashed 200 times."[15] Such an accusation, because of who said it and to whom it was intended, caused a terrible impression on the faithful people, since it rebuked a devotion that was already universally popular, and it also displayed to all an internal dispute within the hierarchy, and if that were not enough, we have to take into account that at the time, idolatry was not punished with 100 or 200 lashes, but with death. Thus the Franciscan provincial,

---

[9] "Testimonio de Gonzalo de Alarcón," in *Información de 1556*, p. 61.

[10] "Testimonio de Juan de Salazar," in *Información de 1556*, p. 51.

[11] "Testimonio de Juan de Salazar," in *Información de 1556*, p. 51.

[12] "Testimonio de Juan de Salazar," in *Información de 1556*, p. 50.

[13] "Testimonio de Francisco de Salazar," in *Información de 1556*, p. 50.

[14] "It would be better if the alms given there were for the hospitals of the city, especially that of buboes, after they had taken the majority of its donations, and he did not know what the alms that were received in this Hermitage of Guadalupe were spent on or consumed." "Testimonio de Juan de Masseguer," in *Información de 1556*, p. 50. His reference to the hospital for buboes was particularly caustic, since it had been founded and supported by Zumárraga. So it implied then that the new Dominican archbishop was greedy and miserable, very different from the previous Franciscan.

[15] "Testimonio de Juan de Salazar," in *Información de 1556*, p. 58.

the highest moral authority of the Church in Mexico, was publicly recommending that the Dominican archbishop, the highest hierarchical authority, be put to death.

But let us go on with the events. The following day, the Archbishop of Mexico, Alonso de Montúfar, started a process, which remained in a mere introductory stage.[16] He called witnesses and made them declare under oath[17] all that they had seen and heard in reference to Friar Francisco de Bustamante's preaching. This process has been called *Información de 1556*.

The Franciscan provincial's accusations were extremely delicate and serious, particularly because Montúfar presided over the First Mexican Provincial Council in 1555, where it was determined that severe punishments were set against those who sustained a false or uncertain devotion. The archbishop was perfectly aware of the legislation since he had been an examiner in the Holy Office in Spain before becoming Archbishop of Mexico. For this reason he could not just accept the ungrounded attacks by the Franciscan, having been the one who had promoted the elimination of all false devotions with punishments as great as that of excommunication. All of this is testified by Juan de Salazar, who had personally heard the archbishop say that "it was declared in the Council that preaching a false or uncertain miracle had been prohibited and the punishment for this was excommunication."[18]

In effect, a little before that fierce attack by the Franciscan Bustamante, Archbishop Montúfar, on June 29, 1555, headed the First Mexican Council, which ended on November 17 of that same year. In that meeting, among other things, the initial alignments were drawn up for the consolidation of a diocesan Church, some projects of which would displease the Franciscans. Likewise, very clear norms were given in order to banish the Indigenous idolatry. It is interesting to verify this in chapter 72 of the council proceedings,

---

[16] It seems that *Información de 1556* on Bustamante's sermon became a real Canon process against Bustamante, even though Montúfar did not follow it through in this way. Esteban Anticoli, *Historia de la Aparición de la Virgen de Guadalupe en México desde el año MMDXXXI al MDCCCXCV*, Ed. La Europea, Mexico 1887, T. XIV, pp. 203–28. José de Jesús Cuevas, *La Santísima Virgen de Guadalupe*, Ed. Círculo Católico, Mexico 1897, T. XIV, pp. 54–55; T. XXII, p. 119. Fidel de Jesús Chauvet, *Historia del Culto Guadalupano*, in José Ignacio Echegaray, *Álbum Conmemorativo del 450 aniversario de las apariciones de Nuestra Señora de Guadalupe*, Ed. Buena Prensa, Mexico 1981, pp. 30–34, all think so, while Edmundo O'Gorman believes that there was no Canon process: Cfr. Edmundo O'Gorman, *Destierro de Sombras. Luz en el origen de la imagen y culto de Nuestra Señora de Guadalupe en el Tepeyac*, UNAM, Mexico 1986, pp. 81–107.

[17] An example of the oath is that carried out by the Royal Attorney of the Audience, who was a witness and swore "by God and by Saint Mary and by the sign of the Cross, on which he placed his right hand, whose charge he promised to say the truth about what he knew and was asked." "Testimonio de Juan de Salazar," in *Información de 1556*, p. 49.

[18] "Testimonio de Juan de Salazar," in *Información de 1556*, pp. 51–52.

where it reads, "The Indigenous are not to sing rituals or old story songs without them first being examined by religious, or persons who understand the language very well, and the Gospel ministers are to try to keep them from singing profane things in those songs." With this, many of the Indigenous customs were banned, especially their songs, which presented dubious orthodoxy or clear idolatry. However, the songs composed to the Virgin of Guadalupe, exalting their devotion, were not hindered.

In addition, in chapter 34 of the council proceedings it is stated that images were not to be painted without the painter and the paintings in question being examined. The priests of the council declared that

> The Council wishes to separate everything that goes against the authentic devotion from the Church of God, and other problems, like painting absurdities and indecent images, which cause misunderstandings to the simple people; and because it is more convenient to take necessary measures in this place than in other places because the Indigenous, without knowing how to paint correctly or understand what they are painting, paint images whether they know how or not, which results in underestimating our Holy Faith; therefore, the Holy Council establishes and orders that no Spaniard or Indigenous paint images or altarpieces in any Church of our Archdiocese, nor Province, nor sell images, without first being examined and a license be issued by us, or by our Vicar Generals, so that he can paint, and that it be what is suitable for the devotion of the faithful. The images he thus paints are to be first examined and appraised by our judges for their price and value, under penalty of losing the painting and image that he made if the painter were to do the contrary. And we will send our inspectors to see and examine thoroughly the stories and images that are being painted in the Churches and holy places that they visit; and those that they find doubtful, wrong or indecent, are to be removed from those places.[19]

In this context of the council, where very clear norms with regard to paintings as well as the stories within the images are presented to painters, whether Spaniards or Indigenous, one may have the accurate impression that if the Image of Our Lady of Guadalupe had been painted by an Indigenous or even a Spaniard before September 8, 1556, the date on which Friar Francisco de Bustamante preached the sermon in reply to the one given by Archbishop Alonso de Montúfar only two days before, it would have been destroyed and obviously the veneration to Our Lady of Guadalupe in Tepeyac would have

---

[19] *Concilios Provinciales. Primero y Segundo, celebrados en la muy noble y leal Ciudad de México, presididos por el Illmo. y Rmo. Señor D. Fr. Alonso de Montúfar, en los años de 1555 y 1565, publicados por el arzobispo de México, Francisco Antonio Lorenzana*, Imprenta del Superior Gobierno del Br. D. Joseph Antonio de Hogal, Mexico 1769, p. 171.

never been supported and promoted by the Archbishop of Mexico, Montúfar. Furthermore, within this precept, if it had been a painting done by a
Spaniard or an Indigenous, several questions could have been answered; the
identity of the artist and many more details would have been known. But
Bustamante only threw in that it had been a certain Indigenous by the name
of Marcos who painted it, at the moment of anger in his sermon; he did not
present any proof or show anything or anyone more in this respect. The identity of who ordered such an image to be painted would also have been
known, its story could have been known and, as we said, if the painting had
not been authorized, it is obvious that it would have been removed from veneration, even more so having the influential Franciscans openly against it.
The truth is that the veneration to the Virgin of Guadalupe of Mexico continued without anyone being able to stop it, regardless of the Franciscans'
opposition. For example, the witness Alonso Sánchez de Cisneros declared
that he had been in the house of the Franciscan religious, who claimed to be
against the Image of Guadalupe, "and that he felt that all of them were of the
same opinion as the Provincial."[20]

Well, for the historian Edmundo O'Gorman, the Image of Guadalupe is a
painting ordered by Archbishop Montúfar, who had been presumed responsible for starting that devotion; because the council did not say one single word
about the devotion of Guadalupe, O'Gorman concludes that "It appears valid
to surmise that on November 6, 1555, the day in which the results of the council were announced, the Image of the Virgin still had not appeared on the historical horizon of Mexico."[21] But one must remember that the council not only
saw the things that took place in the past, and did not necessarily need to name
them in order for them to exist, but was a norm which was put into practice in
the present and the future.

For example, the council did not say a single word about the Sanctuary of
Our Lady of Remedies, and nevertheless the devotion continued because it
was in accordance with the norms dictated by the council; no one thought
of saying that that devotion never existed simply because the council never
mentioned it.

On the other hand, it is difficult to believe that the Image was invented
in order to place it precisely in such an inappropriate place if this choice had
been left to man's criteria, considering the demands of sixteenth-century
Spaniards, who gave so much importance to the purity of race, under the
pressure of the Inquisition. However, the Sanctuary was founded on this site,

---

[20] "Testimonio de Alonso Sánchez de Cisneros," in *Información de 1556*, p. 64.
[21] Edmundo O'Gorman, *Destierro de Sombras*, p. 21.

on the hill of Tepeyac, which did not seem appropriate, as other sources that will be analyzed later point out. In addition, as we have already seen, the declarations of the witnesses who participated in *Información*, drawn up after September 8, 1556, present us a devotion which was deeply rooted in all social classes, as much among the Spaniards as among the Indigenous; Juan de Salazar's testimony tells us that

> There is a great devotion which the people of this city have given to this blessed Image, including the Indigenous; important and well-dressed ladies go barefooted, walking with their canes in their hands, to visit and pray to Our Lady, and from them the natives have received a great example and follow it as well . . . many ladies and young girls, of great status as well as of great age, went barefooted, with their canes in their hands, to the Hermitage of Our Lady, and thus this witness has seen it because he has gone many times to this Hermitage, which astonishes this witness very much, having seen many old women and young girls, in great numbers, walking with their canes in their hands, to visit this Image.[22]

This same witness adds all the different offerings and celebrations that they had in the Sanctuary, "where those who go continuously find Masses, as the faithful and devotees have said, and some solemn holidays."[23] It even got to the point that "No one talked about anything else, only 'Where shall we go?' 'Let's go to Our Lady of Guadalupe.'"[24]

Furthermore, a large amount of alms had been collected, but Bustamante also found there one more reason to attack the archbishop, because, according to Salazar's oath, Bustamante had said "It would be better to use them in favor of the hospitals of this city, especially in the one for the buboes since most of the hospital's donations were taken from it, and that he did not know what those alms that were given in that Hermitage of Guadalupe were spent on nor used for, and that to remedy all this, and so it would not continue, the solution was up to the Viceroy and all the council."[25] That means that the alms were so generous as to wish the viceroy and the council to take up the

---

[22] "Testimonio de Juan de Salazar," in *Información de 1556*, p. 51.
[23] "Testimonio de Juan de Salazar," in *Información de 1556*, p. 51.
[24] "Testimonio de Juan de Salazar," in *Información de 1556*, p. 53.
[25] "Testimonio de Juan de Salazar," in *Información de 1556*, p. 49–50. The great popularity of the devotion is also manifested in other testimonies: "This witness being in the Hermitage has seen Spaniards as well as natives enter there with great devotion, and many on their knees, from the door to the altar where the Image of Our Lady of Guadalupe is placed, and it seems to him that is fundament enough to sustain this Hermitage, and that wanting to remove this devotion would be against all Christianity." "Testimonio de Juan de Salazar," in *Información de 1556*, p. 71. Another testimony: "He ran into many well-to-do ladies walking, and other people, men and women of all types, going

case. All this shows the strong roots that the devotion had, that not only the Indigenous made pilgrimages there but also the Spaniards and all social classes, and great celebrations and offerings took place there. It was an extensive devotion, so strong that many went barefooted and praying to Her Hermitage, a beloved devotion which was within their hearts, and the great scandal, provoked by Friar Francisco de Bustamante's words, was visible in all the city[26] and he lost the prestige that he had obtained. It is difficult to agree with Edmundo O'Gorman when he concludes that the devotion to the Image of Guadalupe happened within ten months. O'Gorman said, "In conclusion, let us say that we have proposed a lapse between the beginning of November 1555 and September 6, 1556, during which time the Image of Our Lady of Guadalupe must have been placed in the old Franciscan Hermitage of Tepeyac."[27]

But let us continue analyzing *Información de 1556*. The witnesses answered each one of the questions, and their responses clearly showed what the provincial had expressed and the scandal that he had provoked. The anti-Apparitionist historian Edmundo O'Gorman affirmed in his book *Destierro de Sombras* that "It is very obvious that almost all of the witnesses declared that, in fact, Father Bustamante attributed the Image of Our Lady of Guadalupe, found in the Hermitage, to an Indigenous painter; but none of them seemed surprised or offered an objection, not even one comment to the preacher was heard; otherwise, the witnesses of *Información*, or at least one of them, would have included it in his disposition. It is obvious that the matter was known, or in any case, for those that it was something new to them, it was acceptable and in no way extravagant or impudent."[28]

But investigating and analyzing directly in historical sources we confirm that this is not true. The witnesses clearly stated that it had been a true scandal: in Juan de Mesa's testimony, it can be read that "This witness said that he heard someone say after the sermon finished that there was a scandal and

---

and coming, and that he saw many alms being given there, and that it seemed to him that it was with great devotion." "Testimonio de Alvar Gómez de León," in *Información de 1556*, p. 67.

[26] "There was a great scandal in the auditorium; and it has been in the city, and he has heard many righteous people say that he seemed passionate and that he was scandalized." "Testimonio de Juan de Masseguer," in *Información de 1556*, p. 71.

[27] Edmundo O'Gorman, *Destierro de Sombras*, p. 21. Stafford Poole, C.M., agrees with O'Gorman's position: "There is some plausibility, however, to the theory advanced by some anti-Apparitionists, such as O'Gorman, that it was Montufar who installed the original Image in the Hermitage." Stafford Poole, *Our Lady of Guadalupe. The Origins and Sources of a Mexican National Symbol, 1531–1971*, Ed. Tucson, Arizona: The University of Arizona Press. 1995, p. 68. This last author, who is an anti-Apparitionist and continues along the line of O'Gorman, did not even analyze the important *Información de 1556*, he only points out his approval of O'Gorman's hypothesis.

[28] Edmundo O'Gorman, *Destierro de Sombras*, p. 13.

groups of people talking."[29] In Juan de Salazar's testimony it confirms that "Some neighbors from this city who were next to him, listening to the sermon, were scandalized and were embarrassed with what the Provincial said."[30] The witness Marcial de Contreras declared, "In the city there is great scandal, from what he has heard about what this Provincial preached."[31] The testimony from the Bachelor from Puebla was that "It is true that here in the Church, and later in the city, there has been a great scandal about the things that the Provincial preached. And, thus, many people, scandalized about what they had heard, came to ask this witness what he thought, and he said not well and that it had been scandalous."[32] The Bachelor Francisco de Salazar testified that "He saw that many people were scandalized by this Provincial's words."[33] The witness Gonzalo de Alarcón swore that "The most important people that were at that sermon were upset."[34] The witness Juan de Masseguer declared, "There was a great scandal in the auditorium, and there was a scandal in the city and he heard many well-to-do people say that he seemed passionate, and that they were scandalized. And this witness says that Bustamante has lost much of the credibility which he had in this city because of what Bustamante said against the Image. The devotion has not stopped, but better still, it has grown more, and every time that this witness goes there, he sees more people than he used to."[35]

The witnesses not only confirmed that there was a great scandal because of Friar Francisco de Bustamante's speech, but they also confirmed the great devotion to Our Lady of Guadalupe; for example, the Bachelor Francisco de Salazar swore "not only persons who without health problems and without body ailments can walk, but also very old and sick men and women, with this devotion, go to the Hermitage."[36] In his testimony, Juan de Masseguer tells us, "All of the people in general have a great devotion to this Image of Our Lady, people of all types, nobles, citizens and Indigenous."[37]

From what they attest, it is clearly seen that the devotion counted with the support of the episcopacy, but it had great popular roots from before. Francisco de Salazar declared, "Many have a great devotion, going on horseback and others walking . . . women and men, old and sick . . . young children that

[29] "Testimonio de Juan de Mesa," in *Información de 1556*, p. 48.
[30] "Testimonio de Juan de Salazar," in *Información de 1556*, p. 50.
[31] "Testimonio de Marcial de Contreras," in *Información de 1556*, p. 54.
[32] "Testimonio del Bachiller de Puebla," in *Información de 1556*, pp. 56–57.
[33] "Testimonio de Francisco de Salazar," in *Información de 1556*, p. 59.
[34] "Testimonio de Gonzalo de Alarcón," in *Información de 1556*, p. 62.
[35] "Testimonio de Juan de Masseguer," in *Información de 1556*, p. 71.
[36] "Testimonio de Francisco de Salazar," in *Información de 1556*, p. 59.
[37] "Testimonio de Juan de Masseguer," in *Información de 1556*, p. 71.

understand, see that their parents and older people practice this devotion, and they like to go there."[38] Alvar Gómez testified that

> It is true that he has gone there once, and that he ran into many important ladies walking, and other people, men and women, of all classes, going and coming; there he saw that they gave generous alms, and that it seemed that it was with great devotion; he did not see anything that would seem wrong, but that led to a devotion to Our Lady, and that this witness, seeing the others with so much devotion incited him to a greater devotion. It seemed to him that this was something that should be supported and promoted, especially because in this land there is no other devotion known where the people have had so much devotion and that with this Holy devotion many do not bother going to the orchards, as was the custom in this land, now they go there where there are no orchard arrangements nor any other benefits; instead, they go before Our Lady, in contemplation and in devotion.[39]

With this testimony one can clearly see not only the great devotion to the Most Holy Mary of Guadalupe, but also the enormous conversion of so many who manifested a change in their life, and, at the same time, through these witnesses we prove that the devotion to Holy Mary of Guadalupe was not implanted by the Franciscans, thanks to their testimonies that verify the initial opposition of the Franciscans to the devotion and the fact that they attacked it openly. Some witnesses of this process initiated by the archbishop of Mexico talked about a conversation among the Franciscan Friars Antonio de Huete and Alonso de Santiago, as well as with other members of that same order. Both friars seemed hostile. Friar Alonso de Santiago went so far as to say that the devotion to Our Lady of Guadalupe was dangerous because the Indigenous believed that the Image of Tepeyac was in fact the Virgin Herself and they would adore Her as an idol. Also in this testimony one can see such a rejection from the first missionaries, that it is clear that it was not the Franciscans who tried to impose the Virgin of Guadalupe as an extension of the one in Extremadura, Spain, or to dominate the Indigenous with this devotion; Friar Alonso de Santiago, upset by the promotion that Archbishop Montúfar made for the Virgin of Guadalupe of Tepeyac, said, "Since the illustrious Archbishop wanted the people to go to that Hermitage as a devotion, he should order that She not be named Lady of Guadalupe, but of Tepeaca or Tepeaquilla, because if in Spain Our Lady of Guadalupe had that name it was because that same town was called Guadalupe."[40]

---

[38] "Testimonio de Francisco de Salazar," in *Información de 1556*, p. 59.
[39] "Testimonio de Alvar Gómez de León," in *Información de 1556*, p. 67.
[40] "Testimonio de Gonzalo de Alarcón," in *Información de 1556*, p. 62.

Finally, there was one witness, Juan de Masseguer, who said that a friar from the convent in Tlaltelolco, called Luis,[41] told him, frankly, "this is a devotion in which we are all wrong."[42] But just as Masseguer transmits Friar Luis's opinion to us, he also confirms the great devotion that the people had to the Virgin of Tepeyac. Masseguer said, "All the people have a true devotion to this Image of Our Lady and many people go to visit Her very frequently with profound devotion, all types of people, Spaniards, Creoles, and Indigenous, although some Indigenous have grown cold in such devotion because the Friars have ordered it."[43] The overarching conflict between the Franciscans and the archbishop had become clear; they publicly called him greedy and inept, and they affirmed that they had to remove him from office and make him return to Spain, "and if the Archbishop says what he says, it is because of his own interest at heart; he is over sixty and he is delirious already . . . we will make the Archbishop go back across the sea."[44]

As we have seen, this intervention by the Franciscan Bustamante caused an enormous scandal and it discredited its author. It was a fact that the devotion to the Virgin of Guadalupe had great force, that She enjoyed the esteem of most of the Spaniards and the veneration of the Indigenous, that generous alms were given, and that the reputation of the Image had been spread, thanks to the prodigious miracles that She performed. But it was also clear that the Franciscans absolutely opposed this devotion born on Tepeyac. In the end, the result was self-defeating for the Franciscans, because the devotion increased and Bustamante was very much discredited, as Francisco de Salazar's testimony confirms: "In regard to the scandal that there was about the contradiction which he made, now no one talks about anything else but to say that even if it hurts Bustamante, we are to go serve Our Lady wherever Her Image may be, and he may contradict the devotion all he wants. It is understood that he regrets that Spaniards go there. From now on, if before we went once, now we shall go four times."[45]

We do not know how the fight between Bustamante and Montúfar ended, in which the king had to intervene, but we do know that the statements were interrupted "ex abrupto" and that the process was dismissed on September 24

---

[41] The Franciscan and expert in Guadalupe Friar Fidel de Jesús Chauvet identifies Friar Luis as Luis Cal, Cfr. Friar Fidel de Jesús Chauvet, *El Culto Guadalupano del Tepeyac. Sus Orígenes y sus Críticos en el Siglo XVI*, in Appendix, *La Información de 1556*, Ed. Centro de Estudios Bernardino de Sahagún, A.C., Mexico 1978, pp. 99–100.

[42] "Testimonio de Juan de Masseguer," in *Información de 1556*, p. 69.

[43] "Testimonio de Juan de Masseguer," in *Información de 1556*, p. 71.

[44] "Testimonio de Juan de Masseguer," in *Información de 1556*, p. 69.

[45] "Testimonio de Francisco de Salazar," in *Información de 1556*, p. 60.

with an attestation written by Montúfar that said "Suspend it and party is without verdict."[46] We also know that this subject was never discussed again, that Montúfar was not lashed, that Bustamante was removed from provincial and sent, apparently punished, to Cuernavaca, where he lived "cloistered," a punishment which he endured "with great humility and self-contempt,"[47] a humility which must have been sincere because in 1560 he was reelected provincial and in 1561 was sent to Spain with the Dominican and Augustine provincials, Friar Pedro de la Peña and Friar Agustín de la Coruña respectively, although this might have been a diplomatic move in order to banish him, because the other two were promoted to the episcopacy, whereas he remained in a convent in Madrid until his death in 1562.

As we have seen, this *Información de 1556* is so important that if we did not have the documentation about the Bustamante-Montúfar controversy, we would not have known about the issue, because the Franciscan writers do not mention it.

On the other hand, it is true that this era was characterized by strong tension, and the same circumstances caused the religious writers to keep understandably silent. The Franciscans continued believing, in good faith, that the Image and the devotion were "a satanic invention," and they were not going to change their opinion because a viceroy ordered it, and least of all because their provincial ended up looking so bad. Nor was it false that they considered Montúfar harmful and inept, also in good faith; however, they could not help noticing the self-defeating results from all that had happened because the devotion "which everyone on earth would follow"[48] and which alarmed them so because of its profound roots among the Indigenous, did nothing but increase, with pilgrimages which they considered suspicious for their numbers and the great distances that many covered.[49]

In conclusion, the Bustamante-Montúfar controversy clearly showed the reasons for the Franciscans' silence, originating in their theological position and derived from pastoral concepts, mixed with the beggar-bishops controversy and seasoned with other elements of the jurisdictional controversies of the time. Montúfar's position on Guadalupe showed the bishops' total support of the Guadalupan Event from then on, as important to the ecclesial life of New Spain. It can also be said that, regardless of the little or no support of

---

[46] "Testimonio de Juan de Masseguer," in *Información de 1556*, p. 72.

[47] Friar Gerónimo de Mendieta, *Historia Eclesiástica*, p. 705.

[48] Juan Suárez de Peralta, *Tratado del descubrimiento de las Indias*, Ed. SEP, Mexico 1949, p. 161.

[49] The distances covered by the Indigenous pilgrims were truly amazing. Torquemada mentioned that they went from Guatemala to the Sanctuary in Tianquizmanalco, the equivalent to Guadalupe. Cfr. Friar Juan de Torquemada, *Monarquía*, T.III, p. 357.

the clergy, 25 years after the Apparitions, the devotion was already so profoundly rooted as to provoke all of the viceroyalty to take part in it, dividing itself by in favor or against. Besides, someone as suspicious as Montúfar (who saw heresies everywhere, who had been an examiner in the Holy Office, and who had declared the punishment of excommunication against those who promoted false devotions with false tales) favored and defended the devotion, and regarded the profound devotion, not only of the Indigenous but also of the Spaniards, as a true miracle. It is clearly seen how the Indigenous were unconditionally devoted to Her, no matter how much the Franciscans explicitly fought against Her, fearing they would return to their idolatry. There is no doubt that the devotion to Our Lady of Guadalupe of Tepeyac also enjoyed the favor of the Spanish laity, favors that increased as a reaction to Bustamante's abuses. As these witnesses confirm, there was a multitude that went on pilgrimages, made sacrifices, and even did penance. With all of this and the other historic documented proofs, one can conclude that the hypothesis that it was a fraud, consciously put together by the same Franciscans in order to control the Indigenous better, or that it was Archbishop Montúfar's invention, lacks historical foundation.[50]

Archbishop Montúfar continued his pastoral projects, not only giving the archdiocese an installed and stable clergy, but also the support and promotion of the veneration of the Virgin of Guadalupe, for which he enlarged the Hermitage,[51] aware of the need to do so because of the great flow of devout pilgrims.

[50] Cfr. Friar Fidel de Jesús Chauvet, *El Culto Guadalupano del Tepeyac*. Also José Bravo Ugarte, *Cuestiones Históricas Guadalupanas*, Ed. Jus, Mexico 1966, pp. 15–45. Robert Ricard, *La conquista espiritual de México*, translation by Ángel María Garibay, Ed. Jus, Mexico 1947, pp. 348–52. "Información de 1556," in Ernesto de la Torre Villar and Ramiro Navarro de Anda, *Testimonios Históricos Guadalupanos*, pp. 36–141. Jacques Lafaye, *Quetzalcóatl y Guadalupe*. Ed. Gallimard, Paris 1974, pp. 315–20. This last one, although an unfavorable theory of the supernaturalness of the Apparition, exposes accompanying elements that influenced the hostility of the Franciscans.

[51] Cfr. Francisco Antonio Lorenzana, *Concilios Provinciales. Serie de los Arzobispos de México*, Imp. Joseph Antonio de Hogal, Mexico 1769, T. I., p. 214. Also in Luis T. Montes de Oca, *Las Tres primeras ermitas guadalupanas del Tepeyac*, Mexico [1935?].

CHAPTER SEVEN

~

The People Marked in Their History the Guadalupan Event

Besides the interesting testimonies given by the old Indigenous from Cuauhtitlán, Juan Diego's birthplace, the surprising conversion of the Indigenous, and the *Información de 1556* which offers us a clear reference to the deeply rooted devotion to Guadalupe in the Indigenous as well as in the Spaniards, there are various other historical documents where the people marked the Guadalupan Event and its protagonists as one of the most important historical moments. Juan Diego's evident and constant reputation is made known in them, as a virtuous and holy Indigenous, a reputation that has lasted up to now.

Let us see how, since 1531, the Tepeyac Sanctuary has been of great importance, not only for the Indigenous but also for the Spaniards, and a little later for the Creoles and *mestizos*. As we know, the first temple constructed as home of the Virgin of Guadalupe was the Hermitage built in the time of Friar Juan de Zumárraga, which was very humble, "of adobes, not finished nor adorned,"[1] which the Indigenous from Cuauhtitlán continued fixing and improving: "Many Indigenous men and women from this town would go work at this Hermitage, to perfume it and sweep it, the natives of this town were more devoted than the Indigenous from other towns, being that Juan Diego was from it and that She had appeared to him."[2]

---

[1] "Testimonio de Gabriel Xuárez," in *Informaciones Jurídicas de 1666*, f. 20r.
[2] "Testimonio de Gabriel Xuárez," in *Informaciones Jurídicas de 1666*, f. 20r.

Until the arrival of the second archbishop of Mexico, Alonso de Montúfar, the Sanctuary was no more than an "*ermitilla*" (little Hermitage), as the
viceroy, Enríquez de Almanza, classified it in his letter of September 23,
1575, directed to King Philip II: "There was an *ermitilla* in which the Image
that is now in the Church used to be."[3] Initially, Montúfar improved the *ermitilla* but later he constructed another one on the same spot, entirely new,
which he consecrated in 1566, and which the Viceroy Enríquez de Almanza
called "Church," but regardless of the enormous veneration that it had and
the generous alms that it collected, it was still modest, even poor, at least for
the opulent Hieronymus monk, Diego de Santa María, who had arrived in
Mexico after being sent by the wealthy convent in Extremadura in order to
investigate the situation of the Tepeyac Sanctuary that apparently had an
usurped name. This friar said in 1574, "It is not adorned and the building is
very poor."[4] But, as the historic documents record it, if it is true that the Tepeyac Sanctuary was simple and humble, nonetheless it was rich in devotion,
splendorous in conversions, embellished by many alms and donations. It was
a place where people of all conditions and all levels were attracted in a surprising manner, as in our days.

This unusual devotion, as it has been mentioned, stands out in the documents called "Annals," which are writings that contain, in a communal manner, the news about the fundamental facts of each year and, in some of these,
the people pointed out the Guadalupan Event. Even though some of these
have mistakes and discrepancies, since they are written with an Indigenous
mentality, which they tried to lay out and corroborate with a Spanish calen-
dar, that is what makes them authentic in their contents.

Several annals were elaborated in Puebla. These were the people's records,
which pointed out the Guadalupan Event, such as, for example, *Los Anales
de Puebla y Tlaxcala*, also known as *Anónimo B*. This is a document whose
text is important for us because it says, "1510 Year of the Stone Dagger.
Again President . . . came here in this year to govern Mexico and also Our
Precious Little Mother of Guadalupe deigned to appear, over there in Mexico, She deigned to appear to a little Indigenous Juan Diego."[5]

---

[3] "Carta del Virrey de la Nueva España, don Martín Enríquez, al rey don Felipe II, dándole cuenta
del estado de varios asuntos, de la solución que había dado a otros e informando sobre algunos puntos que se le consultaban," Mexico, September 23, 1575, in *Cartas de Indias*, Ed. Secretaría de Hacienda y Crédito Público, Mexico 1980, p. 39.

[4] "Carta de fray Diego de Santa María a Su Majestad," Mexico City, December 12, 1574, AGI,
Seville, Spain. Document Mexico no. 69, no. 3, in Xavier Noguez, *Documentos Guadalupanos. Un Estudio sobre las fuentes de información tempranas en torno a las mariofanías en el Tepeyac*, Ed. FCE, Mexico 1993, p. 230.

[5] *Anales de Puebla y Tlaxcala* or *Anónimo B* (1524–1674), AHMNA, AAMC, no. 19, 2.

Another of these documents elaborated in Puebla is the *Códice Gómez de Orozco* or the *Anales de Cuetlaxcoapan* or *Anónimo C*, which says, "1510 Year of the Stone Dagger. It was when President came again to govern Mexico; also in this year Our Beloved María of Hualolope deigned to appear, there in Mexico, She deigned to appear to a little Indigenous named Juan Diego."[6]

Another example that also came from Puebla is that called *Anales de Tlaltelolco y México*, which says, "1530. In this year the President [of the Second Audience] came recently to govern Mexico. In this same year the governing Bishop priest recently came, his reverend name is Friar Juan de Zumárraga, a Saint Francis priest. Our Precious Little Mother of Guadalupe deigned to appear."[7] As one can see in these last examples, true facts are mentioned with confused dates: none of these events occurred in the Spanish years of 1510 or 1530. President Ramirez de Fuenleal arrived in Mexico on September 23, 1531. Zumárraga arrived, without having been consecrated as bishop, on December 9, 1528 and returned in October 1534, already consecrated. What is more, the last example also spoke about the foundation of Puebla, which was also in 1531. However, it is the facts which are objective.

Another example from Puebla is the *Anales de Puebla y Tlaxcala* or *Anales de los Sabios Tlaxcaltecas* or *Anales de la Catedral*, which is totally trustworthy within its kind, even though its chronology is only within the Christian era. This codex extends until 1739. The important text is "The year of 1531. The Christians made Cuelaxcoapan, City of Angels [Puebla], even [made the ground level]. In this same year Our Precious Lady of Guadalupe of Mexico deigned to appear to Juan Diego. . . . Year of 1548. Juan Diego, to whom the precious Lady of Guadalupe of Mexico appeared, died with dignity."[8]

Taking into account that the original is lost and we only know a copy, it is fitting to add the following information that Xavier Noguez indicated:

> The text which Galicia Chimalpopoca copied comes with simple drawings of the sun, the moon, a star, two crossed bones, and two Indigenous looking at the sky in the first part. In addition, there was a small explanation which reads: "*Ixtlamatque tlaxcalteca*" (the wise Tlaxcaltecas). Also, at the beginning of the text, before 1519, a brief description of the Image of Guadalupe is included. The height, the number of stars on the mantle, and the splendor around Her body were mentioned there: 'Motecuzoma being Emperor, don Fernando

---

[6] *Anales de Puebla y Tlaxcala* or *Códice Gómez de Orozco* or *Anales de Cuetlaxcoapan* or *Anónimo C* (1519–1720), BNAH, *Historic Archives*, no. 1040.

[7] *Anales de Tlaltelolco y México* (1524–1686), AHMNA, AAMC, no. 13, 1–2.

[8] *Anales de Puebla y Tlaxcala* or *Anales de los Sabios Tlaxcaltecas* or *Anales de Catedral* (1519–1739), AHMNA, AAMC, no. 18, 1.

Cortés arrived. A little after having reigned in Mexico, Cuitlahuac died. The Christian faith was received during the time or reign of King Cuauhtemotzin. The height of Our Venerated Mother of Guadalupe of Mexico measures six quarters and a half. She is embellished with 46 stars and surrounded by 50 rays' . . . Because of the loss of the original manuscript we cannot know if the drawings mentioned previously complemented any of the information contained in the Annals, or if Galicia Chimalpopoca mentioned them at the beginning, arbitrarily. The inclusion of the brief description of the Image of Guadalupe is particularly strange in a section which is about the years previous to the Spanish conquest. Perhaps in the original the information was connected in some way to the information of 1531 or some later year.[9]

Another important document of this type is the *Añalejo de Bartolache* or *Manuscrito de la Universidad*, in which the date is given, as in the previous document, not only of the Apparition of the Virgin of Guadalupe, but also of the death of Juan Diego. The text says, "Year Cane 1531. The Castilians settled (founded) Cuetlaxocoapan, City of Angels, and the precious Lady of Guadalupe of Mexico deigned to appear to Juan Diego where they call it [the town] Tepeyac. . . . Year Tecpatl, 1548. Juan Diego, to whom the beloved Lady of Guadalupe of Mexico deigned to appear, died with dignity. It hailed on the white hill."[10]

Through the so-called *Cantares* the Indigenous also kept a record of important events, those which had marked their history. This same method was used to keep the experience of the Guadalupan Event alive. P. Luis Becerra Tanco stated that since before 1629 he used to hear these *Cantares*:

> With regard to the second method that the natives had so that they would not forget the memorable events, and which was by the use of their *Cantares*, I state and certify having heard some old Indigenous in the *mitotes* and *saraos*, which the natives used to have, before the flood in this city, when the feast of Our Lady of Guadalupe was celebrated in Her holy temple. This *mitote* took place in the plaza on the west side, outside of the temple; dancing in a circle, and in the center of the circle were two old men, standing and singing the song that referred to the miraculous Apparitions of this blessed Image, which were represented on the mantle that served Juan Diego as a cape.[11]

---

[9] Xavier Noguez, *Documentos Guadalupanos*, pp. 55–56.

[10] *Añalejo de Bartolache* or *Manuscrito de la Universidad* (1454–1737), BNAH, Historic Archives, Archivo de Sucs. Gómez de Orozco.

[11] "Testimonio del P. Luis Becerra Tanco," in *Informaciones Jurídicas de 1666*, ff. 151v–152r. He also states it in his manuscript published in 1675, which is titled *Felicidad de México*, introduction, notes, and version by José Roberto Mendirichaga, Monterrey, Mexico 1995, pp. 30–31. Also in Francisco de Florencia, *La Estrella del Norte*, 1688, Ed. Lorenzo de San Martín, Mexico 1785, pp. 376–79.

Also, these *Cantares* that narrated the history of Guadalupe were approved implicitly by the first three Mexican councils, in the years 1555, 1565, and 1585. In the first, as we saw in the year 1555, chapter 72 stated, "The Indigenous are not to sing *Cantares* of their rituals and old history without those *Cantares* first being examined by religious, or people who understand the language very well, and that the ministers of the Gospel see to it that they do not sing profane things in those *Cantares*." In the second, of the year 1565, the priests at the council ordered that "The inspectors who visit churches and pious places must see and examine the stories and images painted there very well, and those that they find apocryphal, bad, or indecently painted they must have removed from those places, etc." They also point out that "The Indigenous must not sing *Cantares* without the story being reviewed and its orthodoxy checked." Finally, in the third council, in the year 1585, they completely banned the Indigenous canticles from their heathen history and they only permitted those approved by the parishioners and vicars; likewise, the images that had false stories had to be removed.

Besides, in the First Mexican Provincial Council in 1555, with regard to the temple itself, chapter 35 says that

> no one could build a church, monastery, or Hermitage without a license, nor can there be hermits in the land. Even though it is prohibited by the disposition of the Law, that anyone build a church, monastery, or Hermitage without a license and authority of the Ordinary Prelate, some dare to do them without license and authority and because it is not suitable to God's service, nor to the decency, reverence, or ornament that the churches must have, nor to the good of the Indigenous Republic,; in S.A.C. [Your Majesty], we prohibit and forbid, under penalty of excommunication, that anyone from our Archdiocese and Province build a church, monastery, or chapel without this license and authority, and we order, under this penalty, that no clergy or religious celebrate Mass in them. [We ask that] our inspectors have the churches thus built without a license demolished, but the ones of a good building and decency, as well built in such a good place, must not be demolished because in the building of those monasteries and churches one must have a respect for the good, and the good spiritual habits of the natives, but not happiness and consolation of the clergymen and religious inhabitants of them. I order that monasteries and churches first be built with the Diocese's license, for good use and good teaching of the native Indigenous, who could participate in the catechism and sacraments, but to a fresh place, or to the happiness of the religious men or ministers, according to what your Majesty has ordered in your Royal Documents, and in doing so, we do not pretend to eliminate any of the privileges regarded to the religious men.

Furthermore, because the many churches that are constructed in our Arch-bishopric and Province cause great disorder, and many of them are not suffi-ciently decent or situated in convenient places, and it is very difficult for the people to sustain them, we state and order that with diligence and the ap-proval of the Bishop, you will determine which ones are necessary, keeping only those and no others; the rest are to be demolished. Those that remain must have the necessary decency and ornamentation, in them there must be no Indigenous under the pretence of singers, no guards more than necessary, and they should be few, of good reputation, well educated in regard to mat-ters of our Holy Faith, have good habits, married and not single, and be teachers in Christian doctrine for those who do not know it. Those churches that have to be demolished must be done so with an order from the Bishop of those dioceses.

Likewise, to avoid many difficulties and new fads introduced by Indigenous or Spaniards, so that this new church may not cause any misunderstanding, we state and order that in this land, from now on, there are to be no hermits, nor persons with a different habit, living in solitude outside of their approved reli-gious monastery.[12]

One can clearly see that the devotion to the Virgin of Guadalupe was an exception to the rule and that Juan Diego's wish to construct a small hut next to the Hermitage and to live there, demonstrating to everyone the message of his Little Girl from Heaven, continued with the full approval of the ec-clesiastical hierarchy.

As has been pointed out, around this Hermitage, which from the oro-graphic perspective was situated in a totally unsuitable place, but it was specifically there that the Virgin of Guadalupe wanted Her temple, a strong spiritual way of life developed with force and growth, as we saw, with sur-prising conversions, constant pilgrimages, prayer, oaths, donations, and the elaboration of codexes and annals that recorded Her in history. Moreover, on the part of the Spaniards there were also great manifestations of devotion. Later the Creoles and the *mestizos* were born loving Her, with the indis-putable support of all of the bishops of Mexico. Likewise, around the Her-mitage fellowships, Jesuit dormitories, and later homes for nuns, orphanages, and pious places were founded.[13] Guadalupe would also be a significant and important place through which the new viceroys would enter the capital of New Spain.

---

[12] *Concilios Provinciales Primero y Segundo*, pp. 91–94.
[13] Cfr. Manuel Ramos Medina (Coord.). *El Monacato Femenino en el Imperio Español. Monasterios, Beaterios, Recogimientos y Colegios*. Memoria del Segundo Congreso Internacional, Ed. Condumex, Mexico 1995.

A very important aspect in regard to its development is that the Sanctuary always remained administratively and pastorally united to the diocesan Church of Mexico. Even though on May 1, 1543, the king permitted a house for the Franciscans to be built in Tlaltelolco, he agreed that the church would continue being linked to the bishop, and as Tepeyac was on the territory of Tlaltelolco's church, therefore, the Chapel always remained under the administration of the diocese. The king said, "The Church of Santiago in this town is to remain subject to the Prelate, as it is now, without any rights being obtained for the religious of that Church because of that building."[14]

Since the first dawning, this event was continuously transmitted by various channels or sources; for example, this is what Becerra Tanco testified in 1666, when he said,

Gaspar de Prabes, a Diocesan Priest who belonged to the town of San Mateo Texcaliacac, and later to that of Tenango de Taxco, very well known in Mexico City for his prudence and circumspection and honored obligations, grandson of one of the first conquerors of this kingdom, authority in the Mexican Language [Náhuatl], affirmed having heard the narration of the Virgin of Guadalupe from don Juan [Antonio] Valeriano, a very outstanding Indigenous from the royal lineage of the monarchs of this kingdom, who was one of the outstanding natives raised in the Santa Cruz de Santiago, a convent in Tlaltelolco, and who graduated fluent in Latin. Valeriano understood and spoke our Castilian language correctly and was a great rhetorician in his own language. For his great talent he was kept in his office as Governor of the natives of Mexico City by the secular government of this New Spain for 40 years, in which time he always responded honestly. Father Friar Juan de Torquemada gives witness to this in his *Monarquía Indiana* book 2 with regard to [Valeriano] his teacher in the Mexican language. I [Becerra] then say, I heard what I have referred to Gaspar de Prabes, presbyter, with whom I had close communication since childhood because he was my uncle on my mother's side, he died in 1628 at the age of 80. As one can see, [Prabes] was born before the year 1550, 20 years after the Apparition and 30 after the conquest of Mexico City, and two years after the death of don Friar Juan de Zumárraga and the Indigenous Juan Diego, both of whom died in 1548. So he must have heard what he affirmed from those who knew them and also from the first religious who taught the natives the faith in Christ Our Lord, and from other trustworthy persons in his family who had been eyewitnesses of the miracle.[15]

---

[14] *Cedulario de Puga*, published in Pedro Ocharte's house, Mexico 1563, T.I, p. 444.

[15] "Testimonio de Becerra Tanco," in *Informaciones Jurídicas de 1666*, ff. 156r–157r. Even though he says that the erudite Indigenous, raised in the convent of the Santa Cruz de Santiago, in Tlaltelolco, and governor of the natives of Mexico City was named Juan Valeriano, in reality he is writing about Antonio Valeriano.

The previous testimony converges with the documents that we have already mentioned, pointing out the date of the death of the archbishop of Mexico, Friar Juan de Zumárraga, who died on June 3, 1548, at the age of 72, and which coincides with Juan Diego's death the same year, as the historical sources indicate.[16] Meanwhile, in Cuauhtitlán, Juan Diego's birthplace, as well as in Tulpetlac, the place where he lived at the time of the Apparitions, the people started to construct Hermitages next to the buildings that they knew had belonged to Juan Diego,[17] and a special devotion began for this Indigenous who had a reputation of being a saint. The offerings, the implements, and even the tombs within these Hermitages were set in such a way so that they would be as close as possible to the walls adjacent to Juan Diego's houses. Later, churches were erected over the ruins of what had been Juan Diego's houses as well as over the ruins of those first Hermitages, places of worship that expressed the uninterrupted tradition which the people greatly esteemed.[18]

Around the middle of the sixteenth century was when the Indigenous Antonio Valeriano,[19] the Colegio de Santa Cruz de Tlaltelolco's greatest scholar, wrote his famous *Nican Mopohua*[20] or *Huey Tlamahuizoltica*, "The Great Event," in which the Apparitions of Our Lady of Guadalupe to Juan Diego are narrated. Valeriano wrote it in the best Náhuatl and the most refined style. Most likely Valeriano gathered what he must have heard his protagonist, Juan Diego, narrate several times during his youth, leaving us not only

---

[16] Cfr. *Añalejo de Bartolache* or *Manuscrito de la Universidad* (1454–1737), BNAH, Historic Archives, Archivo Sucs. Gómez de Orozco. Also Luis Becerra Tanco, *Felicidad de México*, 1666, pp. 36 and 39; *Los Anales de Puebla y Tlaxcala* or *Anales de los Sabios Tlaxcaltecas* or *Anales de Catedral*, AHMNA, AAMC, no. 18, I.; and in *Códice 1548*, in *Enciclopedia Guadalupana*, directed by Xavier Escalada, S.J., Ed. Enciclopedia Guadalupana, Mexico 1997, T.V.

[17] Discoveries confirmed by Manuel García de la Torre, Secretary of the National Patrimony, December 3, 1963, INAH and Dept. of Pre-Hispanic Monuments.

[18] For example, the eighteenth-century church in Cuauhtitlán was erected by using its foundations as a trunk which protected the original adobe walls of the house that had always been considered Juan Diego's.

[19] The writer Antonio Valeriano (we do not know his Indigenous name) was Bernardino de Sahagún's most important collaborator, and the most brilliant student in the *Colegio de Santa Cruz de Tlaltelolco*, later to be professor and director. He was not of noble descent, but after marrying the princess Isabel Huanitzin, he became part of the most high-ranking Indigenous aristocracy, and relative to the royal houses of Mexico and Texcoco. Being lord of Atzcapotzalco, he gave asylum to his nephew-in-law, Francisco Verdugo Quetzalmamalitzin, ancestor of Fernando de Alva Ixtlilxóchitl, through whom this document got to P. Sigüenza y Góngora's hands, who then transmitted it to our general knowledge. Miguel León-Portilla confirmed that this manuscript was written by Antonio Valeriano about 1556, Cfr. *Carta de Miguel León-Portilla al P. Fidel González*, Mexico, August 12, 1998, ACCID, in CCS.

[20] The oldest known copy of the *Nican Mopohua* of the sixteenth century is kept in the New York Library, Sec. Manuscripts, Col. Lenox.

that account but also an account of the lifestyle of the Indigenous world. It is clear that many writers base their works on this writing, which is a treasure of Náhuatl literature and a perfect example of the style of that time. Due to the Indigenous ability to memorize, it is certain that Juan Diego recalled perfectly all the words which he transmitted to thousands of listeners during the years that he lived after the Apparitions and was caring for the Hermitage; among these listeners was, without a doubt, Valeriano. The care for the chronological and topological precision is typical of a true historical narration within the Indigenous style; we can affirm this because of the similarity of many other historical and documentary sources, such as the *Relación Primitiva*, the *Testamento de Juana Martín*, the *Códice 1548*, codexes and Indigenous *Annals*, Juan Suárez de Peralta's mention in the *Nican Motecpana*, the Virgin of Guadalupe and the painted *tilma* by Baltasar de Echave, Ozumba's mural, the journal of the Clare nun Ana de Cristo, the image printed by Diego Garrido, the *Informaciones Jurídicas de 1666*, the *totonac* tradition of Saint Miguel Zozocolco, Veracruz, and others.

A particular manifestation of the popular devotion of the common people is to leave donations, alms, and bequests in official documents as in testaments, which are notarized. In the Mexican archives, especially in the Archives of the Basilica of Guadalupe, abundant documentation is preserved, since the sixteenth century, of these donations, testaments, and other acts which reveal a growing devotion to the Virgin of Guadalupe who appeared to the Indigenous Juan Diego on Tepeyac.[21]

For example, there is the *Testamento de la Hija de Juan García Martín*, mentioned before, also known as *Testamento de Juana Martín* or *Testamento de Gregorio Morales*, which was written on Saturday, March 11, 1559, the writer being Mr. Morales. The name of the woman of this document not being known, it has been called different names, taking some names from the text, so it appears that this testament is from Juana Martín, or Gregoria María, or Gregoria Morales. Reading the text, the most appropriate name[22]

---

[21] In fact, Lorenzo Boturini, in his *Catálogo*, gives us the news of "a big bequest of old titles and documents of a pious manuscript of embarrassing poor people, that was connected to the first Hermitage and Sanctuary of Guadalupe. In this bequest there are documents that prove the veneration from times immediately after the Apparitions and much later (originals)." Lorenzo Boturini Benaduci, *Catálogo de Obras Guadalupanas*, in Ernesto de la Torre Villar and Ramiro Navarro de Anda, *Testimonios Históricos Guadalupanos*, p. 410.

[22] *El Testamento de la Hija de Juan García Martín* is kept in the Public Library of New York, Manuscript Section, Col. Lenox, Guadalupe Archives, a copy of the original and its translation in Col. Aubin-Goupil, National Library of Paris, and in the Historical Archives of the Basilica of Guadalupe, Mexico City. The translation of the text was done by Faustino Galicia Chimalpopoca. Cfr. Mariano Cuevas, *Álbum Histórico Guadalupano del IV Centenario*, Escuela Tipográfica Salesiana, Mexico 1930, pp. 85–86.

is that of the *Testamento de la Hija de Juan García Martín*. An essential part of the text says,

> Everyone must know and understand what this document contains and will be kept carefully so that no one takes my estate against my will, and will know how I have lived in this city of Cuauhtitlán and its neighborhood of San José Millán, where the young Juan Diego was raised, then went to get married in Santa Cruz el Alto [Tlacpac], close to San Pedro, with the young lady Doña Malintzin, who soon died, leaving Juan Diego alone. A few days later, through this young man, something prodigious occurred there in Tepeyacac. To him the Beautiful Lady, Our Holy Mary [*initech campaomo nexiti in tlazocihuapili Santa María*] uncovered Herself or appeared. Her Image we saw there in Guadalupe, which belongs to us, those of this city of Cuauhtitlán. Now, with all my soul, with all my heart and with all my will I leave to the same Lady all the grove of Pirú which goes as far as the tree next to the group of houses. I leave it all and I turn it over to the Virgin of Tepeyacac. I also warn that the house, or hut in which I find myself [*Ca xacal izca*] I leave to all my children, and grandchildren if they were to have them, so that they will have something settled and will serve the beautiful Lady; and I order that they do not argue or fight over the portion of this land [*amo quimo quimilizque ini tlatzin*] I hand it over to them so that they will joyfully dedicate themselves to Her service. Thus do so and keep it and make the authorities of Cuauhtitlán and everyone of this neighborhood respect this. Now, whoever you may be, gentleman or lord, native of Cuauhtitlán or not, you must take charge of this donation immediately so that you will defend it as something that belongs to the beautiful Lady, just as She will defend you after your death.

Through historical documentation we know that not only was the Hermitage enlarged, but also its surroundings were fixed so that there would be more space given to the great number of pilgrims who were attracted by the Guadalupan Event[23] and the news of the miracles.

As we had pointed out, Juan Suárez de Peralta also offers us important information, not only about the arrival of the Viceroy Martín Enríquez de Almanza, but also about the great devotion, that "all the people would go." He also spoke of the news of the miracles which Our Lady of Guadalupe had performed and the knowledge of the narration of the Apparitions: "She appeared among some cliffs." The viceroy passed by the Sanctuary of Guadalupe on November 5, 1568.[24] "To every town which he arrived—Suárez de Peralta

---

[23] Cfr. *Actas de Cabildo de la Cd. de México*, Acta 3121–3271.

[24] Cfr. Niceto de Zamacois, *Historia de Mexico desde sus tiempos más remotos hasta nuestros días*, Ed. J. F. Parres y Compañía, Barcelona-Madrid [date of the Introduction: 1876]. T.V, p. 149.

narrated—they gave many receptions, as is customary for all the Viceroys who come here. Thus he arrived at Our Lady of Guadalupe, which is a most venerated Image about two leagues from Mexico who had performed many miracles (She appeared among some cliffs and all the people go to this devotion). From there he entered Mexico City, and on that day a great party was given for him, with servants dressed in silk, a skirmish of many on horseback, very costly."[25]

Various artists of all kinds expressed their devotion through their art, and it is in these artistic manifestations that they exposed the history of the Guadalupan Event. In this way countless works of art of the Image of Our Lady of Guadalupe came forth, and in some of them the moment in which the Virgin met Juan Diego was represented. It is a fact that some artists painted, drew, or rendered in sculpture Juan Diego's image with a halo,[26] obviously expressing this humble Indigenous's holiness by this, because his reputation among the people was constant.

If the Church had seen that there was some incorrect detail in the Image of Our Lady of Guadalupe, or that it was inconsistent with its strict orthodoxy, the Image would have been destroyed, due to the first missionaries' constant fear that the Indigenous would return to their idolatry, as it is expressed in 1585 by the Third Mexican Provincial Council, in their *Libro Primero, Título I* [*Book 1, Title 1*], which says, "So that the Indigenous persevere in the Catholic faith that they received through a unique benefit from God, there must be no trace whatsoever of their old ungodliness impressed on them, of which the Indigenous could take advantage, and, thus deceived by the devil's cunnings, go back again as dogs to the vomit of idolatry."[27]

The Spaniards continuously organized expeditions to the north of the New Spanish territory, in order to settle towns; in some regions, such as what is now the state of Georgia in the United States of America, religious objects from the later part of the sixteenth century and the beginning of the seventeenth century have been found among the remains of old villages. One of these objects has strongly called our attention, since it is a medallion, surely made in Mexico, where the Virgin of Guadalupe is represented on one side,

---

[25] Juan Suárez de Peralta, *Tratado del Descubrimiento de las Indias*, Public Library of Madrid, manuscript no. 302, f. 163v. Also in *Noticias Históricas de la Nueva España. Tratado del Descubrimiento de las Indias*, Madrid 1878, chap. 41. Also in Fortino Hipólito Vera, *Tesoro Guadalupano*, T. I, p. 68. Also there has been an edition by the Secretariá de Educacion Pública, Juan Suárez de Peralta, *Tratado del Descubrimiento de las Indias*, Ed. SEP, Mexico 1949.

[26] AA. VV., *Álbum de los 450 Aniversario de las Apariciones*, Ed. Buena Prensa, Mexico 1981.

[27] *Concilio III Provincial Mexicano Celebrado en México el Año de 1585*, published by Mariano Galván Rivera, Ed. Eugenio Maillefert, Mexico 1859, L. I, T. I, p. 23.

and on the opposite side Juan Diego is represented, kneeling in veneration, but it has a very particular characteristic, which is a halo over his head, as a sign of holiness.

On the other hand, it is known that people continued giving donations constantly in the Hermitage, and that there were so many alms that some-one tried to steal them, as Fernando de Álvarez, person in charge of the Her-mitage, reported.[28] Pilgrimages also were constantly taking place, such as one organized by the Jesuit priests in 1599, asking for rain. Friar Francisco Javier Alegre made an interesting comment on that: "Never was there that soft smell of piety as in that [pilgrimage] they went on in this same year to the fa-mous Sanctuary of Our Lady of Guadalupe."[29] Certain towns had the purpose of keeping the Guadalupan Event always alive, so they decided to paint the walls of their churches, their atriums, or their entrances; an example of this is the parish of San Francisco, in Ozumba, Chimalhuacan, in the state of Mexico, where the most important events of the First Evangelization were painted on the frontal part of the atrium, approximately in 1613. Among the most important events are the arrival of the first Franciscan missionaries, the martyrdom of children in Tlaxcala, and the Apparitions of Our Lady of Guadalupe. In the part of the fresco which represents Friar Juan de Zumár-raga on his knees, venerating the Sacred Image on Juan Diego's *tilma*, it is precisely Juan Diego's image that is very deteriorated, though his image can still be appreciated. At the right angle of the fresco the whole event is com-plemented with the representation of the scenes of the Apparitions of the Virgin of Guadalupe in Tepeyac.

In a very short time the devotion to the Virgin of Guadalupe of Tepeyac was reaching unthinkable dimensions, as in the surrounding sites of Mexico City, state of Mexico, Colima, and Campeche; Guatemala; the state of Geor-gia; and Parris Island in the United States of North America, and others. The flow of all types of people on pilgrimages to the Sanctuary was so great that the metropolitan canon thought seriously about the construction of a larger Sanctuary and decided that the first stone would be laid on September 10, 1600.[30]

It was also estimated that the surroundings of Guadalupe needed repairs and amplifications urgently, so on March 2, 1600, the bridge was repaired.[31] In 1604, Friar Juan de Torquemada offers very interesting information on the

---

[28] Cfr. *Informe de Fernando Álvarez*, AGN, Ramo Bienes Nacionales, v. 78, file 111.

[29] Francisco Javier Alegre, *Historia de la Compañía de Jesús*, T. I. Lib. IV, p. 374.

[30] *Actas del Cabildo*, ACC, L-4-1600, f.246. Also in Cayetano de Cabrera, *Escudo de Armas*, Lib. III, Chap. XVII, n. 707, p. 358.

[31] Cfr. *Actas de Cabildo de la C. de México*, Acta 6065.

repairs that took place on the Calzada de Guadalupe (Road of Guadalupe), which he was commissioned to be in charge of: "This that is called Guadalupe was begun . . . which I was to be in charge of. . . . The construction of this 'Calzada de Nuestra Señora' lasted more than five months, where daily there were 1,500 to 2,000 men who worked immensely hard, and it is incredible to see what they did in such a few months."[32] The best administrators and foremen were called for the Hermitage, such as Diego López de Montoya and Alonso López de Cárdenas.[33]

Surely, the construction of a new Sanctuary implied a great cost, and in 1602, no less than the King of Spain, Philip III, donated the sum of 20,000 ducats for this Church of Guadalupe of Mexico. In addition, great campaigns were organized in order to collect sufficient money, some very inspired and creative ones, in order to be able to face the project; one of these was to make an artistic engraving in which the Virgin of Guadalupe was represented that would be sold in order to gather funds. This engraving was made by Samuel Stradanus, whose masterpiece is a testimony of devotion. The engraving contains a narration of the miracles that favored the Spaniards, miracles that coincide with the ones narrated by P. Miguel Sánchez in his book, *Imagen de la Virgen María*, written in 1648, and which are the same that are narrated in *Nican Motecpana*, written about 1590, only omitting the Indigenous aspects that specify the life of Juan Diego. The engraving is one more testimony out of the many in relation to the devotion to the Image of Guadalupe, appearing on Juan Diego's *tilma*, that are still preserved.

Finally, in 1609, the first stone was placed for the new Church of the Sanctuary of Guadalupe, and two commemorative lead plaques were placed in a wooden case. On one it said in Latin: "Beatisimae Virginae Mariae, Reginae Caelorum et Mexicanae Provinciae singularissimae Patronae sacellum, interveniente elemosynarum copiosissima . . . tione . . . Anno Domini 1609."[34] It is interesting that these plaques were decayed by the humidity and saltpetrous deposits in that place, and Juan Diego's *ayate* where the Image of Our Lady of Guadalupe is impressed is preserved until our days. These plaques show us that Mary of Guadalupe was recognized as patroness and that because of the great devotion to Her, the alms were very generous, coming from all types of people, from the king as well as from humble and poor persons.

---

[32] Friar Juan de Torquemada, *Monarqúia Indiana*, T. I, 727.

[33] Cfr. Jesús García Gutiérrez, *Primer Siglo*, p. 116.

[34] Cayetano de Cabrera, *Escudo de Armas*, Lib. III, Chap. XCII, n. 708, p. 359. Also in Patricio Uribe, *Disertación*, no. 8, p. 59.

At this same time, as we have also already pointed out, 1619 was when Ana de Cristo, a Clare nun, accompanied Mother Superior Jerónima de la Asunción as her secretary. She was on her way to the Philippines as abbess and founder of the new monastery of her order in those islands. The nuns arrived in Mexico, which was the only route at the time to get to the Philippine Islands, at the end of September 1620, and stayed until April 1, 1621. On their trip to Mexico City the nuns passed through the Sanctuary of Guadalupe. Ana de Cristo narrated the most important events of that trip in a certain type of diary. In that narration she said, "The last day's journey in New Spain was to a Hermitage that they call Our Lady of Guadalupe. We were there one night. It is a paradise and there is a great devotion to the Image. She was seen throwing dirt into the eyes of the enemy when Mexico was beaten, She appeared to an Indigenous in the place where She is, which is among some rocks, and She told him to make a house on the place where She stood, on that place a little clear water flows through there and we saw it, and it was boiling as though it were with a great flame, and they gave us a little cup of it and it was salty, but some pious women who take care of the Hermitage told us that the Virgin Herself asked the Indigenous for his mantle and She measured it from head to foot."[35] The statement is purely incidental, and precisely because of that it is more valuable, because it narrates the happenings of the trip and going through Guadalupe is just one more of them. One perceives that in the short time that they were there, they only heard the Spanish version of the events. Also it is noticeable that she was more impressed by the water's saltiness than by the devotion itself, and she makes a very curious mention of the imprint: "the Virgin Herself asked the Indigenous for his mantle and She measured it from head to foot." It is obvious that she refers to Juan Diego, that in substance and in essentials of the story, the narration of the Apparitions on the cliff, Her message of wanting a temple in that place, and the miraculous apparition on Juan Diego's *tilma*, are present.

Some of the more distinguished historical authors were Carlos de Sigüenza y Góngora, who informs us about Juan Diego's Indigenous name, which is Cuauhtlatoatzin; Mateo de la Cruz, whose work written in 1660 was judged by P. Francisco de Florencia as "the best edited narration that has come out"; P. Baltazar González, censor who authorized the translation of the *Nican Mopohua*, by Luis Lasso de la Vega, in the name of the Jesuit Province; P. Francisco de Florencia with his works, *Estrella del Norte* and *Zodiaco Guadalupano*, where he tries to demonstrate the history of the Event. The or-

---

[35] Congregatio de Causis Sanctorum, Prot. 1720, Manilen. *Beatificationis . . . Hieronymae ab Assumptione* (in Saec. H. Yañez) . . . *Positio super vita et virtutibus*, Rome MCMXCI, pp. 648–56; 726.

ator Luis Becerra Tanco gathered all of these writings in a collection that has been the source of later literature on Guadalupe.

Of course there was no lack of poets to manifest their love for the Virgin of Guadalupe and their veneration of Juan Diego; an example of this is Capitan Luis Ángel de Betancourt's poem. He came to Mexico in 1608 and before 1621 he wrote this poem in hendecasyllabic octaves in honor of the Virgin of Remedies,[36] which contains a verse with a most clear reference to the Virgin of Guadalupe, "painted by God Himself," "Grande Apeles," "Verdadero Praxiteles," and in which Juan Diego is represented as the mediator and messenger of Guadalupe. The importance of this allusion derives from the fact that it constitutes a testimony previous to P. Miguel Sánchez's book, which was written about the Apparitions in 1648, for which reason he could not have influenced Betancourt, nor either could Betancourt have influenced Sánchez because his poem remained unpublished.

The poet sings that a bird tells Juan Diego:

Look at the blood of the sacrifices;
that in this idolism is hot;
it will come to purify Christianity
of its vices of my rose orient;

and so that you have beginnings of your glory
go down to Tepeaquilla diligently,
and among tiled and round rocks
you will see my image close to the ripples.

Not as here [in Remedies] of sculpture and paintbrushes
that the great Apeles piles on white canvas
because God, true Praxiteles,
there will advocate me from Guadalupe.

You will make me a temple there, when the faithful
lift the cross, and occupy this hemisphere,
after the conquest of this land,
because there is nothing good in war.

---

[36] According to Jesús García Gutiérrez, the manuscript of this poem is found in the Archivo General de la Nación, in a series of manuscript volumes about historical matters of Mexico: *Colección de Memorias de Nueva España, quien de virtud de órdenes de Su Majestad del Excmo. Sr. Conde de Revillagigedo y del M.R.P. Ministro Fray Francisco García Figueroa, colectó, extractó y dispuso en 32 tomos, un religioso de la Provincia del Santo Evangelio de México, por el año de 1792, tomo I. Comprenden las piezas del Museo de Boturini y otras, de las que pidió Su Majestad en su real orden del 21 de Febrero de 1790,* Cfr. Jesús García Gutiérrez, *Primer Siglo,* p. 120.

She said, and the imperious crane
and the devout *cacique* went down to the valley;
he found the precious canvas of the rose,
and he was, as the first, to keep Her.

Until the majestic city
dressed by Spain to our size,
and for Her from Guadalupe, blessed flower,
don Juan wrought from pines a Hermitage.[37]

As we see, the allusion is unmistakably clear in regard to classifying the Image as a painting by God. The manner of describing Juan Diego is as a protagonist in this great Event.

In this way we see that the Guadalupan Event has been an inspiration from the sixteenth century until now, and if it is true that the Virgin of Guadalupe constitutes its main character, it also manifests plainly the veneration of the humble messenger of the Lady from Heaven, Juan Diego. As we have said, Juan Diego is represented in several paintings, sculptures, and monuments as a messenger, as a pillar holding up the pulpit in the Church of the *Pocito* (the spring of water at Guadalupe); as a column holding up all the altarpiece of Guadalupe in the Church of San Lorenzo Ríotenco; as a pillar holding up a chalice for the Eucharistic celebration. He appears with a halo not only in a sixteenth-century drawing, but also on a medallion from the beginning of the seventeenth century and in poetry, as in the one we saw by Luis Ángel Betancourt. As we can see, there are several artistic works in which the figure of Juan Diego, the humble and obedient messenger of the Virgin of Guadalupe, is also represented.

In these few historical details that we have sketched, it is clear that the Guadalupan Event left its mark, and continues leaving its mark, on the history and identity of a whole nation, but at the same time it is an Event that is intended for the whole world. Through Juan Diego, we have the Virgin of Guadalupe's central message, by which She manifests Herself as the Mother of God who asks to be our Mother and show us all the same Love, which is so needed by humankind.

---

[37] Luis Ángel Betancourt, *Poema*, in Francisco de la Maza, *El Guadalupanismo Mexicano*, Eds. FCE y SEP (=Col. Lecturas Mexicanas no. 37), Mexico 1984, pp. 41–42.

CHAPTER EIGHT

~

The Guadalupan Event Spreads Rapidly

Various documental sources that speak directly about the devotion to Our Lady of Guadalupe and that complement the history of the great Event are shown here. One of the principal protagonists in that Event was Juan Diego, who, with his holy life, marked history.

This devotion reached the far-off land of Colima, Mexico, where, at an early date, an interesting document was elaborated: the Testimony of Bartolomé López. It was spoken in the valley of Colima, on November 15, 1537, before the notary Juan de la Torre. Bartolomé López dictates his bequests for Guadalupe in clauses 23 and 24: "I order to Our Lady of Guadalupe, for my soul, 100 Masses, and order that they be paid with my estate." Then, "I order that they say 100 Masses for my soul in the House of Our Lady of Guadalupe and that they be paid with my estate." The historian Jesús García Gutiérrez[1] points out the difference in the clauses, as one says "Our Lady of Guadalupe" in general, and the other, "in the House of Our Lady of Guadalupe," so it is logical to think that it was referring to two different orders; it would not make sense to divide the bequest if it were not so. It is a very early reference, barely six years after the Apparitions, and in a far-off place, recently founded by the people of Mexico. The testator is not an Indigenous, but a Spaniard who evidently was influenced by the Guadalupan Event.

---

[1] Jesús García Gutiérrez, *Primer Siglo*, p. 72.

Francisco Verdugo Quetzalmamalintzin, lord of Teotihuacan, also made his testament, on March 2, 1563, where he indicated, "First I order, that if God were to take me from this life, four pesos be taken then to Our Lady of Guadalupe as alms, so that the priest who resides in that Church will use them to say Masses for me."[2]

Also Esteban or Sabastián Tomelín, born in Villa de Guadacanal, legitimate son of Sabastián García and Isabel García and living in the city of Puebla de los Ángeles, being ill and feeling that his end drew near, ordered his testament on April 4, 1572,[3] leaving bequests in favor of Our Lady of Guadalupe. He explicitly mentions the one in Mexico City: "I send to Our Lady of Guadalupe in Mexico City ten pesos in gold, which is to be paid from my estate." This testament is catalogued and published by Lorenzo Boturini, who tells us in the third volume of his *Catálogo*, "In addition, in his testament, Esteban Tomilín (father of the venerated nun, María de Jesús, from the convent of the *Limpia Concepción de la Puebla*, and whose canonization is now being processed) left a bequest of some pesos to the Blessed Image of Guadalupe in 1575. This serves as proof of the notoriety of the Apparitions and the successive veneration that was given to the Most Holy Lady."

Also in Villa de Colima, on April 30, 1577, Elvira Ramírez dictated her testament before the notary Francisco López, and in it she unmistakably mentions Our Lady of Guadalupe in Mexico. This document is interesting precisely because, as in the *Testamento de Bartolomé López*, the devotion to Our Lady of Guadalupe is noticeable in a distant land and only a few years after the Apparitions. The main text is that "I order that in the city of Mexico, in Our Lady of Guadalupe, three Masses be said, one in the Incarnation, another one in the Conception of Our Lady, and the other to the Holy Spirit, and that the customary alms be paid." And in another place it says, "I order that they be said in the same House of Our Lady of Guadalupe, five Masses: one to Blessed [Saint] Blas and Saint Anthony, and three Masses for the souls in Purgatory, and that they be paid from my

---

[2] *Testamento de Francisco Quetzalmamalintzin*, in the Archives of the Royal Academy of History, Madrid, Col. de Manuscritos, Guía de Fuentes para la Historia de I-A, vol. II, p. 406. Also in the National Library of Paris, Mexicains, 243. Quoted by Lorenzo Boturini Benaduci, "Museo Indiano," in *Idea de una Nueva Historia General de la América Septentrional*, Ed. Porrúa (=Col. "Sepan Cuantos" no. 278), paragraph 2, Mexico 1986, pp. 148–49.

[3] Cfr. *Testamento de Sebastián or Esteban Tomelin*, in Fortino Hipólito Vera, *Tesoro Guadalupano*, Appendix pp. 13–22. Also Cfr. Jesús García Gutiérrez, *Primer Siglo*, pp. 70–71. Also Cfr. Lorenzo Boturini Benaduci, "Catálogo del Museo Indiano. Guadalupe, Instrumentos Públicos y otros Monumentos, Párrafo XXXVI," in Ernesto de la Torre Villar and Ramiro Navarro de Anda, *Testimonios Históricos Guadalupanos*, pp. 409–11.

estate."[4] Explicit reference is also made to the "house" of Guadalupe in Mexico City.

Alonso Hernández de Siles dictated his testament in Sultepec, Mexico, on April 9, 1577. The important text in his bequest is "I send the Church of Our Lady of Guadalupe that is in Tepeaquilla, outside of Mexico, 20 pesos of *tepuzque* for the construction being done and it should be paid from my estate."[5] The Spaniards called Tepeyac "Tepeaquilla," so as not to confuse it with Tepeaca in the state of Puebla.

Another testament was that of Anna Sánchez, who dictated her document in Mexico City on February 17, 1580, and it has an important bequest: "That four Masses be said for my soul and those of my deceased ones, two in the house and Hermitage of Our Lady of Guadalupe and the other two in the house and Hermitage of Our Lady of Remedies, and that they be paid for with the customary alms."[6]

Just as there were these expressions of devotion, such as testaments, donations, and alms, there was also a good organization to help orphan girls who were unprotected. It is proven that at an early time, there was a cofraternity in the Hermitage, as appears in Alonso Montabte's testament, which was dictated in Mexico City on July 16, 1564, and whose text reads, "Give Our Lady of Guadalupe in this city two pesos of *tepuzque* as alms because I am a member of the cofraternity of her house."[7] As we can see, he declares the devotion he has for Our Lady of Guadalupe, leaving alms for the Hermitage, but also he tells us that he is a member of the Hermitage's cofraternity, which means that already there was this devotional organization in the important Sanctuary of Guadalupe. The devotion was becoming more and more important and the great and numerous miracles that were verified in Tepeyac were very clearly extending out to other places.

Several documents testify in particular to the devotion and confirmation of great and wonderful miracles that were verified in the Sanctuary of Guadalupe on Tepeyac. One of the most eminent examples was that of the Spaniard Bernal Díaz del Castillo,[8] a soldier and companion of Hernán Cortés. He

---

[4] *Testamento de Elvira Ramírez*, Archivo General del Estado de Colima, Registro de Escrituras Públicas ante Francisco López (1577), box 4, file 10. All the Registro has 56 fs. The original document takes up only 5 folders.

[5] *Testamento de Alonso Hernández de Siles*, AGN, Bienes Nacionales, vol. 391, file 16, s.n.f.

[6] *Testamento de Anna Sánchez*, AGN, Bienes Nacionales, vol. 391, file 11, s.n.f.

[7] *Testamento de Alonso Montabte*, AGN, Bienes Nacionales, vol. 391, file 10.

[8] Bernal Díaz del Castillo was born in Medina del Campo, Spain, between 1492 and 1493; he came to the New World as a soldier under Pedrarias Dávila, and died in Guatemala in 1585. He went to Cuba in expeditions with Hernández de Córdoba, Juan de Grijalva, and then with Cortés, under Pedro de Alvarado. He participated in the unfortunate expedition of Las Hibueras. He participated in

attributes the success of the conquerors to "the grace and help of the Virgin of Guadalupe" and in two texts he speaks of the miracle of Tepeyac in his book titled *Historia Verdadera de la Conquista de la Nueva España*, written in about 1560. The first text says, "Then Cortés ordered Gonzalo de Sandoval to leave what he was doing in Ixtapalapa, and to go by land to fence off all the road that goes from Mexico to a town they called Tepeaquilla, which they now call Our Lady of Guadalupe, where She does and has done many miracles."[9] In the second text he says, "There are many hospitals, and they have great benefits, and the holy house of Our Lady of Guadalupe that is in Tepeaquilla, where Gonzalo de Sandoval's estate used to be when we beat Mexico. She has performed many holy miracles, and does so every day. Let us give thanks to God and his blessed Mother, Our Lady, for this. She gave us grace and helped us win this land where there is so much Christianity."[10]

Bernal Díaz del Castillo was not in Mexico in 1531, and all that he says in reference to the Virgin of Guadalupe and of "the holy miracles that She performed every day" he knew because in Guatemala, where he lived, they received news about the devotion. The great distance that exists between Mexico City and Guatemala must be pointed out in noting that the reputation of the miracles of Guadalupe had arrived there. In addition, he gives some concrete information about the area of Tepeyac, or Tepeaquilla, as the Spanish call it so as to distinguish it from Puebla's Tepeaca. His testimony is more powerful because he did not believe in miracles easily, as he shows in his chronicle, where he writes ironically and mocks some people who saw the Apostle James fighting in favor of the Spaniards against the Indigenous during the Conquest.

Just as Díaz del Castillo describes the Sanctuary as an important point of the devotion, confirmed by the miracles of the Virgin of Guadalupe, there are others in literature, like Francisco Cervantes de Salazar, who, when describing Mexico City in his book *México en 1554*, also points out the Hermitage on Tepeyac: "From the hills to the city (something that brings out its merit), more than thirty kilometers of irrigated lands extend out in all directions, bathed by the waters from canals, rivers, and springs. Great cities of the Indigenous are settled there, like Texcoco, Tacuba, Tepeaquilla, Azcapozalco, Coyoacan, Ixtapalapa, and many others. These temples that shine and look

---

the principal events. He went to Spain in 1539, obtained a title of magistrate in Soconusco, returned to Mexico in 1541 and decided to go to Santiago de Guatemala. In 1551 he went back to Spain for a second time and obtained a title as magistrate in Guatemala. Around 1560 he wrote a book, *Historia Verdadera de la Conquista de la Nueva España*. It was published in Madrid in 1632 by Friar Alonso Ramón, General Reporter in the Order of Merced, who used a copy sent by the author to Spain. The original manuscript of his work is now found in the National Archives of Guatemala.

[9] Bernal Díaz del Castillo, *Historia Verdadera*, T. I, p. 373.
[10] Bernal Díaz del Castillo, *Historia Verdadera*, T. I, p. 651.

toward Mexico are theirs."[11] Another commentator, Alonso de la Santa Cruz, in approximately 1555 drew this Sanctuary on a map.[12]

The arrivals of the viceroys, as well as their departures, were official and solemn events of great importance. A feast was celebrated in which the whole city participated with great enthusiasm. It became a great occasion for the most important city of the viceroyalty. From the fact that the town of Guadalupe and its Sanctuary were chosen for the performance of these solemn events, one can understand the importance of this sacred place.

We know that when Gastón de Peralta, Marquis of Falces,[13] arrived in Mexico on September 17, 1566, a supreme celebration was held. There was a canopy of gold fabric with gold and silver fringe and crimson velvet decorated with the coat of arms of the city. In addition, a new wardrobe was commissioned for the judges, the councilmen, the chief notary, and the treasurer. Inside the Hermitage was the venerated Image on Juan Diego's *tilma* and a shining full-size sculpture of the Virgin, made of silver and covered in gold, which was a special offering from the richest man in New Spain, Alonso de Villaseca, donated for his beloved Guadalupe on September 15, 1566, only two days before the arrival of the viceroy. The historian José Ignacio Rubio Mañé complements this information: "It was also authorized, at the expense of the government, that the necessary allowances would be made for the accommodations of the new Viceroy in the town of Guadalupe. This is the first time that this town was mentioned in connection with receptions of this nature. Perhaps it was the first time that Guadalupe was chosen as a place for the Viceroy to rest after the fatigue of the trip from Veracruz before entering the city, and also in order to have a chance to plan the details for the ceremonies with him."[14]

Two years later, in October 1568, a new viceroy arrived in Mexico, Martín Enríquez de Almanza,[15] who was also received with great celebrations in the

---

[11] Francisco Cervantes de Salazar, *México en 1554*, E. Antigua Librería de Andrade y Morales, Mexico 1875. Also in Fortino Hipólito Vera, *Tesoro Guadalupano*, T. I, p. 15.

[12] It is a polychrome parchment 78 cm. by 114 cm; now kept in the University of Uppsala, Sweden. How it got to Sweden is a mystery; it seems that after its keeper, Alonso de la Santa Cruz, died in Prague in 1572, it was purchased by the collector Rudolph II of Germany and then ended up in Prague where it "probably became part of the booty in the pillage of Prague in 1648 by the Swedish army." Sigvald Linne, *El Valle de la Ciudad de México en 1550*, in José Irurriaga de la Fuente, *Anecdotario de Viajeros Extranjeros en México, Siglos XVI–XX*, presentation by Andrés Henestrosa, Ed. FCE, Mexico 1989 [republished in 1991], T. I, p. 67.

[13] Gastón de Peralta, Marquis of Falces, was viceroy in the New Spain from 1566 to 1567.

[14] José Ignacio Rubio Mañé, *El Virreinato. Orígenes y Jurisdicciones, y Dinámica Social de los Virreyes*, UNAM, Instituto de Investigaciones Históricas, y FCE, Mexico 1983 [Reprinted in 1992], T. I, p. 124.

[15] Martín Enríquez de Almanza was viceroy in the New Spain from 1568 to 1580.

Sanctuary of Guadalupe in November of that same year. But when he had barely arrived at the Mexican coast with a complete convoying fleet, he surprised the pirate Hawkins. With this, Hawkins had no choice but to abandon some of his companions on the coast at Pánuco, and among these was the English Protestant, Miles Philips, who was captured and sent to Mexico City. Thanks to the fact that he had the custom of writing down his adventures, we can learn important details about the Sanctuary of Our Lady of Guadalupe at that time. The sculpture made of silver and gold, donated to the Hermitage by the rich miner Alonso de Villaseca in 1566, called his attention more than the venerated Image on Juan Diego's *tilma*. The pirate said,

> The next day in the morning we walked to Mexico, until we got within two leagues of the city, to a place where the Spaniards have erected a magnificent Church dedicated to the Virgin. There they have Her image in gold-covered silver, as tall as a tall woman, and in front of Her and in all the rest of the Church there are as many silver lamps as there are days in the year, all of which are lit during solemn feasts. Always when the Spaniards pass next to this Church, even on horseback, they get off, go inside the Church, kneel down before the Image and pray to Our Lady to free them from all evil, so that, if they are walking or on horseback, they would not pass without going inside the Church and praying, as I said, because they believe that if they do not do so, they would not have good luck in anything. The Spaniards call this Image Our Lady of Guadalupe. There are some cold baths here that gush out as if the water were boiling and it is salty to the taste, but very good for those who have wounds or sores, because they say many have been cured. Every year, the day of the feast of Our Lady, people are used to coming to offer and pray before the Image and they say that Our Lady of Guadalupe does many miracles.[16]

As one can see in this fresh and spontaneous narration by someone that did not profess the Catholic religion, there is important information about the magnificent gifts and devotional offerings that were made to the Hermitage, the strong devotion of the Spaniards who tried to obtain a blessing, kneeling before the Image, the salty water from the surroundings which caused the atmosphere not to be the most adequate for the preservation of the Image, about the devotion of the people, their offerings, their prayers, and their pilgrimages, and the reputation that Our Lady of Guadalupe had for the "many miracles" that She performed.

---

[16] *A discourse written by one Miles Philips, Englishman*, p. 143.

The devotion to Our Lady of Guadalupe was such that not only the people but the clergy themselves, specially the diocesan, looked for a way to celebrate liturgical acts in the Sanctuary, even at the cost of neglecting their obligations. For example, the canons in the metropolitan cathedral were absent from their services in the cathedral while going to celebrate in the Sanctuary of Guadalupe, especially on the day of the Nativity of the Virgin Mary, which was the date on which Our Lady of Guadalupe was liturgically celebrated at that time. Evidently this got to be a problem, especially with those who did not give notice, so on September 14, 1568, a formal act was passed and it imposed a severe sanction on those who went to the Hermitage of Guadalupe without permission. It declared that "With regard to going to Our Lady of Guadalupe on the day of the Nativity of Our Lady, he that has to go, from now on, is to get permission if he were to ask for it; but if he were to go with the Archbishop he would go 'without justification.'"[17] But this did not solve the problem, so one year later, anticipating what could happen, two days before the liturgical feast of the Nativity of Mary, on September 6, 1569, another act was drawn up that revealed how the canons who were to go to Our Lady of Guadalupe could make up a "justification."[18]

As we have pointed out, there was a well-organized cofraternity of Our Lady of Guadalupe which had many members and a good sum of money to cover any celebration or feast of Guadalupe, so much money that on May 8, 1571, the treasurer Cristóbal de Aguilar was permitted to take 2,200 pesos as a loan from the cofraternity.[19] Years later more cofraternities of the Sanctuary would be founded.

The Jesuits who arrived in Mexico on September 28, 1572, immediately understood the importance of the devotion to Our Lady of Guadalupe, so they became Her great promoters among the youth in their schools, as well as in their own missions. Through literary contests in all of their schools they were able to get several young students to take the devotion to Guadalupe very seriously. The sermons on Guadalupe elaborated by the sons of Saint Ignatius are famous. As we pointed out, the Jesuits also motivated the devotion among the people. When drought hit the country in 1599, the Jesuits promoted a famous pilgrimage to the Sanctuary of Guadalupe.[20]

---

[17] Archivo del Cabildo y Catedral Metropolitana, *Actas de Cabildo*, 2nd book, laser copy. Also published by Jesús García Gutiérrez, *Primer Siglo*, p. 85.

[18] Archivo del Cabildo y Catedral Metropolitana, *Actas de Cabildo*, 2nd book, laser copy. Also published by Jesús García Gutiérrez, *Primer Siglo*, p. 85.

[19] Actas de Cabildo de la Catedral de México, Act 3513.

[20] Cfr. Francisco Javier Alegre, *Historia de la Provincia Compañía de Jesús en la Nueva España*, Ed. Institutum Historicum, S.J., Rome 1959, T. I, p. 374.

Just as Bernal Díaz del Castillo, Suárez de Peralta, and Miles Philips made testimony to the devotion to and of the great reputation of the miracles of the Virgin of Guadalupe on Tepeyac, the Jesuits also testified to them. The superior of the Jesuits in Mexico, P. Francisco Baez, sent the Jesuit General, who resided in Rome, the annual report, titled *Annuae Literae*, which covered April 1600 to April 1602, giving the most relevant aspects of each of their schools and community houses. When it mentioned the Colegio de Mexico that they had in the capital of New Spain, it said, "Even though our students and priests have shown their devotion and fervor, they have been more fervent because of their affection shown to the Most Holy Virgin, Our Lady, using many holidays to go visit two Images and Churches of Hers, one at a long league from this city and the other three leagues. They go and come on foot as in a pilgrimage and they receive the Most Holy Sacrament at the altar of the Image which they visit, opening the case of the Image that is of great veneration in this land, because of the great miracles She has done since the beginning of these Indies."[21] It is obvious that one of these images and "the great miracles She had done since the beginning of these Indies" is precisely the Image of Our Lady of Guadalupe, whose church "is one long league from this city." The reputation of the Chapel of Guadalupe is also proven by P. Pedro Flores, S.J., who in 1609 called it the "famous sanctuary."[22] In the history of the Jesuit missions in northern Mexico, California, and other regions which today are part of the United States, they took the devotion to the Virgin of Guadalupe, dedicating churches and missions to Her and hanging paintings of Guadalupe everywhere.[23]

A series of documents summing up its importance are those that derive from the indulgences and privileges that the Holy Father gave to the Hermitage at its beginning. The Archbishop of Mexico, Pedro Moya de Contreras, requested benefits and indulgences for the Hermitage of Guadalupe from Pope Gregory XIII through the General Prelate of the Jesuits, Everardo Mercuriano. The Holy Father agreed to such a petition in February 1573, granting the faithful who visited the church of "Saint Mary of Guadalupe from Tepeaquilla in the Mexican province" plenary indulgence and other benefits

---

[21] P. Francisco Baez, S.J., *Annuae Literae de la Provincia de Mexico y Philipinas*, from April 1600 to April 1602, AHSI, Rome, Mexican, *Annuae 1574–1614* (Mexico 14), vol. I, f. 268v.

[22] P. Pedro Flores, S.J., *Annuae Literae Provinciae Mexicanae*, 1609, AHSI, Rome, Mexican, *Annuae 1574–1614* (Mexico 14), vol. 1, f. 502v.

[23] A synthesis of the Jesuits' devotion to Guadalupe and of their propagation can be seen in the sermon by Friar Antonio López Murto, Franciscan in Propaganda Fidei, pronounced on May 7, 1791, 24 years after the Jesuits were expelled. In it he praised the Jesuits' missionary work and how the most reluctant Indigenous of northern Mexico lived their devotion to Guadalupe.

according to the customary manner.[24] Later, Father Everardo Mercuriano, S.J., wrote to Archbishop Moya de Contreras on March 12, 1576; the Jesuit said "The prorogation of the indulgences granted to the Hermitage of Our Lady of Guadalupe and the substitution of the day, as ordered, have been obtained and the Brief goes with this."[25] Father Mercuriano wrote from Rome to the Provincial of New Spain, Pedro Sánchez, on March 31, 1576, and, among other things related to Mexico, he reported that the pope had granted "the prorogation of the jubilee that the cofraternities requested for the Hermitage of Our Lady of Guadalupe of Tepeaquilla."[26] It seems, from Pope Gregory XIII's brief, *Ut Deiparae semper Virginis*, of March 28, 1576,[27] that he had direct information about the Hermitage of Guadalupe, which had become a fundamental center for pilgrimages for Indigenous and Spaniards of Mexico City and its surroundings, especially during the great feasts in which indulgences were specified. This, without a doubt, provoked a request to extend those indulgences temporarily, and extend them also to the metropolitan cathedral in order to avoid the faithful leaving the cathedral on those holidays to go visit the Sanctuary of Guadalupe instead.[28] Different spiritual and pastoral activities were already organized; for example, the Spaniards would keep vigil in the Sanctuary and pray novenas. In a report from Friar Alonso Ponce, on approximately July 23, 1585, he said, "by a stone bridge, near a little Indigenous town, and in it, next to a hill, a Hermitage and Church called Our Lady of Guadalupe, where the Spaniards from Mexico go to keep vigil and pray novenas, and a clergy lives there who celebrates Mass."[29]

This confirms once again that already at that time, the faithful, not only the Indigenous but also the Spaniards, would go more to the Sanctuary of

---

[24] In the Vatican's Secret Archives two chronological indices are kept, one on the commissions expedited from 1569 to 1571, another one on the briefs expedited between 1569 and 1575. The pontifical indulgences in favor of the Sanctuary of "Our Lady of Guadalupe de Tepeaquilla in the Mexican province" are registered, February 1573. ASV, Sec. Brev. Lat. 81, p. 165.

[25] *Carta de Everardo Mercuriano, S.J., al arzobispo de Mexico, Pedro Moya de Contreras*, ARSI, Mexican, 1, f. 9r; published also in *Monumenta Mexicana*, vol. I (1570–1580), (=Col. Monumenta Historica Societatis Iesu no. 77), editing directed by Félix Zubillaga, Ed. Monumenta Historica Societatis Iesu, Rome 1956, pp. 192–93, note 3. Cfr. *Cartas de Indias*, p. 310; Francisco del Paso y Troncoso, *Epistolario de Nueva España*, XI, p. 266. Some information offered by Stafford Poole, *Our Lady*, p. 76, is wrong.

[26] *Monumenta Mexicana*, vol. I, p. 213.

[27] Cfr. Gregory XIII, *Ut Deiparae semper Virginis*, March 28, 1576, ASV, Sec. Brief 69, fs. 537r–538v; Sec. Brief 70 f. 532–533v. This brief is published in *America Pontificia*, coordinated and edited by Joseph Metzler, Libreria Editrice Vaticana, Vatican City 1991, vol. 2, pp. 1051–53.

[28] Cfr. Gregory III, *Ut Deiparae semper Virginis*, March 28, 1576, Sec. Brief 69, fs. 537r–538v; Sec. Brief 70, ff. 532r–533v.

[29] Friar Alonso Ponce, *Relación*, in Miguel Salva y Marqués Fuensanta del Valle, *Relación Breve y Verdadera*, Imp. Viuda de Calero, Madrid 1875, vol. 1, p. 107.

Guadalupe than to the cathedral, with a deeply rooted devotion that was be-coming part of their identity. This fact contradicts some historians' theses when they affirm that in the middle of the seventeenth century Guadalupe was practically unknown.[30] Moya de Contreras's episcopacy was rich in ref-erences and juridical acts that confirm the fact of Guadalupe in Mexico and that should be interpreted according to all the documents and controversies. For example, Moya de Contreras decided that all the revenues and alms that the Church of Our Lady of Guadalupe received, excluding all the necessary expenses for it, should be used to marry orphaned and poor young ladies, thus encouraging the generosity of the devotees of Guadalupe. This he wrote in his *Constituciones de Tepozotlan* on September 10, 1576.[31]

The chapel and its surroundings were frequently restored. Its enormous pilgrimages, its important policy, and its social strength were a clear and con-stant reality. Diverse documents where we find information on these types of restorations are what draw us near to the reality that was lived in the six-teenth century. For example, on February 19, 1574, the contractor García de Albornoz repaired the bridge on the road to Guadalupe.[32] On September 4, 1574, Gerónimo López and the builder, Diego Hernández, visited the road being built from el Barrio de Santa Lucía to the road to Guadalupe.[33] On November 8, 1591, the wooden bridge on the road to Guadalupe was re-paired.[34] And these constant repairs and amplifications continue even today.

During the repairs and adaptations in the Hermitage as well as in its sur-roundings, the Hieronymus monk, Diego de Santa María, arrived in Mexico, having been sent from the Monastery of Guadalupe in Extremadura, Spain. Showing his displeasure at the Hermitage of Tepeyac having detached itself from the Spanish devotion, he came to Mexico in order to inspect the Sanc-tuary of Tepeyac, since its reputation had transcended borders and because, according to him, part of the alms received in the Hermitage had to go to the Hieronymus monks. Friar Diego de Santa María wrote his first report on De-cember 12, 1574, to King Philip II, in which he confirmed the many be-quests, donations, and alms that the Hermitage received: "Today this Her-mitage has 2,000 pesos in revenues and almost another 2,000 is gathered in alms, and I do not see how they can spend that because it is not adorned and

---

[30] For example: Stafford Poole, *Our Lady*, pp. 76–77.
[31] In the archives of the Basilica of Guadalupe they keep diverse documents with the information about all the orphan girls who were aided by the archbishop of Mexico's disposition. Also, Patricio Uribe published it in *Disertación Histórico-Crítica sobre la Aparición*, no. 8, p. 60.
[32] Cfr. *Actas de Cabildo de la C. de México*, Act. 3743.
[33] Cfr. *Actas de Cabildo de la C. de México*, Act. 4154.
[34] Cfr. *Actas de Cabildo de la C. de México*, Act. 5266.

the building itself is very poor. These alms have been gathered under the name and shadow of Our Lady of Guadalupe and, if Your Majesty sees it convenient, an account will be made of the administrators and persons who have held positions in this house during the time that it has been called Guadalupe so that Your Majesty may put it in order."[35] He also noticed that the terrain was inappropriate for having a Sanctuary built there, and he even thought that it would have been better if it had been built in the beautiful forested area of Chapultepec.[36] "The place where the Hermitage was founded is very bad—it has saltpeter deposits and is up against the lake, unhealthy and without water. For this and for many other reasons . . . if Your Majesty sees it convenient that this Hermitage be moved to a good place, a monastery for the Order could be made, as others have been founded in this way by the Order of the monastery of Our Lady of Guadalupe. The most convenient place found close to this city is a farm called Chapultepec."[37]

The Hieronymus monk confirmed the great devotion that existed: "I found in this city a Hermitage under the name of Our Lady of Guadalupe, half a league from the city, where many people gather."[38]

On one hand, the monk Diego de Santa María gives us important information, such as the facts about the constant donations and alms, the testaments directing bequests to the Hermitage, the inappropriateness of the area because of the saltpeter deposits and the aridity, and the great devotion that existed in Tepeyac, "where many people gathered." But, at the same time, his imprecisions are not few and he commits obvious errors, showing that he knows absolutely nothing about the facts of Guadalupe, since in his second letter, on March 24, 1575, sent to the President of the Council of Indies, Juan de Ovando, as a response to a letter from him, he dares to say that the Hermitage had received its name after 1560, while in another, preceding letter he said that in 1562 it had another name. However, historical sources, such

---

[35] "Carta de Fray Diego de Santa María a su Majestad," Mexico City, December 12, 1574, AGI, Sevilla, Spain, Document Mexico no. 69, no. 3, in Xavier Noguez, *Documentos Guadalupanos*, pp. 230–31.

[36] Diego de Santa María's testimony of December 12, 1574, with the results of his visit and his propositions, sent on that date to Philip II, were discovered by P. Mariano Cuevas in the General Archives of Indies and published in his *Historia de la Iglesia en México*. vol. 2, pp. 493–97. The letters were directed to Philip II and not to Carlos V, who had died by that time. Sometimes this monk commits small errors of appreciation and judgment about the place.

[37] "Carta de fray Diego de Santa María a su Majestad," Mexico City, December 12, 1574, AGI, Sevilla, Spain, Document Mexico no. 69, no. 3, in Xavier Noguez, *Documentos Guadalupanos*, pp. 230–31.

[38] "Carta de fray Diego de Santa María a su Majestad," Mexico City, December 12, 1574, AGI, Sevilla, Spain, Document Mexico no. 69, no. 3, in Xavier Noguez, *Documentos Guadalupanos*, pp. 230–31.

as *Información de 1556*, demonstrate that as early as then the devotion of the Tepeyac was denominated "Guadalupe."

In this second report what stands out is his preoccupation about the Spaniards forgetting the Sanctuary in Extremadura because of their attraction to that of Tepeyac, to which they made offerings and gave alms, and that there were several testaments that contained bequests precisely for the one in Mexico. The Hieronymus monk declared, "The inconvenience of having given the name of Guadalupe to the Image that is venerated in Mexico is that the Spaniards have begun to forget the Virgin of Guadalupe that is venerated in Extremadura, Spain, to whom many Spaniards used to grant their bequests. But now it seems that it is the Spaniards who grant the Virgin of Guadalupe of Tepeyac their bequests and estates in Mexico."[39] Thus the Hieronymus monk, Friar Diego de Santa María, confirmed that it was the Virgin of Guadalupe in Mexico whom the Spaniards venerated "and give alms to."

Friar Diego de Santa María thinks that it is a mistake, because he supposes that the Spanish think they offer their bequests to the Virgin of Spain. He analyzes the economical aspects, and he expresses his opinion about the Sanctuary's destiny, looking for the jurisdiction, direction, and administration of the Hermitage of Tepeyac to the one of Extremadura, Spain. The Hieronymus monk did not obtain anything of that which he was hoping for, and the administration and the direction of the Hermitage continued being the same. But, as we said, the details that are contained in this information also help us to see objectively that the Hermitage of Our Lady of Guadalupe of Tepeyac had nothing to do with the one in Extremadura, in addition to proving the strong Mexican devotion, not only of the Indigenous but of the Spaniards as well, with its manifestations in alms, donations, bequests, and so on. Again, the inadequate ground with saltpeter deposits where the Hermitage was located, which made the preservation of the Image more surprising, is confirmed. Another detail to take into account is the ecclesiastical and civil power that the Hieronymus order had at the time in the realm of the Spanish Crown. However, even with all its great political power, it accomplished absolutely nothing.

The Spanish Crown showed a greater interest in knowing about this devotion to Our Lady of Guadalupe who had appeared in Tepeyac. And so, with King Philip II's request for information, the Viceroy Enríquez de Almanza wrote on September 23, 1575, saying, "What is commonly known about the foundation of the Church that is now standing, is that in 1555 or

---

[39] "Carta de fray Diego de Santa María a su Majestad," Mexico City, March 24, 1575, AGI, Sevilla, Spain, Signature México, no. 283, in Xavier Noguez, *Documentos Guadalupanos*, pp. 232–36.

1556 there was a small Hermitage in which there was the Image that is now in the Church."[40] Obviously the viceroy meant the Hermitage that the second archbishop of Mexico, Alonso de Montufar, had enlarged. He also wrote about other interesting details, such as confirming the inadequacy of the place for founding any monastery, as well as the fact that there were 400 members in one of the cofraternities of the Hermitage.[41]

Alonso de Villaseca, who was a great benefactor of the Sanctuary, died on September 8, 1580. He was remembered for his great donations to the Virgin of Guadalupe, particularly the life-size sculpture of gold-covered silver that was one of his most important gifts. His son-in-law, Agustín Guerrero, knowing the great devotion that his father-in-law professed to the Virgin of Guadalupe, arranged a great ceremony where his father-in-law's body was displayed for three days in his beloved Sanctuary of Guadalupe.[42]

More ceremonies were to be held in the Sanctuary since they were starting the preparations for the traditional reception of the new viceroy for New Spain, Lorenzo Suárez de Mendoza, Count of Coruña.[43] On September 26, 1580, it was decided that the festivities for the welcoming be extended, among which stood out "that the Very Excellent Lord, Viceroy, Count of Coruña be served abundantly in the house of Our Lady of Guadalupe."[44] Later, the new viceroy named by Philip II, on February 26, 1585, was Álvaro Manríque de Zúñiga, Marquis of Villamanrique.[45] When this news was known in Mexico, on July 29, the canon got together and decided in a solemn act, no. 4679, that a skirmish be organized in the valley of Our Lady of Guadalupe, in honor of the new viceroy. A committee was named to carry out all the preparations for the welcoming, among which was this event: "For the first time the flatlands of Guadalupe are mentioned, to do the skirmish there. . . . Lastly, that the road to Guadalupe be straightened as far as Santiago. However, in the October 2 session it was agreed to suspend all the projects for the festivities in Santiago, since everything had to be done in Guadalupe, the Viceroy being hosted there before his entrance."[46] And so it

---

[40] Historic Archives of Madrid, *Documentos de Indias*, no. 235. Published in *Cartas de Indias*, LVI, p. 310. Also in Fortino Hipólito Vera, *Tesoro Guadalupano*, p. 34.

[41] Cfr. Historic Archives of Madrid, *Documentos de Indias*, no. 235. Published in *Cartas de Indias*, LVI, p. 310, Also in Fortino Hipólito Vera, *Tesoro Guadalupano*, p. 46 and p. 48.

[42] Cfr. Francisco de Florencia, *La Estrella del Norte*, Imp. D. María de Benavides, Mexico 1688, p. 197. Also in Fortino Hipólito Vera, *Tesoro Guadalupano*, pp. 57–58.

[43] Lorenzo Suárez de Mendoza, Count of Coruña, was viceroy of New Spain from 1580 to 1583.

[44] José Ignacio Rubio Mañé, *El Virreinato*, vol. I, p. 128.

[45] Álvaro Manríque de Zúñiga, Marquis of Villamanrique, was viceroy of New Spain from 1585 to 1589.

[46] José Ignacio Rubio Mañé, *El Virreinato*, vol. I, p. 129.

was: the Viceroy Manríque de Zúñiga had a long and pleasant stay in Guadalupe, where he was able to enjoy the festivities of his arrival.

It was precisely at this time, October 16, 1585, when the Third Provincial Council of Mexico took place, one of the most important ecclesial reunions where, in addition to many articles that directed the steps of the Church in Mexico, some issues were decided, such as that they specifically prohibited the Indigenous songs of the time and the type of their paganism, and that only those approved by the parishioners and the vicars would be permitted, and the same was said about the images, that if one of these had a false story it should be destroyed. The narration about the Virgin of Guadalupe continued with the approval of its history, and the miraculous Image was still much venerated, and the Hermitage, as we have seen, was the official meeting place for the most important personalities of New Spain. For the archbishop of Mexico, Pedro Moya de Contreras, it was one of the last important acts in which he participated, because in April 1586 he left the archbishopric and went straight to Guadalupe where he spent some days contemplating and saying good-bye to the Sacred Image of Our Lady of Guadalupe whom he loved so much.

Nearly three years later, on July 19, 1589, King Philip II ordered the Viceroy Manríque de Zúñiga to hand over his office to the new viceroy, Luis de Velasco, son of the second viceroy of New Spain, who had borne the same name.[47]

On December 24 of that same year, Luis de Velasco disembarked on the Mexican coast. Quickly those in charge of the welcoming committee went into action and prepared the details for the solemn festivities of entrance: "also 'Mr. Baltasar Mejía Salmerón was commissioned to accommodate and receive him, to make the house and bed comfortable, and the rest would be at Our Lady of Guadalupe, where this city makes the arrangements. That which is spent, what is convenient and the responsibility of the Treasurer of this city, the Treasurer is to give it to him and the Steward is to pay for it.' . . . Likewise, a very costly arch of triumph was ordered, and a gold key that the Magistrate Pablo de Torres was to give him. He, the Mayors of the orders, and the Chief Justice were designated to take the reins of the stallion and thus be the ones to introduce the Viceroy into Mexico City in a symbolic act. . . . The preparations continued in the session of January 2, 1590. They tried to do the skirmish then in Guadalupe, as before, thus eliminating Plaza Mayor."[48]

---

[47] Luis de Velasco, the son, was viceroy of New Spain from 1589 to 1595.
[48] José Ignacio Rubio Mañé, *El Virreinato*, vol. I, p. 132.

Viceroy Manríque de Zúñiga went to receive Luis de Velasco, meeting him at Acolman where, "after being together for nearly two hours, Manríque de Zúñiga went on to Texcoco. The next day the new Viceroy headed toward Mexico City, and spent the night at Our Lady of Guadalupe (the place where all of the Viceroys stop and where some festivities are made for them). From there he entered the city, so on January 25, he was received."[49]

King Philip II appointed another viceroy for New Spain on May 28, 1595. He extended the title to Gaspar Acevedo y Zúñiga, Count of Monterrey,[50] while Luis de Velasco was appointed viceroy for Peru. On September 15, 1595, the preparations to receive the new viceroy were begun. In addition to appointing the welcoming committee,

> they did not forget the silk for the gowns that were made for each occasion; to prepare the reception at Guadalupe; "to buy the horse along with the rich harness and bridle so that the Viceroy would enter from Guadalupe"; that the arch of triumph was made, "using what was left of the one before"; to dress all the street from Santa Ana to Guadalupe; to make a gold key to give to Gaspar Acevedo y Zúñiga, Count of Monterrey, in respect from the city government; the pallium for the reception; the infantry and the cavalry for the military honors; the comedy and the skirmish that must be made in Guadalupe; as well as the game with sugarcanes. . . . The Count of Monterrey was received with great festivities, and as it was planned, he solemnly entered the Capital that Sunday, on November 5, 1595.[51]

In 1603, the king appointed a new viceroy for Mexico, Juan de Mendoza y Luna, Marquis of Montesclaros;[52] who, accompanied by his wife and many servants, disembarked in Veracruz on September 5, 1603. Not until September 14 was the arrival of the new mandatory known. When the news got to Mexico City, there was jubilation for the new viceroy, but at the same time there was anxiety because, after the splendid reception the time before, there was no money to organize a reception as was the custom. So they had to take from other funds. At the session of September 15, it was agreed to give "2,000 pesos for the repair of the house in the town of Guadalupe where the Marchioness was to be accommodated, and to dress the road and the bridges on the way from Mexico City to Guadalupe before the exit of the Count of Monterrey. As in the previous occasions, the skirmish and the game with

---

[49] Friar Juan de Torquemada, *Monarquía Indiana*, vol. I, p. 652.
[50] Gaspar Acevedo y Zúñiga, Count of Monterrey, was viceroy in New Spain from 1595 to 1603.
[51] José Ignacio Rubio Mañé, *El Virreinato*, vol. I, p. 134.
[52] Juan de Mendoza y Luna, Marquis of Montesclaros, viceroy in New Spain from 1603 to 1607.

sugarcanes had to take place on the field of the town of Guadalupe. . . . Finally, on October 16, the Canon was advised that everything was ready so that the new Viceroy could arrive in Guadalupe on Monday, October 20, and that the pompous festivities of his entrance into Mexico City were prepared for the following Wednesday."[53] The viceroy arrived in Guadalupe, where he was received very well, but as the place where he was going to reside in Mexico City was not ready, "he had to stay more time in Guadalupe, constantly entertained, until finally on Sunday, October 26, he entered the city with great solemnity."[54]

In September 1608 arrived the new archbishop of Mexico, García Guerra, who is famous for the great love that he immediately had for the Holy Image.[55] On June 12, 1611, that same archbishop was named viceroy of New Spain, and the traditional reception took place in Guadalupe, as for any other viceroy, but in addition to the festivities dedicated to him, he chose to stay a good time in a spiritual retreat, praying and reflecting on the well-known novenas that were performed in the Sanctuary. Juan de Torquemada tells us that "He was received as a Viceroy, with the appearance and the circumstances of all the other Viceroys before him. For this reception he went out of the Hermitage of Our Lady of Guadalupe, where he had been before at novenas, and he entered the city and palace houses with majesty."[56] Archbishop García Guerra had the strong conviction that the donations and alms which arrived to the Sanctuary were not only to receive great personages, but also for needy people, so he donated monthly alms to the shy beggars of the Church of Our Lady of Guadalupe.[57]

On January 23, 1612, the new viceroy of Mexico, Diego Fernández de Córdova, Marquis of Guadalcazar, was named.[58] His welcome was organized for September: "1,500 pesos had to be given to the Steward of Mexico City, Hernando de Rosas, for the expenses of reconditioning the house in the town of Guadalupe, and the meals that would be served to him, his wife, and family members accompanying him."[59] On this occasion the Audience that governed the viceroyalty again tried to limit the additional expenses. But on

[53] José Ignacio Rubio Mané, El Virreinato, vol. I, pp. 136–37.
[54] José Ignacio Rubio Mané, El Virreinato, vol. I, p. 137.
[55] Mateo Alemán, Sucesos de Fr. García Guerra, Arzobispo de México, Mexico 1613, in Fortino Hipólito Vera, Tesoro Guadalupano, p. 285.
[56] Friar Juan de Torquemada, Monarquía Indiana, vol. I, book I, chap. LXXIV, p. 767.
[57] Cfr. Francisco Antonio Lorenzana, Concilios Mexicanos, vol. I, Serie de los Ilmos. Sres Arzobispos de la Santa Iglesia de México, p. 216.
[58] Diego Fernández de Córdova, Marquis of Guadalcazar, was viceroy of New Spain from 1612 to 1621.
[59] José Ignacio Rubio Mañé, El Virreinato, vol. I, p. 140.

October 16, 1612, they insisted on the need to perform the solemn receptions that were customary, so, "they agreed to insist on the skirmishes in Guadalupe, for which they asked for authorization to spend 2,000 pesos more."[60]

Surely the viceroys were shown the joy and the hope of the people, precisely in the most significant and important place for them: the place where the Mother of God, the Lady from Heaven, had shown Herself to a humble Indigenous.

There were also several authors who gave proof of this Sanctuary's reputation; for example, in 1616, Friar Luis de Cisneros finished his work titled *Historia de la Imagen de Nuestra Señora de los Remedios*, which was printed in Mexico in 1621. In book 1, chapter 5, when he came to the subject of the sanctuaries of Mexico, he had no doubt when he said, "The oldest one is that of Guadalupe, which is at one league from this city, to the north, and which has an Image of great devotion and consensus that, almost since the land was won, She has done, and does, many miracles."[61] In the same manner, Diego de Cisneros, in his work approved in 1617, which he titled *Sitio, Naturaleza y Propiedades de la Ciudad de México*, and published in Mexico, spoke of the new temple that was being built and the roads of Mexico. He said, "and there is another main one to the north which they call Guadalupe, because the Church and the most venerated Image of Our Lady of Guadalupe is on the side of this road, on the skirts of some mountains, and its construction has grown with the unique devotion and infinite care of the most Illustrious Juan de la Serna, Archbishop of this city."[62]

Meanwhile, the order that great expenses not be made in the entertainments to receive the viceroys remained. So when the new Viceroy Diego de Pimentel, Count of Priego and Marquis of Gelves, arrived in 1621,[63] even though there was enthusiasm and readiness to do the festivities, they continued the view that the "expenses of the welcoming committee, and most of all, the accommodations and the entertainments in the town of Guadalupe" were not to be paid for by the treasurer.[64] And although there were objections, the organizers had to give in, due to the precise orders that came from the Spanish Court. But on August 20, 1621, in the Canon session on the custom of great festivities taking place for the receptions of the new viceroys,

---

[60] José Ignacio Rubio Mañé, *El Virreinato*, vol. I, p. 141.

[61] Also published by Cayetano de Cabrera, *Escudo de Armas*, book III, chap. XV, n. 677, p. 342.

[62] This was also published by Fortino Hipólito Vera, *Tesoro Guadalupano*, p. 94.

[63] Diego de Pimentel, Count of Priego and Marquis of Gelves, was viceroy of New Spain from 1621 to 1624.

[64] José Ignacio Rubio Mañé, *El Virreinato*, vol. I, p. 142.

they determined that they were "against those orders that were so opposed to the tradition of nearly 100 years 'of receiving their Viceroys with pomp and majesty, naming commissionaires in the name of the city to go to receive them in Puebla de los Ángeles, accommodating them in Guadalupe, where it is obligatory to spend the night, making arches of triumph and other preparations like those seen in the past.'"[65]

By that time, the new temple for the Lady from Heaven was about to be finished and it had even been used for such special celebrations as the one made by Archbishop Juan de la Serna, who presented himself before the Hermitage of Guadalupe when he arrived to the archdiocese of Mexico in 1613 so that She would bless him in his ministry, and he did not even hesitate to ordain priests in the Sanctuary of Guadalupe, as in 1616 when he gave this sacrament to P. Alonso Cuevas y Dávalos.[66] In this way liturgical acts and important pilgrimages were performed and offerings and sacrifices increased.

Finally, in November 1622, Archbishop de la Serna dedicated and blessed the new temple of Our Lady of Guadalupe. The transition to the new enclosure of the sacred Image was extremely emotional. There were eight days of festivities, great pilgrimages, solemn celebrations, and magnificent sermons such as that published by Juan de Cepeda, which he called *Sermón de la Natividad de la Virgen María Señora Nuestra, predicado en la Ermita de la Guadalupana, extramuros de la Ciudad de México en la fiesta de la misma Iglesia* [*Sermon for the Nativity of the Virgin Mary Our Lady, preached in the Chapel of Guadalupe, outside of Mexico City on the feast of the same Church*].[67] Surely, it was one of the most important moments for the whole city.

Nevertheless, the Sanctuary of Guadalupe would be a silent witness of the tremendous problems among the highest authorities of New Spain. Misunderstandings reigned for various causes, so much so that at one moment serious tension between Viceroy Marquis of Gelves and Archbishop de la Serna got to the point that on January 11, 1624, the viceroy's magistrates sentenced the archbishop to be deported to Spain. The archbishop "got into his carriage and, in the first part of his trip toward Veracruz, was escorted by a detachment of soldiers and an immense and very sad multitude of people followed him through the streets of Mexico City as far as the Sanctuary of Guadalupe. There he managed to find a way of lingering for a certain time: he celebrated

---

[65] José Ignacio Rubio Mañé, *El Virreinato*, vol. I, p. 142.

[66] Cfr. "Resguardo contra el Olvido," chap. III, p. 20, in Fortino Hipólito Vera, *Tesoro Guadalupano*, pp. 287–88.

[67] Also published in Fortino Hipólito Vera, *Tesoro Guadalupano*, p. 96. Also printed by Bachelor Juan de Alcazar, Mexico 1622.

Mass there and he sent his clergy the order to reinforce the edicts of excommunication against Viceroy Marquis of Gelves and his collaborators. Not long after that the viceroy had to hand in his office and a new viceroy was named, Rodrigo Pacheco Osorio, Marquis of Cerralvo. So on September 18, there was talk about restoring the Sanctuary of Guadalupe in order to receive the new viceroy, as was customary.

The historian José Ignacio Rubio Mañé offers us interesting information, quoting the Canon session: "In September 1624, it was known in Mexico that this new Viceroy was coming to Mexico. In the Canon session held on Wednesday, the eighteenth of that same month, they gave the notice and the capitularies began to look for a way to make a solemn reception, regardless of everything, more so with the report that 'because it is obligatory for Your Excellence to spend the night in the Hermitage of Our Lady of Guadalupe where it is a custom. But that place is so indecent that it is fitting to arrange to receive and accommodate Your Excellence that night since it is inexcusable.'"[68] But because of the tensions and the extravagance that was often the case in these festivities in order to entertain the new viceroy, they decided not to do it in Guadalupe. In regard to this same procedure we have an interesting detail, transmitted by Rubio Mañé and based on the Canon Acts. It says that

> In the session of September 29, they continued dealing with the reception that they aspired to make with great demonstrations of rejoicing. As the men commissioned for the reception in the town of Guadalupe had resigned because of illness and other causes, "because even though it is true that since this city was won, Viceroys have been received and accommodated in that place of Guadalupe at the expense of the government of this city," . . . so appointments were made for new commissioners, in effect. However, the magistrate, Francisco Enriquez Dávila, said, "today Diego de Astudillo, chamberlain of Your Excellency told me how the Viceroy had let him know that since the place and accommodation in Guadalupe was not fit, that he thought it was best to stay in Chapultepec, even if he had to go around the city and even if it was far. He asked to stay in that area; that from there he would go to Guadalupe the day of his reception in order to maintain the ordinary procedure of everything." So it was agreed.[69]

As we can see, even though the viceroy could not be accommodated in Guadalupe, he wanted to go there to venerate Juan Diego's sacred *tilma*.

---

[68] José Ignacio Rubio Mañé, *El Virreinato*, vol. I, p. 143.
[69] José Ignacio Rubio Mañé, *El Virreinato*, vol. I, pp. 143–44.

More information about the importance that the Sanctuary had in the reception of the viceroys appears later. When Philip IV named García Sarmiento de Sotomayor, Count of Salvatierra,[70] as viceroy, on July 1, 1642, the government of Mexico City insisted that "the reception and entrance of the Viceroys be in the town of Guadalupe and not in Chapultepec, as it had been implanted lately."[71] And later, Francisco Fernández de la Cueva, Duke of Alburquerque,[72] and his family were bidden farewell on March 26, 1661, by the new viceroy and his wife, right at the Sanctuary: "The Counts of Baths accompanied them to see them off at the Hermitage of Our Lady of Guadalupe."[73]

José Guadalupe Victoria's opinion is worthy of being taken into account: "The idea of placing cities and towns under the patronage of a saint or of the Virgin, in one of Her advocations, was a frequent practice in the West since ancient times. Mexico City was no exception, and even though, long after the Conquest, it counted with various patron saints, it is significant that after the middle of the seventeenth century, the Virgin of Guadalupe continued being considered the most important Patroness."[74]

In all solemn celebrations eloquent sermons were also preached. It must be pointed out that in this field of sermons, the Jesuits were great writers and specialists dedicated to the devotion of Our Lady of Guadalupe, especially in the period from the seventeenth century to the eighteenth. As we have pointed out, in 1600 Father Juan de Tovar, S.J., had already included a beautiful sermon in his *Sermonario*,[75] while in 1611, Francisco Colín wrote exalting the work performed by the Jesuits, *Labor evangélica, ministerios apostólicos de los obreros de la Cia. de Jesús, fundación y progresos de su provincia en las Islas Filipinas* [*Evangelic Labor, apostolic ministries of the workers of the Jesuits, founding and progress of their Province in the Philippine Islands*]. This manuscript was printed by José Fernández in Madrid in 1663, and in chapter 19, in one

---

[70] García Sarmiento de Sotomayor, Count of Salvatierra, was viceroy of New Spain from 1642 to 1647.

[71] José Ignacio Rubio Mañé, *El Virreinato*, vol. I, p. 148.

[72] Francisco Fernández de la Cueva, Duke of Alburquerque, was viceroy of New Spain from 1653 to 1660.

[73] José Ignacio Rubio Mañé, *El Virreinato*, vol. I, p. 151. Also in Gregorio Martín de Guijo, *Diario de Sucesos Notables. 1665–1703*, in *Documentos para la Historia de México*, Mexico 1853, vol. I, pp. 446–47 and 455.

[74] José Guadalupe Victoria, "Un singular ejemplo de piedad Mariana, Notas en torno a una Pintura de la Virgen de Guadalupe," in *Anales del Instituto de Investigaciones Estéticas*, UNAM, Mexico 1989, p. 71.

[75] "Sermón Guadalupano," in Juan de Tovar, S.J., *Sermonario*, National Library of Mexico, Fondo Reservado, MS. 1475, ff. 51r–53r.

of its notes on the Virgin of Guadalupe, he refers to the miracles that She had performed in the Philippines, no less![76]

As you can see, there are many and very different historical documents that refer to this great Guadalupan Event; surely there are many more that exist, but those noted here serve to give an idea of the magnitude of the Event which marked history.

---

[76] Also published in Fortino Hipólito Vera, *Tesoro Guadalupano*, p. 263.

CHAPTER NINE

The Holiness of Juan Diego

Juan Diego was a man of his time, a turbulent time; he lived in a moment of fundamental changes; his personal change, his conversion to Christianity, was, without a doubt, the most important change in his life. The Indigenous education that he received before his conversion was summed up in him, as well as the saving message of the Gospel, receiving divine Grace, in addition to the direct election to being the humble and faithful messenger of Our Lady of Guadalupe.

As we have seen, Juan Diego was considered by his neighbors as "a very good Indigenous and a very good Christian." The first part, "a very good Indigenous," would have been enough to classify him as virtuous, though not in the complete sense of the word that the Church gives to it, but, it does in the sense of someone who is profoundly coherent in his principles and perseveringly faithful to them to the point of heroism. We have glimpsed at how close the principles that ruled the Indigenous formation were to the Christian ones. Furthermore, we know that this chosen soul received the sacrament of baptism, and we have proof of his exemplary conduct after his conversion.

Certainly the Indigenous culture was very different from the Spanish one; however, not only the Spaniards but also the Indigenous realized that many things coincided, or were very similar. These similarities made the Spaniards express their confusion, and when they tried to explain them, some went so far as to say that probably an ancient apostle had appeared in those distant lands of the New World and had given some religious guidelines that had been preserved, although some of their expressions had changed because of time. On the other hand, the Indigenous could also appreciate that they shared with the Spaniards certain principles, such as love for God above all things, love for their fellow men, chastity, penance, the calling to sacrifice their life for God and for the world, yet other aspects, like offering the blood and hearts of their prisoners to the gods, were totally contrary to the Spanish way of thinking. But something that the Indigenous could not accept was the total rejection of their ancestral values, nor that all of their ancestors were in hell, although they were willing to accept one god more, as it would be Jesus Christ; surely they could not accept the destruction of their gods, their beliefs, their temples, to that extent.

Above all, the Indigenous were experiencing the destruction of their culture, of their religion, of their people; a deep depression, we have seen, became common. However, God acted as Friar Juan de Zumárraga, head of the Church in Mexico, urged him. And he acted in an unexpected manner, healing the wounds of the people who were born out of labor pains.

That is to say, almost five centuries ago, and under totally adverse circumstances, God performed something that we, after the Second Vatican Council, want to apply in all evangelic announcements, especially in our missions.[1] He preached Jesus Christ starting from the listener's culture, the preacher adapting to them and not pretending that they adapted, or adopted, his culture.

Now we think that this is very obvious, but in the mentality of that era, it was simply impossible. Educated and formed according to a medieval theology, and with the experience of having been able to recover their land from the hands of the Arabs, who had it for nearly eight centuries, and with the certainty that they were the defenders of Christ, the Spanish missionaries considered themselves indebted to His freeing power. They were assured by the Crown of the Catholic kings who, in their eagerness for blood purity, drove both the Arabs and the Jews from their territory, not caring about the financial crisis that this provoked, since their eyes were placed on being God's knights, called to defend Catholicism, which was suffering the Protestants' attacks in central Europe with Luther's disturbing force. For the missionaries, in their vocation of finding a perfect life and in their constant mission of preaching Jesus Christ, the Savior of the world, and baptizing all

---

[1] Cfr. especially the Decree of the Second Vatican Council, *Ad Gentes Divinitus*, on the missionary activity of the Church.

pagans, the incisive idea that the "Parusia" [the second Advent of Jesus Christ], the second coming of Jesus Christ sitting on the throne in order to perform the Final Judgment, was imminent. It was simply impossible that the missionaries and the good Christians could ever imagine the possibility of accepting some part of what they called idolatry.

And on the other hand, the Indigenous vision was totally consecrated by their gods, with the conviction that their sacrifices were vital so that the harmony of the cosmos would continue and in that way, humanity would survive. With a total and complete relationship with their gods and the cosmos, their gods could continue, thanks to the hearts and the blood of the valuable prisoners. The Indigenous could not imagine the collapse that their reason to exist would suffer, and as a consequence, they became immersed in a tremendous depression, because when their gods died, it would be better to let themselves die. It was impossible for them to accept what was happening. For the Indigenous the idea of a "new religion" was inconceivable, since, by definition, nothing that was new could be true, and much less anything related to the essence of stability, as is God. And that, of course, extended on to the moral issue: If true is synonymous of stability, nothing that changes can be true, nor good, either, since stability is also a supreme guarantee of all moral law,[2] for which reason the *Huehuetlamanitiliztli*, "the Elders' Rule for Life," was untouchable,[3] and that was not just because they had decided not to change it, but because that is the way it was essentially. What was traditional, that which was according to what had always been taught and done, was the only thing true and the only thing correct. *Yancuic*, new, came to be synonymous not only of "false" but also "immoral," and as a consequence, the very concept of a "new" religion was for them, in that sense, also contradictory in its same terms.

The circumstances made it impossible for the Indigenous people to convert, but regardless of that, one cannot deny that they converted. That was due largely to the message, strong and direct, and at the same time tender and loving, that was given by Our Lady of Guadalupe, leaving a sign of Her presence on an Image appearing on Juan Diego's *tilma*, a sign that was given in

---

[2] Cfr. Miguel León-Portilla, *La Filosofía Náhuatl Estudiada en sus Fuentes*, UNAM, Instituto de Investigaciones Históricas, Mexico 1974, pp. 234–35.

[3] "There is no one in the world, nor has there been, who honored their elders with more fear and reverence than these people, and so, those who lacked respect for the elders, fathers, or mothers, paid for it with their life. So what these people most recommended to their children and taught them was reverence to the elders, of any type, dignity, or condition that they might be." Friar Diego Durán, *Historia de las Indias de la Nueva España e Islas de Tierra Firme*, Ed. Porrúa (=Col. Biblioteca Porrúa no. 36), Mexico 1967, T.I, p. 36.

search for the approval of the missionary bishop, head of the Church in Mexico, Friar Juan de Zumárraga, so that he would do the will of the Lady from Heaven, erecting a temple in order to manifest God's love. That Image is still in its place, and some aspects of its composition and preservation are still a challenge for human science; but even if this were not so, what is truly unexplainable, and as a consequence, what is more convincing, is that today a theologian finds such wonders of enculturation and theological synthesis, so superior in that era that not even today would we be able to reproduce them.

This is the argument on which the present archbishop of Mexico, Norberto Rivera, offers us his reflection: "Whoever penetrates into the profoundness already made of this our history, must ask himself, How could we exist if Her maternal love had not reconciled and united the antagonism of our Spanish and Indigenous parents? How could our Indigenous ancestors have accepted Christ if She had not complemented what the missionaries had preached, explaining it to them in a magisterially adapted manner, according to their mentality and their culture?"[4]

It is totally true that "the overwhelming Indigenous piety and their search for cosmic and metaphysic security was what led them to such a bloody cult that horrified the not very delicate Spaniards, convincing them that they were facing the most abominable collective diabolic possession in history, which made them give up any possibility of understanding or dialogue, without even having intended to do so. Notice that this would have been enough to create an unsolvable problem for their Evangelization."[5]

Even though the Indigenous were convinced that divinity was stable, they also knew about the changing fragility of humanity; in this aspect they had some approximation of the Catholic belief which contemplated divine values as irremovable, but at the same time, understanding that for the limited man, it is impossible to know and understand them completely. So they were willing to develop, to improve, their religion, but never to change it, for "in regard to our gods, we will sooner die than to leave their service and worship."[6]

This presented a real and unsolvable problem for Evangelization, since no sixteenth-century Spanish missionary, whose rigid orthodoxy did not turn

---

[4] Norberto Rivera Carrera, *¿No estoy yo aquí que soy tu madre? Palabras de la Santísima Virgen de Guadalupe al Beato Juan Diego en el Tepeyac* [*Am I not here, I who am your mother? Words of the Most Holy Virgin of Guadalupe to the blessed Juan Diego in Tepeyac*]. December 1531, Ed. Arquidiócesis Primada de Mexico, México 1996, p. 4.

[5] Fidel González, Eduardo Chávez, and José Luis Guerrero, *El Encuentro de la Virgen de Guadalupe y Juan Diego*, Ed. Porrúa, Mexico 2002, p. 526.

[6] *Colloquios y Doctrina Christiana*, ff. 3r–41v.

away from even the worst inquisitorial extremes, would have ever accepted proposing Christianity as anything other than radically new, diverse, and opposite, and even more, as incompatible with their "diabolic" culture. That proposition was not acceptable, not only in the Indigenous feelings, but also in their very minds.

The admiration for the good things which were undeniably present in the Indigenous culture turned into distrust, and it was even stated that these things were apparently good, for they believed in the deceptive way that the devil disguised his evilness. For example, the very understanding and tolerant Friar José de Acosta, S.J., instead of admiring that the Mexican religiousness knew how to find convergence with the most profound human soul, when they acquired rituals and concepts analogous to the Christian ones, he commented in chapter 11 of his book "How the devil has tried to resemble God in the way of sacrifices, and religion and sacraments . . . there is hardly anything that Jesus Christ, Our God and Lord, has instituted in His Gospel Law, that the Devil has not in some manner complicated and passed on to the gentiles."[7] With this, he did not think that God had seen the Indigenous surrender in totally good faith, but rather, according to him, Satan had managed to deceive and subjugate his victims, as Friar José de Acosta expressed: "It is truly incredible that the false religious opinion can do so much in these boys and girls of Mexico that with such great harshness they can do in the service of Satan what many of us do not do in the service of God the Highest."[8]

We see this problem today, but no one saw it then, or even imagined it; nevertheless, it existed and it mattered then as it does today. As always, it was and is totally real, for as Pope John Paul II said in 1986, there can be no true Evangelization if the culture is not evangelized. The Holy Father said,

> Culture, a typically human demand, is one of the fundamental elements that constitute the identity of people. It is the complete expression of its vital reality and it covers it totally: values, structures, persons. For this reason the Evangelization of a culture is the most radical, global, and profound form of evangelizing people. . . . Culture implies and demands an "integral vision of man" understood in the totality of his moral and spiritual capacities, in the plenitude of his vocation. This is where the profound connection is, "the organic and constructive relation" which unites human culture with Christian culture; faith offers man's profound vision that culture needs; moreover, only in faith

[7] Friar José de Acosta, *Historia Natural y Moral de las Indias*, Ed. FCE, Mexico 1979, p. 235.
[8] Friar José de Acosta, *Historia Natural y Moral de las Indias*, p. 244.

can one find definite nourishment and inspiration. But the connection between faith and culture acts in diverse directions, also. Faith is not an ethereal and external reality in history, which in an act of pure freedom, offers its light to culture, remaining indifferent to it. On the contrary, faith is lived out in the concrete reality and takes form in it and through it. The synthesis between culture and faith is not only a demand on the part of culture, but also on the part of faith. A faith that does not become culture is a faith that is not fully rooted, not completely weighed, not faithfully lived out. Faith commits man in the totality of his being and of his aspirations. A faith situated outside of what is human, and thus what is cultural, would be a disloyal faith to the plenitude of all that the Word of God manifests and reveals, a decapitated faith, what is more, a faith in the process of dissolving. Faith, even when it transcends culture and by the same act, transcends and reveals the eternal destiny of man, creates and generates culture.[9]

It is true that lack of understanding among men can be overcome by a true testimony of charity, and this will always be a sufficient argument to understand the religion that motivates this way of being and acting. In Mexico's case, however, it was extremely difficult because if it was true that the first missionaries were saints, and they gave their excellent testimony, not so some other Spaniards, whose abuses multiplied, as we have seen in the statements of Juan de Zumárraga, the bishop of Mexico, and in so many other documents where they gave witness to these abuses. For example, Fernando de Alva Ixtlilxóchitl refers to it, saying,

> For sure Cortés and the other conquerors did a great thing by implanting the Gospel law in this new world, because the Spaniards have committed cruelties and things referred to in this history and all the rest that have been written. . . . I have read many authors who refer to tyrannies and cruelties in other nations, and none are by them, and all are the work and terrible slavery of the natives, who say that they would rather be branded slaves than to live in the way in which they now have to live, in this manner. The Spaniards who treat them badly should have some pity on them at least for economic reasons. The slaves' misfortune is such that if one of them trips and falls and hurts himself, he becomes happy because he no longer has to work for the Spaniards.[10]

---

[9] *Juan Pablo II al mundo intelectual y cultural católico*, July 1986, in FUNDICE, *Órgano informativo de la fundación pro difusión cultural del medio milenio en América A.C.*, I (1987), 2, p. 3.
[10] Fernando de Alva Ixtlilxóchitl, *Obras Históricas*, introductory study by Edmundo O'Gorman; preface by Miguel León-Portilla, UNAM, Instituto de Investigaciones Históricas, Mexico 1975, T. I, p. 505.

It is logical that the Indigenous thought "If you call these Christians, living as they do and doing what they do, I want to be Indigenous, as you call me, and I do not want to be a Christian."[11]

On the other hand, the good missionary friars were convinced that their duty as good priests and good Christians was to destroy the deceptions of the devil who had taken over the Indigenous, of their culture and religion. Remember, as just one example among many, what Friar Diego Durán and Friar Bernardino de Sahagún proclaimed openly at the end of their writings:

> We have decided to take up this occupation, Christian reader, of putting in writing the old idolatries and false religion with which the devil was served before the Holy Gospel was preached in these parts, having understood that we who teach the Indigenous the doctrine, will never finish teaching them to know the true God, if first the superstitions, ceremonies, and false cults to the false gods that they adore are not totally extirpated and erased from their memory, just as it is not possible to grow wheat and fruit in the hilly land, full of bushes and weeds, which it produced naturally, if all the roots and stems are not first removed. . . . We will never be able to make them truly know God while we have not pulled out from the roots everything that smells like their ancestors' old religion.[12]

He goes further when he affirms that "if the Spaniards, who committed the great cruelties and atrocities that they did by killing men and women and children, were to kill every man and woman they found, so that those born after that would not know about the old customs, perhaps it would be a more remissible sin and cruelty, if done in the zeal for God."[13] And Friar Bernardino de Sahagún, on his part, affirmed that "The doctor cannot prescribe the medicines correctly to the patient without first knowing the cause of the illness. . . . The sins of idolatries and idolatrous rituals, and idolatrous superstitions and omens, and ablutions and idolatrous ceremonies have not disappeared completely. In order to preach against these things, and to know if they still exist, it is necessary to know how they were performed at the time of their idolatry."[14]

In a few words, we could summarize that Evangelization, according to the Indigenous perspective, would have been absolutely iniquitous and unacceptable because the behavior of the laical Christians, who attacked them

---

[11] Frair Gerónimo de Mendieta, *Historia Eclesiástica*, p. 506.
[12] Friar Diego Durán, *Historia de las Indias*, T. I, pp. 3 and 5.
[13] Friar Diego Durán, *Historia de las Indias*, T. I, p. 79.
[14] Friar Bernardino de Sahagún, *Historia General*, p. 17.

and exploited them, was a genocide, and the behavior of the missionaries, who defended them and protected them, but who tried to deprive them of their culture, was an ethnocide. Nevertheless, divine love can put some chosen persons in limited situations, in which His Grace makes them live that faith though He asks them to renounce and sacrifice precisely that which they love the most, as was the case of Abraham, whose fidelity He tested by asking him to kill his only son, and at the same time, to continue trusting that He would give him millions of descendants. Today we can see that such was the case of Juan Diego, a sensitive soul who in some manner understood that God was offering him the ultimate gift: to be his son. He discovered that there was no opposition between his culture and his faith, and he "went where his ancestors, his grandparents said, into the land of the flowers," and he was able to be an instrument that his Indigenous brothers would understand and accept.

We are all benefactors and debtors of Abraham's faith, and all of Mexico is of Juan Diego's. If we remember that "the synthesis between culture and faith is not only a demand from culture, but also from faith, that a faith situated outside of what is human, and thus, outside of culture, would be a disloyal faith to the plenitude of that which the Word of God manifests and reveals,"[15] we could ask ourselves, how could the "most radical global and profound" Evangelization going to be possible among people whose culture was their religion? How were they going to be evangelized by other people that neither understood nor could understand that culture, and that in no way aspired to understand it, but rather to destroy it, if God, through His Mother, had not counted on the heroic collaboration of this intermediary prophet? How could we exist if Her maternal love had not reconciled and united the antagonism of our Spanish and Indigenous parents? How could our Indigenous ancestors have accepted Christ if She had not complemented what the missionaries had preached to them, explaining and magisterially adapting to their mentality and to their culture, that She was "'the Mother of the Most True God, for Whom we live, and Who is Creator of persons and the Owner of what is close and what is near, of Heaven and Earth,' and that She was also the perfect Virgin, the kind, marvelous Mother of Our Savior, Our Lord Jesus Christ?"[16]

Taking into account the antecedents and the context at the moment in which the encounter between the Virgin of Guadalupe and Juan Diego took place, expressed authoritatively in *Nican Mopohua*, we realize the theological

---

[15] *Juan Pablo II al mundo intelectual*, p. 3.
[16] Fidel González, Eduardo Chávez, and José Luis Guerrero, *El Encuentro*, pp. 531–32.

purity of the Event, which is a prodigy of enculturization of the Gospel for the Indigenous mind, and a strong calling to conversion for the Spanish heart.

As we said, Mary of Guadalupe leaves it unmistakably clear to the Indigenous, not that She is the mother of a god, but the Mother of God, of their God, whom they had always loved and venerated through all their gods. Far from demanding "to scorn and hate, to do away with, to abominate, to spit" all of their religious world, She assumes it and uses it to share Her own world, a theological concept that is not well expressed until the Second Vatican Council, and that, even now, is difficult to equal. The evidence of a historical nature is undeniable, in that She, respecting their faith, makes it easy for one who has the Grace of having faith to accept naturally all the rest. It is Juan Diego, a humble Indigenous, who corroborates something that is totally true and real, as are the consequences of this Event. Juan Diego, a recent convert, becomes an evangelist in this New World, presenting himself before the ecclesial hierarchy, Juan de Zumárraga, with the Mother of God's message, asking him to build a temple to show and give God's own love in. In the medieval mentality and theology at the beginning of the sixteenth century, it was surely unthinkable that a recent convert, of dubious reliance, would be entrusted with one of the most extraordinary models of the unforeseen enculturation of the Gospel.

Juan Diego was a faithful witness of the message of the Lady from Heaven, the Mother of God, who wished to have the honor of being the Mother of all, as she expressed it. That God is love was not an unknown concept for the Indigenous, but they did not imagine that love was so close and unconditional, and least of all that man is God's son and heir, thanks to a life developed in virtues, not centered on the type of death which the gods could determine according to their caprice. For the Indigenous, the presentation of this reality could not be more beautiful, more direct and precise than by way of the love of a Mother, a concept that was extremely venerated by the Indigenous; in a culture where the most respected father was mostly absent, in a polygamist society, with continuous wars in order to keep the gods alive and so that the universal harmony would continue, its masculine population was reduced, so that there were more women than men. Besides, the boys were turned over to the disciplinary teachers at the *Tepochcalli* or *Calmecac* schools at an early age, so the image that was better integrated as an archetype of tenderness and protection, and as a consequence, authority and government, was the mother. What is more, the male authorities were continuously compared to a mother, and the language that they themselves used was distinctly maternal. A true sovereign was a "father and a mother" to his subjects, and it could not be otherwise. Friar Diego Durán summarizes the image of a ruler: "a luminary that like a sun ray lights us, and a mirror where we all see ourselves, a mother who takes us on her lap, and a father who carries us on his shoulders, a lord who rules and governs the Mexican dominion, and is help and refuge to the poor, the orphans, and the widows, and has compassion on those who search night and day through hills and clefts for food."[17]

Among the Indigenous, the image and concepts of a good mother were that "the virtuous mother is vigilant, light, watchful, solicitous, careful; she raises her children, takes care of them continuously, she is vigilant that they do not need anything, gives gifts, is like a slave to all those in her house, worries about the needs of each one, does not neglect anything that is necessary in her house."[18] But at the same time she must be rigorous and demanding so that her child would be mature in life. Juan Diego saw all this precisely in Holy Mary of Guadalupe, his "Little Girl," his "Lassie"; Most Holy Mary had manifested Herself to him as wishing to put love in practice. On one hand, declaring that She wanted to solve human problems "because I am truly your compassionate Mother, yours, and of all who are one in this land, and the rest of their generations, My beloved, those who cry out for Me, those who look for Me, those who trust in Me, because I will hear their cry, their sadness, in order to remedy, to heal all of their different afflictions, their miseries, and their pains,"[19] and in a complementary manner, on the other hand, She had demanded, "And I beg you very much, my smallest son, and I rigorously order, that you go again tomorrow to see the Bishop."[20]

To believe is always a totally free privilege. We cannot ask for faith from anyone who has not received it as a gift from the Highest. But we can and should discuss reasons, and it is not reasonable to suppose that, in the sixteenth century, even the most brilliant human understanding could have integrated the "Indigenous beliefs" with the "European beliefs." Because of that, the Guadalupan Event expressed in the *Nican Mopohua* is not a theatrical narration, "full of anachronisms, lies, contradictions, and mythological, and idolatrous errors; in one word, that it is a comedy, novel or self-sacrament, in the fashion of that time,"[21] nor just a "Catechesis or a theatrical representation in four acts, with an introduction on the hill with the little birds singing, with the drops of water resembling diamonds."[22] It is

---

[17] Friar Diego Durán, *Historia de las Indias*, T. I, p. 397.
[18] Friar Bernardino de Sahagún, *Historia General*, p. 545.
[19] Antonio Valeriano, *Nican Mopohua*, p. 33.
[20] Antonio Valeriano, *Nican Mopohua*, p. 39.
[21] Friar Servando Teresa de Mier, "Cartas a Juan Bautista Muñoz," 1797, in Ernesto de la Torre Villar and Ramiro Navarro de Anda, *Testimonios Históricos Guadalupanos*, p. 768.
[22] Guillermo Schulenburg Prado, "El Milagro de Guadalupe." Interview with Guillermo Schulenburg Prado, in *Ixtus, Espiritu y Cultura* 3 (1995) 15, p. 34.

a narration of a real fact that encompasses these cultures, so distinct in themselves, giving them the principles of a theology that not until the Second Vatican Council were even evident. This is proven by analyzing, as we have seen, several historical sources that agree among themselves and show us the true history of the Event.

We have already seen that Mendieta recognized the faith in one single God in all of the Indies, but he blamed the Indigenous for having corrupted it. We could think that that misunderstanding was only something particular of that time, but four centuries later, it is still believed. This is stated by the Jesuit historian Mariano Cuevas, who affirmed in the twentieth century that the

> Character, intellectual dispositions, value, laws, richness, and all that the inhabitants of Anáhuac had were profoundly corrupted, because everything was impregnated with their false religion, an immense and continuous sin which one can hardly excuse in any of the adults that professed it, that went against all spiritual and corporal tendencies of each one of them. Along with other authors, Mendieta says, and we believe, that they knew about the true God and in order to refer to Him they had a proper word. This was all the worse for them, because knowing Him they did not adore Him, but fell into the most humiliating and exaggerated idolatry. . . . Their theogonies resembled bloody, terrifying, and dirty nightmares. The image of their idolizing and degraded people is instinctively rejected as fantasy, as one blushes to think that our good Indigenous would have had such ancestors.[23]

But such concepts were what was habitually known and believed about the Indigenous world in the religious and cultural level of Mexico of that time.[24]

We can, therefore, prove how much we can still learn about the marvelous and loving pedagogy from the Guadalupan Event, how much the Church and the world can still benefit from the obedient and humble Juan Diego, whom we can and should recognize as a true evangelist of Guadalupe, who with his life of holiness marked history.

---

[23] Mariano Cuevas, *Historia de la Iglesia en México*, Ed. Patria, Mexico 1947, T. I, pp. 68–69.

[24] Another clear example is the ritual for the baptism of adults in the Roman ritual, which was not modified until a very short time ago. Not only did it treat the convert like an authentic diabolic possessed person, performing exorcisms on him, but also, as they signaled him on the forehead and the heart, they would threaten him on purpose: "Be horrified of idols, rebuke their images . . . Be horrified of the treacherous Jew, rebuke Hebraic superstition! . . . Be horrified of the treacherous Moslem, rebuke the wicked sect of infidelity! . . . Be horrified of the heresy evilness, rebuke the wicked sects of the evil!" *Ordo Baptismi adultorum, in Rituale Romanum. Paulo V Pontificis Maximi iussu editum et a Benedicto XIV auctum et castgatum cui novissima accedit Benedictionum et Instructionum Appendiz*, Ed. Desclée, Rome 1900, pp. 34–35.

Because Juan Diego was real, and truly submitted himself as a docile in-strument of the love of God through His Mother, the Indigenous world con-verted in an instant, they ran in multitudes to ask for baptism, as we saw writ-ten in the testimonies of the missionaries themselves, and that is why we, the Mexican people, were born there, bearing in our blood the glory of both races. This was a great miracle, not magic: She dissipated all the doubts of the Indigenous and reconciled them with the Spaniards, but did not convert either one of the two, or us, their descendants, into saints or scholars in the new law, because we are to achieve that little by little, with effort and by giv-ing ourselves. Nor does it authorize us to brag about being favorites of God; instead, to the contrary, it binds us to share this treasure with all men, our brothers, since "he who receives much, much is asked of" (Lk 12:48).

CHAPTER TEN

A Commitment to the Whole World

Even though it is almost five centuries after the Guadalupan Event, today it is revealed as something wonderful, perfectly appropriate for the needs of an era which wishes to obtain peace, so all men can grow in harmony, sharing the riches of our ancestral cultures. And this, that today seems impossible, has already taken place in the country where we were born. In order to share this richness, first we must know it, and it is so original that this requires effort, as Archbishop Norberto Rivera affirms: "This knowledge, some of it so new that it is still unknown, even among Mexican priests, is not an esoteric exclusiveness of a few initiated persons; it is at the reach of everyone who will make the effort of studying it. . . . Now, with this motive, several books have been published, that are in the reach of everyone and that I do not hesitate to recommend as serious and well-written, that narrate and make known what was done, how it was done, and all the valuable and unexpected knowledge that was discovered."[1]

The Guadalupan Event, in its great and profound dimension, invites us to know it more and better, and in the same manner, to spread it, since it conferred the undeserved distinction to make us, through His Most Holy Mother, "Her ambassadors, in whom She absolutely deposited Her trust," in order to give the world our testimony of God's love.

---

[1] Norberto Rivera Cabrera, *¿No estoy yo aquí que soy tu madre? Palabras*, p. 5.

It is a fact that was lived by the people, from the faith of the simple and humble. It was the simple people who spread the great Guadalupan Event everywhere, through their art, codexes, writings, testimonies, legacies, offerings, alms, pilgrimages, and especially testimonies of conversions. This enriched the oral tradition. The narration of the Guadalupan Event was transmitted by the characteristic memory of the Indigenous, a tradition that was passed on from parents to children, from grandparents to grandchildren.

One of these singular narrations, that has been transmitted from generation to generation, that gathers the most essential and beautiful incidents of the Event of Guadalupe and in which Juan Diego is called "one of ours," is still heard in Zozocolco, Veracruz, a little town lost in the mountains between Papantla and Poza Rica, six hours into the mountains. Father Ismael Olmedo Casas, on December 12, 1995, had the idea of asking the faithful Indigenous what was the reason for the celebration, before preaching about it himself:

Good morning, Great Chiefs! We want you to tell us about the Virgin of Guadalupe. Today is the feast of the Virgin of Guadalupe.

Mister priest, chief servant of the holy things, good morning!

I will tell you what we have heard from the elders, our grandparents. Many Easters [feasts] of Saint Michael ago, almost 1,000 harvests ago [two a year], almost 500 flights of the Flying Pole [one flight each year during a feast], it happened there, in the center, from where they sent us. We were servants of the Emperor Great Lord, who dressed in fine clothes and beautiful feathers, and offered the Good God of the people what the land produced, and the blood of their children so that the order of life would continue. Men with hair of sun arrived, and we already knew about their arrival. But we did not expect those bad treatments from them, because we thought them to be sent by the angels. And they only brought filth, disease, destruction, death, and lies. They talked to us about a God that they loved, but they, with their lives, hated.

The people were already tired, when, in a dark morning of the strong mid-harvest of coffee [mid-December], God's Holy Spirit, gave one of ours a message from Heaven. As the Big Book [the *Popol Vuh*] of our brothers, the Mayans, said, man had misbehaved, and the Great God would send someone to remake the man of corn.

The Big Book of the Spaniards [the Bible] also says that after man destroyed the harmony that existed in the Universe, manifested in the perfect flight of the Flyer, he deserved life without happiness, but God promised that someone born from our race, a woman, would give us back a smile to our faces, She would take away the *mecapal* with our load on the worst slope, and we would have feasts for whole days, without end [eternal life].

A sign from Heaven appeared on the hill of Anáhuac, that is what the chiefs would say, where the Flyer's apple lands: a woman of great importance, more so than the Emperors themselves, that, even though She is a woman Her power is such that She stands in front of the Sun, our giver of life, and She steps on the Moon, which is our guide in the struggle for Light, and She dresses with the Stars, which are the ones that rule our existence and tell us when we must sow, plow, and harvest.

This woman is important, because She stands in front of the Sun, steps on the Moon, and dresses with the Stars, but Her face says that there is someone greater than She, because She is looking down, in a gesture of respect.

Our elders would offer hearts to God so that there would be harmony in life. This woman says that without taking them out [our hearts], place them in Her hands, in order to present them to the true God.

The three volcanoes emerge from Her hands, and on Her chest, those that border Anáhuac and the one that saw the arrival of our conquerors, which for Her must be considered as a new race, that is why Her face is not like theirs nor like ours, but like both. On Her tunic all of the valley of Mexico is painted and centers the attention on that Lady's womb, that, with the joy of a feast, dances because She will give us Her Son, so that with the harmony of the angel that holds Heaven and Earth [mantle and tunic] a new life will be born. This is what we have received from our elders, our grandparents, that our lives will not end, but they have a new significance, and as the Big Book of the Spaniards says [the Bible], a sign appeared in the sky, a woman dressed with the Sun, with the Moon at Her feet and a crown of Stars, and is about to give birth.

That is what we celebrate today, mister priest: the arrival of this sign of unity, of harmony, of new life.[2]

The Holy Father, John Paul II, understood and conveyed also with great force the importance of the message of Guadalupe communicated by Saint Juan Diego and confirmed the perfect Evangelization that has been given to us by Our Mother, Mary of Guadalupe. The pope declared that "America, which historically has been a melting pot for people, has recognized 'in the *mestizo* countenance of the Virgin of Tepeyac' . . . in Holy Mary of Guadalupe, . . . a great example of Evangelization, perfectly enculturated. For

---

[2] The complete text and its judicial ratification are found in the Sacred Congregation for the Causes of the Saints, Archives for the Cause of the Canonization of Juan Diego.

that reason, not only in the center and in the south, but also in the north of the continent, the Virgin of Guadalupe is venerated as the Queen of all America."[3] The Holy Father also reaffirmed the force and the tenderness in God's message through the Star of Evangelization, Mary of Guadalupe, of Her faithful, humble, and true messenger, Juan Diego. The Holy Father said that "The Apparitions of Mary to the Indigenous Juan Diego on the hill of Tepeyac, in the year of 1531, had a decisive repercussion for Evangelization. This influence goes beyond the boundaries of Mexico, reaching out to all the Continent."[4]

Juan Diego continues spreading to all the world the great Guadalupan Event, a great message of peace, unity, and love, which continues being passed on by each one of us, turning our poor history of humanity, full of tragedies, treasons, divisions, hatreds, and wars, into a wonderful history of salvation, full of hope, because at the center of the Sacred Image, at the center of the Guadalupan Event, at the center of the very heart of the Most Holy Virgin Mary of Guadalupe, Jesus Christ, Our Savior, is found. It is only She, the Mother of God, our Mother, who presents Her Son Jesus Christ, to us; She brings Him to us, She turns Him over to us, among flowers and singing, wrapped in the sun, dressed with stars, stepping on the moon, among fog and clouds, as the great Treasure who comes from the invisible and that becomes visible in Her. It is She who chose a humble Indigenous, Juan Diego, who had embraced faith only a short time before, She who invites us to embrace our God and Lord.

Juan Diego fulfills his role completely as intercessor and as a model of holiness, since each one of us that contemplates the Image and the message of Our Lady of Guadalupe is taken to the Love of God, and for that reason we are disposed, like other "Juan Diegos," to treat the Mother of God as our Mother, our Little Girl from Heaven.

---

[3] John Paul II, *Ecclesia in America*, no. 11, p. 20. The Pope literally quotes *The IV General Conference of the Latin American Episcopacy*, Santo Domingo, October 12, 1992, p. 24. Quoted also in *AAS* 85 (1993) p. 826. The Holy Father also mentions the declaration made by the bishops of the United States of North America in National Conference of Catholic Bishops, *Behold Your Mother Woman of Faith*, Washington 1973, p. 37.

[4] John Paul II, *Ecclesia in America*, no. 11, p. 20.

CHAPTER ELEVEN

~

Pope John Paul II Canonizes Saint Juan Diego

On December 18, 2001, it was announced that the Proclamation for the Decree on the Miracle performed by God through Juan Diego's intercession would take place. This meant the approval of the whole canonization process for this humble Indigenous, celebrated for many years until now.

Thus, on December 20, 2001, the Decree for the Miracle was proclaimed before the Holy Father John Paul II. This Great Event took place in the Clementine Hall within Vatican City, where many cardinals and bishops were gathered. Cardinal Norberto Rivera was present, and also Cardinal Javier Lozano Barragán, Mgr. Cipriano Calderón, as well as P. Fidel González, who was part of Saint Juan Diego's Historical Commission, and myself. I had been named Postulator for Saint Juan Diego's Canonization Cause since May 17 of that year.

Pope John Paul II had been invited to return to Mexico in order to canonize Juan Diego—Cardinal Norberto Rivera as well as several Mexican bishops had extended that invitation. As Postulator, I had told the Holy Father that it would be an enormous Grace, an incommensurable gift, for our people, who in the great majority were unable to come to Rome, if he could canonize Juan Diego on Mexican land, considering that he was the first Indigenous saint from the American continent. By the beginning of January 2002, it was heard that it was probable that the Holy Father would canonize Juan Diego in Mexico.

On January 23, 2002, I had an interview in Saint Peter's Square in Rome with Valentina Alazraki and for the first time I showed the document of the Decree of the Miracle, signed by Cardinal Saraiva and the Secretary of the Congregation, Mgr. Novak. This was an important moment to ask for unity, harmony, and love in our continent, to go forward with justice, and to appeal to our grandeur as a nation, always being able to be better.

In Rome, in the middle of February, I was present for the Consistorium. On Tuesday, February 26, 2002, in the presence of 45 cardinals and 55 bishops, various priests, and religious men and women, the Consistorium took place in the Vatican, again in the Clementine Hall, where the Decree of the Miracle had been proclaimed, and now Pope John Paul II declared that he would canonize the blessed Juan Diego in Mexico City on July 30 of that same year. However, the date had to be changed to July 31 for practical reasons.

With an enormous effort on his part because of his delicate health, John Paul II wished to go as far as Tepeyac, in the north of Mexico City, precisely because it was where the Virgin of Guadalupe and Juan Diego had had that marvelous encounter.

When it was confirmed that the canonization was going to be in Tepeyac, Mexico, the following months involved much work and organization and the different commissions worked with great enthusiasm. Cardinal Norberto Rivera named me the executive secretary for the fifth visit of His Holiness John Paul II, a great honor and, at the same time, a great responsibility. Work was carried out with a spirit of unity and collaboration that our nation demonstrates in these great events. Once again our people showed their solidarity in their participation at all levels, from the most simple people to great entrepreneurs, all our nation was one single voice and one single will around the pope, Our Lady of Guadalupe, and Juan Diego.

After an exhausting trip, the pope arrived to Canada for his encounter with the young people. This was the first part of his trip. After this, he went to Guatemala for the canonization of Saint Paul of Betancour. Then he continued on for the last part of the trip to Mexico City for the canonization of Saint Juan Diego.

In the presidential hangar he was received by the president of Mexico, Vicente Fox, by Cardinal Norberto Rivera, archbishop of Mexico, and by all the Mexican Episcopacy, as well as by thousands of people who waved white and yellow banners as a sign of welcome. An orchestra with children singing beautiful melodies, more children and their families with gifts for the Holy Father, welcoming addresses and gratitude followed, with signs of affection and respect for one who no longer was a visitor to Mexico, but a part of a nation which shouted, "John Paul II, you are now a Mexican!"

Among those words which the Holy Father said to the Mexican people who were gathered in that place, as well as so very many who were seeing him on television and hearing him on the radio, was an expression of *Informaciones Jurídicas de 1666*, an expression used by our forefathers when they blessed their loved ones and that now are the same words taken by the Holy Father John Paul II to bless us: "May God make you holy like Juan Diego." This was one of the most important and moving moments. These words carried a mission of sanctification, of a responsibility to live according to the example of holiness of Saint Juan Diego, words which now have a great and strong meaning, words from our ancestors which now come alive, pronounced by the representative and Vicar of Christ among us, giving those words an enormous spiritual force, that holiness to which we are all called.

The great apostle Saint Paul says,

> Praised be the God and Father of our Lord Jesus Christ, who, through Him, has blessed us from Heaven with all the gifts of the Spirit. God chose us in Christ before the world began to be holy and blameless, to be full of love; destined us from all eternity to be His adopted children, through Jesus Christ—according to his will and plan—to be a hymn to His glorious mercy, which He shed on us through His beloved Son, Who, with His blood, has obtained for us freedom, the forgiveness of our sins, to show us His infinite mercy. And He shed it on us with great wisdom and intelligence to reveal to us His secret plan, according to the will and plan which He had in order to complete history to its plenitude: to make unity through Christ in the universe, in Heaven and Earth. (Eph 1:3–10)

We literally see this take place in our country, with the "Star of Evangelization," as the Holy Father calls the Virgin of Guadalupe, and with Juan Diego, Her humble messenger who gave this good news in the first place to the Church, at the time under the orders of Bishop Friar Juan de Zumárraga. It was a message of holiness under the loving affection and maternal direction of God: "Do everything He tells you."

After a well-deserved rest, on the morning of July 31, everything was ready so that the pope would go through the streets from the Apostolic Nunciature to the Basilica of Our Lady of Guadalupe on Tepeyac, in his "popemobile" among the cheers of millions of people who had waited for him for days, in order to canonize Juan Diego. His arrival in the atrium of the basilica thrilled all who had been waiting for him since daybreak; tears of emotion rolled down dark faces, the cheers, the chants, the salutations mixed with the rattles, drums, and trumpets, all in order to make the joy that the people felt known to their pope as he arrived again to his home.

The Holy Father dressed in the sacristy that was specially constructed for him, and the ceremony initiated with music composed precisely for this great festivity.

Seeing and hearing the Holy Father we were able to feel and relive what the old Indigenous priest said to the first Franciscan missionaries: "Among clouds, in the fog, within the immense waters, you have come. You who are His eyes, you who are His ears, you who are His lips, the owner of what is far and near. Here we, in some way, see in a human manner, here we talk as to a human, to the Giver of Life, Who is night and wind, you are His image, His representative. For this reason we gather, we take His breath, His word, from the Lord of far and near, Whom you have come to bring, Who owns the world, the Lord of earth, Who sent you for our sake. For this reason we stand in awe, truly you have come to bring His book, His painting, the heavenly word, the divine word."[1]

In the crucial moment of the liturgy, the Cardinal Joseph Saraiva, Prefect of the Congregation for the Causes of the Saints, and myself as Postulator of the Cause of Canonization of Juan Diego, asked from the Holy Father the canonization of Juan Diego, a wonderful man, model of holiness to all the world.

Then Pope John Paul II pronounced the canonization formula, that "divine word":

In honor of the Most Holy Trinity, for the exaltation of the Catholic faith and the growth of Christian life, with the authority of our Lord Jesus Christ, of the Holy Apostles Peter and Paul, and ours, after having analyzing it at length, praying many times for divine help and hearing the opinions of numerous brothers in the Episcopacy, we state and define the blessed JUAN DIEGO CUAUHTLATOATZIN as Saint, and we enroll him in the catalog of the Saints, and we establish that in all the Church that he be honored devoutly among the Saints. In the name of the Father and of the Son and of the Holy Spirit. Amen.

Truly we felt that, as our forefathers would say, with those words we were enriched, that "he left jades and sapphires planted in our hearts, that he opened his trunks and chests where he keeps his treasures."[2]

The first Indigenous from the American continent to become a saint, Saint Juan Diego Cuauhtlatoatzin was a protagonist and faithful porter of that ultimate gift which the divine love granted us, the Guadalupan Event,

---

[1] *Colloquios y Doctrinas Cristiana*, p. 147.
[2] Fray Bernardino de Sahagún, *Historia General*, p. 338.

which became the bridge that united the Indigenous culture with the Spanish culture, two nations confronted one against the other, and as Cardinal Norberto Rivera stated in his Pastoral Letter, dated February 25, 2002, "everything is the religious axis that gives a new cohesion and identity, and which leads to the formation of a crossbreed race. In this context, Juan Diego shines as one of the protagonists of this amazing synthesis: on one hand, he is an Indigenous among his people with a tradition that came from remote ancestors, and whose presence in time was synonymous of truth; on the other hand, he enters into contact with the world of the "new" which thus had no guarantee of veracity. Nevertheless, he learned to speak with the source of Spanish symbols: the Virgin Mary and the blessed fruit of Her womb, Jesus. He assimilated it in an exceptional manner, in a religious experience that lets us see the power of Grace within this chosen one. The history of the Apparitions is the life testimony of Mary's efficiency as teacher of a laical Indigenous evangelizer"[3] who, placing himself in Her maternal hands, knew how to be "a link between the old Mexican non-Christian world, and the missionary proposition that came through the mediation of Spain. He is the one chosen by God for the encounter of Jesus Christ with the Indigenous culture, through Mary's intervention."[4]

Truly it was a historic moment when the Holy Father recognized and confirmed that Saint Juan Diego is a model of holiness who handed over the gift of the message of Holy Mary of Guadalupe, a message of love, of unity, of harmony, and of peace, a message which helps us understand that we have the first Indigenous on the continent to be recognized as a saint to intercede for us, and especially to live that message.

---

[3] Norberto Rivera Carrera, *Carta Pastoral por la Canonización del Beato Juan Diego Cuauhtlatoazin, Laico*, Archdioces of México, February 25, 2002, *III Juan Diego Evangelizador*, no. 58–59, p. 28.

[4] Norberto Rivera Carrera, *Carta Pastoral . . . Juan Diego y el desafío para la Misión de los Laicos hoy día*, no. 140, p. 51.

~

Historical Sources and Bibliography

"A discourse written by one Miles Philips, Englishman, put on shore in the West Indies by Mr. John Hawkins, 1568," in Richard Hakluyt, *Voyages and Discoveries: The Principal Navigations, Voyages, Traffiques and Discoveries of the English Nation*, Ed. Penguin Group, London 1985.

Aa. Vv., *Libro Anual 1981–1982*. Ed. Instituto Superior de Estudios Eclesiásticos, Mexico 1984.

Acosta, Joseph de, *Historia natural y moral de las Indias*, Ed. FCE, Mexico 1979.

Actas y Decretos del Concilio Plenario de la América Latina celebrado en Roma, Tipografía Vaticana, Rome 1906.

Álbum Commemorativo del 450 aniversario de las apariciones de Nuestra Señora de Guadalupe, Ed. Buena Nueva, Mexico 1981.

Álbum de la Coronación de la Sma. Virgen de Guadalupe, Ed. "El Tiempo," Mexico 1895, 2 vols.

Alcalá Alvarado, Alfonso, "El Milagro del Tepeyac. Objeciones y respuestas desde la historia," in *Libro Anual 1981–1982*, Ed. Instituto Superior de Estudios Eclesiásticos, Mexico 1984.

Alegre, Francisco Javier, *Historia de la Provincia de la Compañía de Jesús en Nueva España*, edited by Ernest J. Burrus, S.J., and Félix Zubillaga, S.J., Ed. Institutum Historicum, Rome 1959, 4 vols.

Altamirano, Ignacio Manuel, *La Fiesta de Guadalupe*, Mexico 1884.

Alva Ixtlilxóchitl, Fernando de, "Nican Motecpana," in Ernesto de la Torre Villar and Ramiro Navarro de Anda, *Testimonios Históricos Guadalupanos*, Ed. FCE, Mexico 1982.

Alva Ixtlilxóchitl, Fernando de, *Obras Históricas*, UNAM, Instituto de Investigaciones Históricas, Mexico 1975, 2 vols.

Alvear Acevedo, Carlos, *La Iglesia en la historia de México*, Ed. Jus, Mexico 1975.

Añalejo de Bartolache or Manuscrito de la Universidad, BNAH, Archives Historic, Archives of Sucs. Gómez de Orozco, Mexico.

Anales de Puebla y Tlaxcala or *Anales de los Sabios Tlaxcaltecas* or *Anales de Catedral*, AHMNA, AAMC, no. 18, 1.

Anticoli, Esteban, *Historia de la aparición de la Santísima Virgen María de Guadalupe en México desde el año MDCCCI al de MDCCCXCV*, Ed. La Europea, Mexico 1897, 2 vols.

Aste Tonsmann, José, *Los ojos de la Virgen de Guadalupe*, Ed. Diana, Mexico 1981.

Bartolache y Díaz de Posadas, José Ignacio, "Manifiesto satisfactorio u Opúsculo Guadalupano," 1790, in Ernesto de la Torre Villar and Ramiro Navarro de Anda, *Testimonios Históricos Guadalupanos*, Ed. FCE, Mexico 1982, pp. 597–651.

Baudot, Georges, *La pugna franciscana por México*, Eds. Alianza Editorial Mexicana y Consejo Nacional para la Cultura y las Artes (=Col. Los Noventa no. 36), Mexico 1990.

Baudot, Georges, and Tzvetan Todorov, *Relatos aztecas de la conquista*, Eds. Grijalvo and Consejo Nacional para la Cultura y las Artes (= Col. Los Noventa no. 7), Mexico 1990.

Becerra Tanco, Luis, *Origen Milagroso del Santuario de Nuestra Señora de Guadalupe*. Mexico 1666. Ed. Imprenta y Litografía Española, Mexico 1883.

Behrens, Helen, *The Virgin and the Serpent-God*, Ed. Progreso, Mexico 1966.

Benedict XV, "Epistolae, Expostulationem ab Episcopis Mexicanis editam in legem illic latam de republica novanda adprobat B. P. et nuntiat se die festo B. M. V. Guadalupensis litaturum pro mexicano populo," in *AAS*, IX (1917), pp. 376–77.

Betancourt, Luis Ángel, "Poema," in Francisco de la Maza, *El Guadalupanismo Mexicano*, Eds. FCE and SEP (= Col. Lecturas Mexicanas no. 37), Mexico 1984.

Boturini Benaduci, Lorenzo, "Cartas para la Coronación de la Virgen de Guadalupe," in Ernesto de la Torre Villar and Ramiro Navarro de Anda, *Testimonios Históricos Guadalupanos*, Ed. FCE, Mexico 1982, pp. 400–5.

———, "Catálogo de obras guadalupanas," in Ernesto de la Torre Villar and Ramiro Navarro de Anda, *Testimonios Históricos Guadalupanos*, Ed. FCE, Mexico 1982, pp. 405–12.

———, Lorenzo, *Idea de una nueva historia general de la América Septentrional*, Ed. Porrúa (= Col. "Sepan cuantos" no. 278), Mexico 1986.

Bravo Ugarte, José, *Cuestiones históricas guadalupanas*, Ed. Jus, Mexico 1966.

Bullarium . . . Discalceatorum, de Franciscus Matritensis, T. I, p. 134; in the Ambrosiana Library of Milan: *Quaedan expectantia ad Baptismum indorum occidentalium*, November 30, 1536. R. 104. Sub.

Burrus, Ernest J., *A Major Guadalupan Question Resolved: Did General Scott Seize the Valeriano Account of the Guadalupan Apparitions?*, Ed. Cara Studies on Popular Devotion, Washington, D.C., 1979.

———, *The Oldest Copy of the* Nican Mopohua, Ed. Cara Studies on Popular Devotion, Washington, D.C., 1981.

Bustamante, Carlos María de, "Elogios y defensa guadalupanos," 1831–1843, in Ernesto de la Torre Villar and Ramiro Navarro de Anda, *Testimonios Históricos Guadalupanos*, Ed. FCE, Mexico 1982, pp. 1007–91.

Cabrera, Miguel, *Maravilla Americana y conjunto de raras maravillas observadas con la dirección de las reglas del Arte de la pintura en la Prodigiosa Imagen de Nuestra Señora de Guadalupe de México*, Imp. del Real y más antiguo Colegio de San Ildefonso, Mexico 1756.

Cabrera y Quintero, Cayetano de, *Escudo de Armas de México*, Imp. por Vda. de D. Joseph Bernardo de Hogal, Mexico 1746.

Calderón, Luis, *Virtudes y méritos de Juan Diego*, Ed. Tradición, Mexico 1989.

Carrillo y Gariel, Abelardo, *El pintor Miguel Cabrera*, INAH, Mexico 1966.

Carta de fray Bernardino de Sahagún al Papa Pío V, in ASV, AA. Arm. I–XVIII, 33 ff.

Carta de fray Jacobo de Testera, Huejotzingo, May 6, 1533, in *Cartas de Indias*, Madrid, 1877.

Carta de fray Juan de Zumárraga al rey de España, Mexico, August, 27, 1529, Archivo de Simancas, Bibl. Miss., III, 339, letter 13. Copy in Col. Muñoz, T. 78.

Carta de la S. Congregación para la Causa de los Santos al Cardenal Ernesto Corripio Ahumada, Mexico 1982, Prot. N. 1408–2/1982, pp. XVI–XXIV; XIX.

Carta del arzobispo de México, Pedro Moya de Contreras, al Papa Gregorio XIII, ASV, AA-Arm. I. XVIII, s.f.

"Carta del obispo de Tlaxcala Julián Garcés al Papa Paulo III," in Ramón Xirau, *Idea y querella de la Nueva España*, Alianza Editorial, Madrid 1973.

"Carta del Virrey de la Nueva España, don Martín Enríquez, al rey don Felipe II, dándole cuenta del estado de varios asuntos, de la solución que había dado a otros e informando sobre algunos puntos que se le consultaban," Mexico, September 23, 1575, in *Cartas de Indias*, Ed. Secretaría de Hacienda y Crédito Público, Mexico 1980.

Cartas de Indias, edition facsimile by Secretaría de Hacienda y Crédito Público, Ed. Miguel Ángel Porrúa, Mexico 1980.

"Catálogo del Museo Histórico Indiano del Caballero Lorenzo Boturini Benaduci, señor de la Torre y Hono," study by Miguel León-Portilla, in Lorenzo Boturini Benaduci, *Idea de una nueva historia general de la América Septentrional*, Ed. Porrúa (= Col. "Sepan cuantos" no. 278), Mexico 1986.

"Censo a favor de la Obra Pía de Nuestra Señora de Guadalupe," 1597, f. 472 ss., in *Colección Antigua del Museo Nacional*, microfilms of the BNAH, R. 37, ff. 473r–483r.

Centro de Estudios Guadalupanos, *Cuarto Encuentro Nacional Guadalupano. 4, 5 y 6 de Diciembre de 1979*, Mexico 1980.

———, *Juan Diego, el vidente del Tepeyac (1474–1548)*, Mexico 1979.

———, *Primer Encuentro Nacional Guadalupano. 7 y 8 de Septiembre de 1976*, Mexico 1978.

———, *Segundo Encuentro Nacional Guadalupano. 2 y 3 de Diciembre de 1977*, Mexico 1979.

———, *Tercer Encuentro Nacional Guadalupano. 5, 6 y 7 de Diciembre de 1978*, Mexico 1979.

Cervantes de Salazar Francisco, *México en 1554 y Túmulo Imperial*, Ed. Porrúa (= Col. "Sepan cuantos" no. 25), Mexico 1982.

Clavijero, Francisco Javier, *Historia Antigua de México*, Ed. Porrúa (= Col. "Sepan cuantos" no. 29), Mexico 1976.

———, "Breve noticia sobre la prodigiosa y renombrada Imagen de Nuestra Señora de Guadalupe," in Ernesto de la Torre Villar and Ramiro Navarro de Anda, *Testimonios Históricos Guadalupanos*, Ed. FCE, Mexico 1982, pp. 578–96.

Codex Vaticanus, in BAV, Fondo Vaticano, Vat. Lat. 3738, f. 94r.

"Códice Escalada" o "Códice 1548," in *Enciclopedia Guadalupana*, directed by Xavier Escalada, S.J., Ed. Enciclopedia Guadalupana, Mexico 1997, T. V.

Códice Franciscano. Siglo XVI, study by Joaquín García Icazbalceta, Ed. Salvador Chávez-Hayhoe, Mexico 1941.

Códice Mendieta, Documentos Franciscanos. Siglos XVI y XVII, Ed. Edmundo Aviña Levy, Guadalajara, Jalisco, 1971, 2 vols.

Colección de Obras y Opúsculos…, Impr. Lorenzo de S. Martín, Madrid 1785.

Colloquios y Doctrina Cristiana conque los doze frayles de san francisco enbiados por el papa Adriano sesto y por el Emperador Carlo qujnto côvertierô a los indios de la Nueva España ê lêgua Mexicana y Española, published by Miguel León-Portilla, UNAM, Instituto de Investigaciones Sociales, Mexico 1986.

fia del Episcopado Latinoamericano (Celam), *Documentos de Puebla*, nn. 445–46.

Congregatio pro Causis Sanctorum. Officium Historicum. *Canonizationis Servi Dei Joannis Didaci Cuauhtlatoatzin. Viri Laici (1474–1548), Positio, Super fama sanctitatis, virtutibus et cultu ab immemoriabili praestito ex officio concinata, Mexicana 184*, Rome 1989.

———. Officium Historicum, *Canonizationis Servi Dei Ioannis Didaci Cuauhtlatoatzin. Viri Laici (1474–1548), Relatio et Vota, Sobre la Reunión de Consultores Históricos del 30 de enero de 1990, Mexicana 185*, Rome 1990.

Congregación para las Causas de los Santos, *Juan Diego Cuauhtlatoatzin, Laico (1474–1548). Relación y Votos*, traducción española ordenada por el Emmo. Sr. Ernesto Cardenal Corripio, Arzobispo Primado de México, como edición especial privada, Ed. *Criterio. Órgano informativo de la arquidiócesis de México y Metropolitana Circundante*, Mexico 1990.

Cortés, Hernán, *Cartas de Relación*, Ed. Porrúa (= Col. "Sepan cuantos" no. 7), Mexico 1985.

Cuadriello, Jaime Genaro, *Maravilla Americana. Variantes de la Iconografía Guadalupana, siglos XVII–XIX*, Ed. Patrimonio Cultural de Occidente, Guadalajara 1989.

Cuevas, José de Jesús, *La Santísima Virgen de Guadalupe*, Ed. Círculo Católico, Mexico 1887.

Cuevas, Mariano, *Álbum Histórico Guadalupano del IV Centenario*, Ed. Tip. Salesiana, Mexico 1930.

———, *Historia de la Iglesia en México*, Ed. Revista Católica, El Paso, Texas, 1928, 5 vols.

———, *Historia de la nación mexicana*, Ed. Porrúa, Mexico 1967.

———, *Notable Documento Guadalupano*, Ed. Comité General de la ACJM (=Col. Estudios Históricos, Serie C, no. 1), Mexico 1919.

Chauvet, Fidel, *Las apariciones guadalupanas del Tepeyac*, Ed. Tradición, Mexico 1978.

———, *Las apariciones de la Virgen de Guadalupe en México*, Ed. Academia Mariana, Rome 1962.

———, *Fray Juan de Zumárraga O.F.M.*, Imp. Beatriz de Silva, Mexico 1948.

———, *El Culto Guadalupano del Tepeyac. Sus Orígenes y sus Críticos del siglo XVI*, Ed. Centro de Estudios Fray Bernardino de Sahagún, Mexico 1978.

Chávez Sánchez, Eduardo, *Juan Diego. El mensajero de Santa María de Guadalupe*, Ed. IMDOSOC, Mexico 2001.

———, *Juan Diego. La Santidad de un indio humilde*, Ed. Basílica de Guadalupe, Mexico 2002.

———, *Juan Diego. Una vida de santidad que marcó la historia*, Ed. Porrúa, Mexico 2002.

———, *La Iglesia de México entre dictaduras, revoluciones y persecuciones*, Ed. Porrúa, Mexico 1998.

———, *La Virgen de Guadalupe y Juan Diego en las Informaciones Jurídicas de 1666*, Eds. BG, UPM, IETHG, NR, PCCJD, Imp. Ángel Servín, Mexico 2002.

Chimalpahin Cuauhtlehuanitzin, Francisco de San Antón Muñón, *Relaciones Originales de Chalco Amaquemecan*, paleografía, traducción y glosa de Silvia Rendón, with a study by Ángel María Garibay, Ed. FCE (= Col. Biblioteca Americana no. 40), Mexico 1965.

De la Torre Villar, Ernesto, and Ramiro Navarro de Anda, *Testimonios Históricos Guadalupanos*, Ed. FCE, Mexico 1982.

Decorme, Gerardo, *La devoción a la Virgen de Guadalupe y los Jesuitas*, Ed. Buena Prensa, Mexico 1945.

Díaz del Castillo, Bernal, *Historia Verdadera de la Conquista de la Nueva España*, Ed. Porrúa (= Col. Biblioteca Porrúa no. 6), Mexico 1977.

Diccionario Porrúa. Historia, Biografía y Geografía de México, Ed. Porrúa, Mexico 1995.

Dibble, Charles E., *Sixteenth-Century Mexico: The Work of Sahagun*, Ed. Munro E. Edmonson, Albuquerque, University Press of New Mexico, New Mexico, U.S., 1974.

Disertación Histórica sobre la Aparición de la Portentosa Imagen de María Santísima de Guadalupe de México por el Sr. Don Francisco Xavier Conde y Oquendo, Canónico de la Santa Iglesia Catedral de Puebla, Biblioteca Nacional de Madrid, Ms. 1260.

Durán, Fray Diego, *Historia de las Indias de la Nueva España e Islas de Tierra Firme*, Ed. Porrúa (= Col. Biblioteca Porrúa nos. 36 y 37), Mexico 1967, 2 vols.

Elizondo, Virgilio, *Guadalupe. Mother of the New Creation*, Ed. Orbis Books, Maryknoll, New York, 2002.

Episcopado Mexicano, *El Acontecimiento Guadalupano hoy En el XXV Aniversario de la Dedicación de la actual Basílica de Guadalupe y el traslado de la Sagrada Imagen*, Mexico, D. F., October 12, 2001.

Epistolario de la Nueva España, by Francisco del Paso y Troncoso, Ed. Antigua Librería de Robredo, Mexico 1939–1942, 16 vols.

Escalada, Xavier, S.J., *Enciclopedia Guadalupana*, Ed. Enciclopedia Guadalupana, Mexico 1997, T. V.

Fernández del Castillo, Francisco, Rafael García Granados, Luis MacGregor, and Lauro E. Rosell, *México y la Guadalupana. Cuatro siglos de Culto a la Patrona de América*, Mexico 1931.

Florencia, Francisco de, *Estrella del Norte de México*, Ed. Antonio Velázquez, Barcelona 1741.

——, *Las Novenas del Santuario de Nuestra Señora de Guadalupe, que se apareció en la Manta de Juan Diego* (1785), edition by Archicofradía Universal de Santa María de Guadalupe, Mexico 1999.

Gacetas de México, introduction by Francisco González de Cossio, Ed. SEP, Mexico 1950.

Galván Rivera, Mariano, *Concilio III Provincial Mexicano celebrado en México el año de 1585*, Ed. Eugenio Maillefert, Mexico 1859.

García Gutiérrez, Jesús, *Apuntamientos para una bibliografía crítica de historiadores guadalupanos*, Zacatecas, Mexico 1939.

——, *Efemérides Guadalupanas*, Ed. Murguía, Mexico 1931.

——, *Juicio crítico sobre la carta de D. Joaquín García Icazbalceta y fuentes históricas de la misma*, Mexico 1931.

——, *Primer Siglo Guadalupano. 1531–1648*, Imp. Patricio Sanz, Mexico 1931.

García Icazbalceta, Joaquín, *Carta acerca del origen de la imagen de Nuestra Señora de Guadalupe de México*, published by the order of the Archbishop of Mexico, Pelagio Antonio de Labastida y Dávalos, Mexico 1896.

Garibay K., Ángel María, "Los hechos del Tepeyac," in *Libro Anual 1981–1982*, Instituto Superior de Estudios Eclesiásticos, Mexico 1984.

González, Fidel, Eduardo Chávez, and José Luis Guerrero, *El Encuentro de la Virgen de Guadalupe y Juan Diego*, Ed. Porrúa, Mexico 2002.

González Fernández, Fidel, "La 'Traditio' guadalupana como clave de lectura de la historia de la evangelización en Latinoamérica," in *Ecclesia Memoria. Miscelanea in onore del R. P. Josef Metzler, OMI, Prefetto del ASV*, Ed. Herder, Rome-Freiburg-Wien 1991, pp. 407–29.

Gregorio XIII, *Ut Deiparae semper Virginis*, March 28, 1576, ASV, Secc. Brev. 69, ff. 537r–538v; Secc. Brev. 70, ff. 532r–533v.

Guerrero Rosado, José Luis, "Contenido Antropológico y evangelizador del *Nican Mopohua*," in *La Madre del Señor en la fe y la cultura. Actas del Segundo Simposio Mariológico de México*, Ed. Librería Parroquial de Clavería, Mexico 1993.

——, *El Manto de Juan Diego*, Ed. Limusa, Mexico 1990.

——, *El Nican Mopohua. Un intento de exégesis*, Ed. Universidad Pontificia de México, Mexico 1996. 2 vols.

——, *Flor y Canto del Nacimiento de México*, Ed. F. Fernández, Mexico 1992.

——, *Los dos mundos de un indio santo. Cuestionario preliminar de la Beatificación de Juan Diego*, Ed. Cimiento, Mexico 1992.

Guillen Precker, Fernando, "Quetzalcoatl y Guadalupe," in *Libro Anual 1981–1982*, Ed. Instituto Superior de Estudios Eclesiásticos, Mexico 1984, pp. 269–95.

Guridi y Alcocer, José Miguel, *Apología de la aparición de Nuestra Señora de Guadalupe de México en respuesta a la disertación que la impugna*, Ed. Alejandro Valdés, Mexico 1820.

Hakluyt, Richard, *Voyages and Discoveries. The Principal Navigations, Voyages, Traffiques and Discoveries of the English Nation*, Ed. Penguin Group (= Col. Penguin Classics), London 1985.

Hernández Illescas, Juan Homero, "La Imagen de la Virgen de Guadalupe un Códice Náhuatl," in *Histórica* (1/2), pp. 7–20.

Hernández Illescas, Juan Homero, Mario Rojas Sánchez, and Enrique R. Salazar S., *La Virgen de Guadalupe y las estrellas*, Ed. Centro de Estudios Guadalupanos, Mexico 1995.

Herrera, Antonio de, *Historia general de los hechos de los castellanos en las Islas y Tierra Firme del Mar Océano*, Ed. Guaranía, Asunción, Paraguay, 1944–1946, 10 vols.

"Huehuetlatolli," in Miguel León-Portilla, *La Filosofía Náhuatl estudiada en sus Fuentes*, UNAM, Instituto de Investigaciones Históricas, Mexico 1974.

Huehuetlatolli. Libro Sexto del Códice Florentino, edition by Salvador Díaz Cintora, UNAM, Coordinación de Humanidades, Mexico 1995.

"Información de 1556, ordenadas realizar por Alonso de Montúfar, arzobispo de México," in Ernesto de la Torre Villar and Ramiro Navarro de Anda, *Testimonios Históricos Guadalupanos*, Ed. FCE, Mexico 1982, pp. 36–141.

Información de legitimidad, libertad, pureza de sangre, vida, costumbres y cacicazgo, Archivo del Convento de Corpus Christi para las Indias Caciques (Monasterio Autónomo de Clarisas de Corpus Christi, in Mexico), Libro I, *Informaciones desde el año de 1724 hasta el de 1741*, T. I, exp. no. 43.

"Informaciones Guadalupanas de 1666 y 1723," edition by Luis Medina Ascencio, S.J., in Ernesto de la Torre Villar and Ramiro Navarro de Anda, *Testimonios Históricos Guadalupanos*, Ed. FCE, Mexico 1982, pp. 309–33.

"Informaciones Guadalupanas de 1666," photograph of the ms., in Ana María Sada Lambretón, *Las Informaciones Jurídicas de 1666 y el Beato Juan Diego*, Ed. Hijas de María Inmaculada de Guadalupe, Mexico 1991.

Informaciones Jurídicas de 1666, copy of April 14, 1666, History of Basilica of Guadalupe Archives, Ramo Histórico, Mexico.

"Informantes de Sahagún: Códice Matritense de la Real Academia," in Miguel León–Portilla, *Los Antiguos Mexicanos a través de sus crónicas y cantares*, Ed. FCE, Mexico 1983.

Inocencio IV, "In Quinque Libros Decretalium commentaria," Venice 1578, f. 188r, in Fabijan Veraja, *La Beatificazione Storia, Problemi, Prospetive*, Ed. S. Congregazione per le Cause dei Santi, Rome 1983.

Inventario de Lorenzo Boturini Benaduci, AGI, S. Indiferente General, leg. 398, f. 101r.

John XXIII, "Ad christifideles qui ex ómnibus Americae nationibus Conventui Mariali secundo Mexici interfuerunt," Rome, October 12, 1961, in AAS, LIII (1961) 12, pp. 685–87.

John Paul II, "Alocución a los Obispos de América Latina," Mexico City, January 27, 1979, in AAS, LXXI (1979) 3, p. 173.

——, "Alocución por la III Conferencia General del Episcopado Latino Americano," January 28, 1979, in AAS, LXXI (1979) 3, p. 205.

——, Ecclesia in America, Libreria Editrice Vaticana, Vatican City 1999.

——, "Discurso para la apertura del 'Novenario' de años promovido por el CELAM: Fidelidad al pasado, mirada a los desafíos del presente, compromiso para una nueva evangelización," Sto. Domingo, December 10, 1984, in Insegnamenti di Giovanni Paolo II, Libreria Ed. Vaticana, VII/2, p. 889.

Junco, Alfonso, El milagro de las Rosas, Ed. Jus, Mexico 1969.

——, Un radical problema guadalupano, Ed. Jus, Mexico 1971.

Lafaye, Jacques, Quetzalcóatl y Guadalupe. La formation de la conscience nationale au Mexique, Ed. Gallimard, Paris 1974.

Lasso de la Vega, Luis, Huey Tlamahuizoltica, Mexico 1649, Ed. Carreño e Hijos Editores, Mexico 1962.

——, "Huey Tlamahuizoltica," Mexico 1649, facsimile edition, in Alfonso Junco, Un radical problema guadalupano, Ed. Jus, Mexico 1971.

León-Portilla, Miguel, El reverso de la conquista, Ed. Joaquín Mortiz, Mexico 1964.

——, Tonantzin Guadalupe. Pensamiento náhuatl y mensaje cristiano en el "Nican Mopohua," Eds. Colegio Nacional y FCE, Mexico 2000.

——, Los Antiguos Mexicanos a través de sus crónicas y cantares, Ed. FCE, Mexico 1983.

——, Visión de los vencidos, UNAM (= Col. Biblioteca del Estudiante Universitario no. 81), Mexico 1969.

——, Un catecismo náhuatl en imágenes, Ed. Privada de Cartón y Papel de México, Mexico 1979.

——, Historia Documental de México, UNAM, Instituto de Investigaciones Históricas, Mexico 1974, 2 vols.

Libro Sexto del Códice Florentino, edition by Salvador Díaz Cintora, UNAM, Coordinación de Humanidades, Mexico 1995.

Los diálogos de 1524 según el texto de fray Bernardino de Sahagún y sus colaboradores indígenas, facsimile edition and study by Miguel León-Portilla, UNAM, Fundación de Investigaciones Sociales, Mexico 1986.

Mendieta, Fray Gerónimo de, Historia Eclesiástica Indiana, Ed. Porrúa (=Col. Biblioteca Porrúa no. 46), Mexico 1980.

Mercuriano, Everardo, Gen., "Carta al arzobispo de México, Pedro Moya de Contreras," Rome, March 12, 1576, ARSI, Mexicana No. 1, f. 9r; published by Félix Zubillaga (editor), Monumenta Mexicana. Monumenta Historica Societatis Iesu, Rome 1956, T. I: 1570–1580, pp. 192–93.

Molina, Alejandro Javier, Química aplicada al manto de la Virgen de Guadalupe, p. 7; in Archivo para la Causa de Canonización de Juan Diego, en la CCS, Holy See.

Montes de Oca, Luis T., *Las tres primeras ermitas guadalupanas del Tepeyac*, Mexico 1934.

Monumenta Mexicana (=Col. Monumenta Historica Societatis Iesu no. 77), T. I (1570–1589), edition by Felix Zubillaga, Ed. Monumenta Historica Societatis Iesu, Rome 1956.

Mota, Ignacio H. de la, *Diccionario Guadalupano*, Ed. Panorama Editorial, Mexico 1997.

Motolinia, Fray Toribio Paredes de Benavente, *Historia de los indios de la Nueva España*, Ed. Porrúa (=Col. "Sepan Cuantos" no. 129), Mexico 1973.

Munch, Guido, *El cacicazgo de San Juan Teotihuacan durante la Colonia*, Ed. INAH (=Col. Científica no. 32), Mexico 1976.

Muñoz, Juan Bautista, "Memoria sobre las Apariciones y el culto de Nuestra Señora de Guadalupe," in Ernesto de la Torre Villar and Ramiro Navarro de Anda, *Testimonios Históricos Guadalupanos*, Ed. FCE, Mexico 1982.

Muriel de González Mariscal, Josefina, *Conventos de monjas en la nueva España*, Ed. Jus, Mexico 1996.

Narración sobre la Misión de los indios Acaxes en la Sierra de San Andrés, sixteenth or seventeenth century, AHSI, Roma, *Mexicana Annuae 1574–1614*, (Mexico 14) T. I.

Nebel, Richard, *Santa María Tonantzin Virgen de Guadalupe. Continuidad y transformación religiosa en México*, original: *Santa Maria Tonantzin Virgen de Guadalupe. Religiöse Kontinuität und Transformation in Mexiko*, Ed. FCE, Mexico 1995.

Nicoselli, Anastasio, *Relación Histórica de la admirable aparición de la Virgen Santísima Madre de Dios bajo el título de Nuestra Señora de Guadalupe, acaecida en México el año de 1531*, Rome 1681, Imprenta de D. Felipe Zúñiga y Ontiveros, Mexico 1781.

Noguez, Xavier, *Documentos Guadalupanos. Un estudio sobre las fuentes de información tempranas en torno a las Mariofanías en el Tepeyac*, Eds. El Colegio Mexiquense y FCE, Mexico 1993.

———, "El culto prehispánico en el Tepeyac," in *Arqueología Mexicana* IV (1996) 20, pp. 50–55.

Ochoterena, Isaac, *Análisis de algunas fibras del ayate de Juan Diego el Icono de nuestra Señora de Guadalupe, realizadas por el Instituto de Biología de la UNAM*, México, June 7, 1946, Departamento de Biología de la UNAM, oficio 242, exp. 812.2/-2.

O'Gorman, Edmundo, *Cuatro historiadores de Indias. Siglo XVI*, Ed. SEP (=Col. SepSetentas no. 51), Mexico 1972.

———, *Destierro de Sombras. Luz en el origen de la imagen y culto de Nuestra Señora de Guadalupe en el Tepeyac*, UNAM, Instituto de Investigaciones Históricas, Mexico 1986.

Oliva de Coll, Josefina, *La resistencia indígena ante la conquista*, Ed. Siglo XXI, Mexico 1974.

Omaecheverria, Ignacio, *Pedro Pérez de Mezquía, OFM (1688–1764). Maestro y Precursor de Fray Junípero Serra en las Misiones*, Ed. Diputación Foral de Alava, Consejo de Cultura, Spain 1963.

Orozco y Berra, Manuel, *Historia antigua y de la conquista de México*, Ed. Porrúa (=Col. Biblioteca Porrúa N 17–20), Mexico 1960, 4 vols.

———, *Historia de la dominación española en México*, Ed. Antigua Librería Robredo, Mexico 1938, 4 vols.

Ortega y Medina, Juan A., *El conflicto anglo-español por el dominio oceánico. Siglos XVI y XVII*, UNAM, Mexico 1994.

Palomera, Esteban J., *Fray Diego Valadés OFM, Evangelizador Humanista de la Nueva España, su obra*, Ed. Jus, Mexico 1962.

Patronato Mexicano del V Centenario de Cortés, *Cortés navegante, político, arquitecto, economista y literato*, Edition Commemorative 1492–1992, Ed. Diana, Mexico 1992.

Paul VI, "Nuntius Radiotelevisificus," October 12, 1970, in *AAS*, LXII (1970) 10, p. 681.

Peñalosa Joaquín, Antonio, *La práctica religiosa en México. Siglo XVI. Asedios de Sociología Religiosa*. Ed. Jus, Mexico 1969.

Perea, Francisco J., *El mundo de Juan Diego*, Ed. Diana, Mexico 1988.

———, *450 Años a la sombra del Tepeyac*, Ed. Universo, Mexico 1981.

Pérez de Salazar y Solana, Javier, *Nuestra Señora la Virgen de Tequatlalope*, Ed. Perpal, Mexico 1992.

Pérez Villanueva, Joaquín, and Bartolomé Escandell Bonet, *Historia de la Inquisición en España y América*, Eds. BAC y Centro de Estudios Inquisitoriales, Madrid 1984.

Perfetti, Claudio, *Guadalupe la tilma della Morenita*, Ed. Paoline, Milano 1987.

Phelan, John L., *El reino milenario de los franciscanos en el Nuevo Mundo*, Ed. UNAM, Instituto de Investigaciones Históricas, Mexico 1972.

Pius XI, Carta Apostólica "B. V. Maria sub titulo de Guadalupa Insularum Philippinarum Coelestis Patrona Declaratur," in *AAS*, XXVIII (1936) 2, pp. 63–64.

Pius XII, "Alocución Radiomensaje," October 12, 1945, en *AAS*, XXXVII (1945) 10, pp. 265–66.

Pomar, Juan Bautista, and Alonso de Zorita, *Relación de Texcoco y de la Nueva España*, Ed. Chávez Hayhoe, Mexico 1941.

Pompa y Pompa, Antonio, *El gran acontecimiento guadalupano*, Ed. Jus, Mexico 1967.

Poole, Stafford, *Our Lady of Guadalupe: The Origins and Sources of a Mexican National Symbol, 1531–1791*, Ed. University of Arizona Press, Tucson, 1995.

Porras Muñoz, Guillermo, *Personas y lugares de la ciudad de México. Siglo XVI*, Ed. UNAM, Instituto de Investigaciones Históricas, Mexico 1988.

Potterie, Ignace de la, *Contra los intentos de una gnosis que renace siempre*, in *30 Giorni*, X (1996), p. 104.

Prescott, William H., *Historia de la conquista de México*, Ed. Porrúa (=Col. "Sepan Cuantos" no. 150), Mexico 1970.

Provisiones Reales para el Gobierno de Indias, de 1541 a 1626, Biblioteca Nacional de Madrid, MS. 2989.

Puente de Guzmán, Alicia, "Promoción y dignidad de la mujer a la luz del evento guadalupano," in *Libro Anual 1981–1982*, Ed. Instituto Superior de Estudios Eclesiásticos, Mexico 1984.

Ramos Medina, Manuel (director), *El monacato femenino en el Imperio Español.*
Monasterios, Beaterios, Recogimientos y Colegios, Memoria del Segundo Congreso Internacional, Ed. Condumex, Mexico 1995.

Rangel Camacho, Manuel, *Virtudes y Fama de Santidad de Juan Diego*, Ed. Jus, Mexico 1984.

"Relación Primitiva o Inin Huey Tlamahuizoltzin," 1541–1545, in Ernesto de la Torre Villar and Ramiro Navarro de Anda, *Testimonios Históricos Guadalupanos*, Ed. FCE, Mexico 1982, pp. 24–25.

Rasmussen, Jorgen Nybo, *Bruder Jakob der däne ofm als verteidiger der religiösen gleichberechtigung der indiarner im Mexiko im XVI jahrhundert*, Ed. Franz Steiner Verlag, Wiesbaden 1974.

Ricard, Robert, *La conquista espiritual de México*, Ed. Jus, Mexico 1947.

Riva Palacio, Vicente, *México a través de los siglos*, Ed. Cumbre, Mexico 1891, 8 vols.

Rivera Carrera, Norberto, *¿No estoy yo aquí que soy tu madre? Palabras de la Santísima Virgen de Guadalupe al Beato Juan Diego en el Tepeyac. Diciembre de 1531*, Ed. Arquidiócesis Primada de México, Mexico 1996.

Robelo, Cecilio, *Diccionario de mitología náhuatl*, Ed. Museo Nacional de Arqueología, Mexico 1911.

Rojas, José Luis de, *México Tenochtitlan, economía y sociedad en el siglo XVI*. Eds. El Colegio de Michoacán y FCE, Mexico 1992.

Rojas Sánchez, Mario, "La Virgen de Guadalupe, la culminación de una pedagogía," in *Ixtus. Espíritu y Cultura* 3 (1995) 15, pp. 12–15.

Romero de Terreros, Manuel, "El convento franciscano de Ozumba y las pinturas de su portería," in *Anales del Instituto de Investigaciones Estéticas*, UNAM, Mexico 1956, pp. 9–21.

Romero Salinas, Joel, *Eclipse guadalupano, la verdad sobre el antiapicionismo*, Ed. El Nacional, Mexico 1992.

———, *Juan Diego, su peregrinar a los altares*, Ed. Paulinas, Mexico 1992.

———, *Precisiones históricas de las tradiciones guadalupana y juandieguina*, Ed. Centro de Estudios Guadalupanos, Mexico 1986.

Rosa, Agustín de la, "La aparición de María Santísima de Guadalupe," in Ernesto de la Torre Villar and Ramiro Navarro de Anda, *Testimonios Históricos Guadalupanos*, Ed. FCE, Mexico 1982, 1211–22.

———, "Defensa de la Aparición de Ntra. Sra. de Guadalupe," in Ernesto de la Torre Villar and Ramiro Navarro de Anda, *Testimonios Históricos Guadalupanos*, Ed. FCE, Mexico 1982, 1222–79.

———, *Dissertatio historico theologica de Apparitione B.M.V. de Guadalupe*, Ed. Narcisi Parga, Guadalajara 1887.

———, *Estudio de la filosofía y riqueza de la Lengua Mexicana*, Tip. del Gobierno, Guadalajara 1889.

Rubio Mañé, José Ignacio, *El Virreinato. Orígenes y jurisdicciones, y dinámica social de los virreyes*, Eds. UNAM, Instituto de Investigaciones Históricas, y FCE, Mexico 1983, 4 vols.

Sada Lambretón, Ana María (director), *Las Informaciones Jurídicas de 1666 y el Beato Juan Diego*, Ed. Hijas de María Inmaculada de Guadalupe, Mexico 1991.

Sahagún, Friar Bernardino de, *Historia General de las Cosas de la Nueva España*, Ed. Porrúa (= Col. "Sepan cuántos" no. 300), Mexico 1982.

Salazar, Enrique Roberto, Maurilio Montemayor Narro, and Luis Medina Ascencio, *Juan Diego, el mensajero del Tepeyac (1474–1548)*, *biografía compendiada*, Ed. Centro de Estudios Guadalupanos, Mexico 1979.

Salinas, Carlos, *Juan Diego en los ojos de la Santísima Virgen de Guadalupe*, Ed. Tradición, Mexico 1974.

Salinas, Carlos, and Manuel de la Mora, *Descubrimiento de un busto humano en los ojos de la Virgen de Guadalupe*, Ed. Tradición, Mexico 1976.

Sánchez Flores, Ramón, *La Virgen de la patria*, Ed. Imagen Pública y Corporativa, Puebla, Mexico 1996.

Sánchez, Miguel, *Imagen de la Virgen María, Madre de Dios de Guadalupe*. *Milagrosamente aparecida en la ciudad de México. Celebrada en su historia, con la profecía del capítulo doce del Apocalipsis*, Imp. Vda. de Bernardo Calderón, Mexico 1648.

Sánchez, Oscar, *Gestación Histórica de la Diócesis de Colima*, Tesis de Licencia in Canon Law, Pontificia Universidad Gregoriana, Rome.

Schulenburg Prado, Guillermo, "El milagro de Guadalupe." Interview of Guillermo Schulenburg Prado, in *Ixtus, Espíritu y Cultura* 3 (1995): 15.

——, *Informe de Actividades de los años 1963 a 1988*, published by Venerable Cabildo de la Basílica de Nuestra Señora de Guadalupe, Mexico 1988.

Sejourne, Laurette, *Pensamiento náhuatl cifrado por los calendarios*, Ed. Siglo Veintiuno (= Col. América Nuestra no. 35), Mexico 1981.

——, *Pensamiento y religión en el México Antiguo*, Ed. FCE, Mexico 1975.

Senties Rodríguez, Horacio, *Genealogía de Juan Diego*, Ed. Tradición, Mexico 1998.

Sermones Guadalupanos del Siglo XVIII, Biblioteca Nacional de Madrid, Ms. 12459.

Sigüenza y Góngora, Carlos de, *Piedad Heroica de don Hernando Cortés*, 1690, Ed. José Porrúa, Madrid 1960.

——, "Primavera Indiana, poema sacro-histórico. Idea de María Santísima de Guadalupe de México, copiada de flores," 1668, in Ernesto de la Torre Villar and Ramiro Navarro de Anda, *Testimonios Históricos Guadalupanos*, Ed. FCE, Mexico 1982, pp. 334–58.

Siller Acuña, Clodomiro L., "Anotaciones y Comentarios," in *Libro Anual 1981–1982*, Ed. Instituto Superior de Estudios Eclesiásticos, Mexico 1984.

——. *Para comprender el mensaje de María de Guadalupe*, Ed. Guadalupe, Buenos Aires 1989.

Simeon, Remy, *Dictionaire de la langue náhuatl ou mexicaine*, Ed. Imprimerie National, Paris 1885.

Smith, Jody Brant, *The Image of Guadalupe*, revised, Ed. Image Books, Garden City, New York 1984.

Sosa, Francisco, *El Episcopado Mexicano. Biografía de los Ilmos. Señores Arzobispos de México*, Ed. Jus, Mexico 1962, 2 vols.

Soustelle, Jacques, *La pensee cosmologique des anciens mexicains*, Ed. Hermann et Cie, Paris 1940.

———, *La vie quotidienne des azteques a la veille de la conquete espagnole*, Ed. Hachette, Paris 1955.

Staehlin, Carlos María, *Apariciones*, Ed. Razón y Fe, Madrid 1954.

Suárez de Peralta, Juan, *Tratado del descubrimiento de las Indias*, Biblioteca Pública de Madrid; manuscript no. 302; published by Ed. SEP, Mexico 1949.

Súplica del Episcopado de América Latina al Papa Pío XI, Imp. Murguía, Mexico 1933.

Taylor, William B., *Drinking, Homicide and Rebellion in Colonial Mexican Villages*, Ed. Stanford University Press, California, 1979.

Téllez Girón, Fray José María, "Impugnación al Manifiesto satisfactorio del Dr. José Ignacio Bartolache," 1792, in Ernesto de la Torre Villar and Ramiro Navarro de Anda, *Testimonios Históricos Guadalupanos*, Ed. FCE, Mexico 1982, pp. 651–88.

Testamento de Elvira Ramírez, Archivo General del Estado de Colima, Registro de Escrituras Públicas ante Francisco López, 1577, box 4, exp. 10.

Testimonio de Andrés de Tapia, publish by Francisco Fernández del Castillo, Publicaciones del Archivo General de la Nación, T. XII, Mexico 1927.

Thomas, Hugh, *The Conquest of Mexico*, Ed. Hutchinson, London 1993.

Tibon, Gutierre, *Historia del nombre y de la fundación de México*, prologue by Jacques Soustelle, Ed. FCE, Mexico 1993.

Tira de Tepechpan. Códice colonial procedente del Valle de México, Instituto Mexiquense de Cultura, Mexico 1996, 2 vols.

Tornielli, Andrea, "Así es si así os parece," in *30 Giorni* XIV (1996).

Torquemada, Friar Juan de, *Monarquía Indiana*, Ed. Porrúa (= Col. Biblioteca Porrúa N 41, 42 y 43), introduction by Miguel León-Portilla, Mexico 1986, 3 vols.

Toussaint, Manuel, *Arte Colonial en México*, UNAM, Instituto de Investigaciones Estéticas, Mexico 1990.

———, *Pintura Colonial en México*, UNAM, Instituto de Investigaciones Estéticas, Mexico 1965.

Valeriano, Antonio, *Nican Mopohua*, traducción y notas de Mario Rojas Sánchez, introduction by Manuel Robledo Gutiérrez, Ed. La Peregrinación, Argentina 1998.

Valero de García Lascuráin, Ana Rita, *Estudio Introductorio*, in Francisco de Florencia, *Las Novenas del Santuario de Nuestra Señora de Guadalupe, que se apareció en la Manta de Juan Diego* (1785), edition by Archicofradía Universal de Santa María de Guadalupe, Mexico 1999.

Vargas Llosa, Mario, *La utopía arcaica. José María Arguedas y las ficciones del indigenismo*, Ed. FCE, Mexico 1996.

Vargas Lugo, Elisa, "Algunas notas más sobre Iconografía Guadalupana," in *Anales del Instituto de Investigaciones Estéticas*, UNAM, Mexico 1989, pp. 59–66.

Vázquez Santa Ana, Higinio, *Juan Diego. Epigrafía, iconografía y literatura popular de Juan Diego*, Ed. Museo Juan Diego, Mexico 1940.

Velázquez, Primo Feliciano, *La Aparición de Santa María de Guadalupe*, Imp. Patricio Sanz, Mexico 1931.

Vera Fortino, Hipólito, *Informaciones sobre la milagrosa aparición de la Santísima Virgen de Guadalupe, recibidas en 1666 y 1723*, Imp. "Colegio Católico," Amecameca, Mexico 1889.

———, *Tesoro Guadalupano, Noticia de los Libros, Documentos, Inscripciones, etc., que tratan, mencionan o aluden a la Aparición y Devoción de Nuestra Señora de Guadalupe*, Imp. Colegio Católico, Amecameca 1887.

Vetancour, Agustín de, *Teatro Mexicano. Crónica de la provincia del Santo Evangelio. Menologio Franciscano*, Ed. Porrúa (= Col. Biblioteca Porrúa no. 45), Mexico 1971.

Xirau, Ramón, *Idea y querella de la Nueva España*, Ed. Alianza, Madrid 1973.

Zamacois, Niceto de, *Historia de México desde sus tiempos más remotos hasta nuestros días*, Ed. J. F. Parrés, Barcelona-Madrid 1876, 6 vols.

Zavala, Silvio, *El servicio personal de los indios en la Nueva España. 1521–1550*, Eds. El Colegio de México and El Colegio Nacional, Mexico 1984, 7 vols.

Zavala, Silvio, *Las instituciones jurídicas en la conquista de América*, Ed. Porrúa (= Col. Biblioteca Porrúa no. 50), Mexico 1971.

———, *La Encomienda Indiana*, Ed. Porrúa (Biblioteca Porrúa no. 53), Mexico 1973.

———, *La filosofía política en la conquista de América*, Ed. FCE, Mexico 1947.

———, *Repaso Histórico de la bula Sublimis Deus de Paulo III*, in *Defensa de los Indios*, Universidad Iberoamericana, Mexico 1991.

Zubillaga, Félix (editor), *Monumenta Mexicana. Monumenta Historica Societatis Iesu*, Rome 1956, T. I: 1570–1580, pp. 192–93.

Zumárraga, Fray Juan de, "Recado urgente a Hernán Cortés," AGI, Est. 51, box 6, leg. 3; published by Mariano Cuevas, *Notable Documento Guadalupano. Informe leído en la Real Academia de la Historia, en sesión de 27 de Junio de 1919*, Ed. Comité General de la ACJM, Mexico 1919.

Index

~

About the Author

Eduardo Chávez is a founding member and rector of the Superior Institute of Guadalupan Studies (ISEG), honorary canon of the Basilica of Guadalupe, first rector of the Catholic University Lumen Gentium of the archdiocese of Mexico, and doctor of history of the Church that lectures frequently on The Virgin of Guadalupe and Saint Juan Diego. He was a member of the historical commission of the Guadalupan Event formed by the Congregation for the Cause of the Saints, and postulator for the Cause of Canonization of Saint Juan Diego. He was also an ordained priest at the archdiocese of Mexico and holds a doctorate in history of the Church from the Pontifical Gregorian University in Rome.

Dr. Chávez is author of several books, including: *El Encuentro de la Virgen de Guadalupe y Juan Diego*; *Il Volto di Cristo Re e la Persecuzione della Chiesa in México*; and *Juan Diego. El mensajero de Santa María de Guadalupe*.